THE
WORLD WARS

THE WORLD WARS

Paul Dowswell, Ruth Brocklehurst & Henry Brook

Designed by Karen Tomlins, Leonard Le Rolland,
Michael Hill & Kate Rimmer

Edited by Jane Chisholm

Consultant: Terry Charman, Historian
Imperial War Museums

CONTENTS

A German U-boat surfaces during the First World War.

THE WORLD WARS

The first half of the 20th century was dominated by worldwide conflict. During the First World War, (1914-1918) and the Second World War (1939-1945), most of the same nations were pitted against each other. To some, this made it seem like one long war, with a 20-year lull between fighting. At stake was the mastery of the world. But the final outcome was not what many of the leading players on either side would have hoped for – or expected. In seeking to defend or increase their power, Britain, France and Germany lost their dominant position to the United States and Soviet Russia.

Bad to worse

Twenty thousand British soldiers died on the first day of the Battle of the Somme – the worst day's slaughter for Britain in the First World War. People were shocked, but there was worse to come. In the Second World War, this many would die every one or two days on the Eastern Front, in savage fighting between German and Soviet forces.

American troops ride into battle on French tanks, during the late stages of the First World War. Early tanks look slightly comical to us now, but they terrified troops who had to defend trenches against them.

Man-made catastrophes

Between them, the First and Second World Wars make up the greatest man-made catastrophes in history. Almost every inhabited region on Earth was drawn into the struggle, which was fought from the deserts of North Africa to the rainforests of New Guinea. Ordinary people were more involved in the hostilities than they had been in any previous conflicts, and far more civilians died than those in the armed forces.

A British *Lancaster* bomber of the Second World War. Bomber aircraft caused massive damage to cities and industry hundreds of miles behind enemy lines.

Into the future

During ten years of global carnage, empires fell, and countries were destroyed or created. At least 76 million people were killed, and many were left homeless. Sixty years after the end of the Second World War, both wars still haunt and fascinate us today. Recent events in world history – from the dissolution of the Soviet Union, to the turmoil of the Middle East and the emergence of the United States as the world's only superpower – all have their roots in these two brutal conflicts. Even in the 21st century, they continue to shape current events.

INTERNET LINK

For links to websites where you can read illustrated accounts of the wars and how they affected people and places around the world, go to **www.usborne-quicklinks.com**

Russian women and children, in 1941, driven from their homes by fighting, cast a wary eye over a German supply column. They have good reason to fear their conquerors, who treated Soviet citizens with great cruelty.

THE FIRST WORLD WAR

The First World War was a human tragedy on a global scale. It began in Europe, but countries from around the world were soon dragged into the fighting. The war lasted for four dark years – from 1914 to 1918 – and a staggering 65 million men were mobilized to fight. Over 21 million people died, including 13 million civilians. The terrible impact of the war sparked revolutions, toppled once-great empires and changed the political map of Europe forever.

One of the poppy fields in northern France, where some of the bloodiest battles of the war took place. Many soldiers were struck by the beauty of the poppies that grew wild on the battlefields, and the poppy became a symbol for remembrance of the people who had died in the war.

THE GREAT WAR

The First World War was fought on such a massive scale that people called it the Great War. Never before had any war been fought on so many battlefields, with such a vast array of powerful and destructive weapons, and resulted in so many deaths.

Mass destruction

The reason the war was so destructive was that it was the first major war between the newly industrialized nations of Europe. In the days before factories, trains and steamships, wars often involved hundreds of men, charging into battle on foot or on horseback, brandishing swords. This time, it was possible to transport millions of men quickly to the front, and to arm them with an almost endless supply of the latest mass-produced weapons and ammunition. Machine guns, poison gas and barbed wire, as well as planes, tanks and submarines, all came into use – some for the first time – with devastating effect.

This map shows how, by August 1917, most of the world had divided into two sides in the war. On one side were the Allied Powers – shaded green on this map – and on the other were the Central Powers – shaded red. Only those places shaded yellow remained neutral.

Clash of empires

The most powerful countries involved had empires, with colonies and influence in every corner of the globe. So, although the war began in Europe, it rapidly spread to the wider world. Soon, men from the colonies were drawn into the fray. Beyond Europe, fighting took place on land – in Africa and Asia – and at sea – in the South Atlantic and the Pacific. Altogether, 28 countries became involved, making it the first war to be called a World War.

A German soldier is thrown from his feet by a powerful blast from a shell. This picture is from a movie made after the war, but with actors who fought in it.

Total war

The war affected the lives of civilians more than any previous war, because for the first time they were expected to help their country in the war effort. Workers had to step up agricultural and industrial production to keep their troops armed, clothed and fed.

All this meant that people far from the fighting became targets for enemy attack. Factories and supply routes were most at risk, but bombs fell on homes, schools and places of worship too. This kind of unrestricted warfare, in which whole populations are involved in the effort, is sometimes called Total War.

INTERNET LINK

For a link to a website where you can explore an interactive timeline of the First World War, go to
www.usborne-quicklinks.com

This map shows the European alliances during the First World War. The same shading is used throughout this book, to show which side each country was on.

Allied Powers
Central Powers
Neutral

SWEDEN

NORWAY

Christiania

Stockholm

Petrograd
(St. Petersburg)

North Sea

DENMARK

Copenhagen

Baltic Sea

RUSSIA

UNITED KINGDOM

London

Amsterdam

The Hague

NETHERLANDS

Berlin

Brussels

English Channel

BELGIUM

LUXEMBOURG

GERMANY

Luxembourg

Paris

Vienna

Budapest

FRANCE

Bern

SWITZERLAND

AUSTRIA-HUNGARY

Bay of Biscay

RUMANIA
(Entered the war August 1916)

PORTUGAL
(Entered the war March 1916)

MONACO

Adriatic Sea

BOSNIA

Sarajevo

Belgrade

Bucharest

Black Sea

ANDORRA

ITALY
(Entered the war May 1915)

SERBIA

BULGARIA
(Entered the war October 1915)

Madrid

Corsica
(Fr.)

MONTENEGRO

Lisbon

SPAIN

Rome

Cetinje

Sofia

Constantinople
(Istanbul)

Sardinia
(Ital.)

Durazzo

ALBANIA

Mediterranean Sea

GREECE
(Entered the war November 1916)

Aegean Sea

TURKISH EMPIRE
(Entered the war November 1914)

Sicily

Athens

Dodecanese Islands
(Ital.)

Malta
(Br.)

Crete

11

BALANCE OF POWER

Kaiser Wilhelm II was fascinated by the army, and loved dressing in uniform

During the decades before 1914, Europe's most powerful nations split into two rival groups. The threat of war hung heavy in the air. Most governments hoped that the sheer size and strength of the two sides would prevent either one from attacking the other. But some began to fear that if Germany became stronger it might just tip this precarious balance of power. Then, a major war would be inevitable.

A nation is born

Until the late 19th century, Germany was made up of 39 small, independent states. In the 1870s, Prussia, the most powerful of them, led the German states in a successful invasion of northeast France, taking Alsace and Lorraine. Then, the Prussians convinced the other German states to unite with them, creating a powerful new nation.

The Central Powers

Fearing retaliation from France, the Germans formed an alliance with Austria-Hungary. They promised each other military aid if Russia attacked either of them, or helped another country, such as France, in a war against them. In 1882, Italy joined them to form a triple alliance known as the Central Powers. But, secretly, the Italians also made a pact with the French, to stay neutral if Germany invaded France.

Industrial superpower

The Germans wasted no time in building up their industries and expanding production of coal, iron and steel in their new nation. They were so ambitious that by 1913 they had outstripped Britain as Europe's leading industrial power.

The new ruler, Kaiser Wilhelm II, also had ambitions for a "place in the sun" to rival the empires of Britain and France. To do this, he expanded his army and ordered the construction of a new fleet of warships. By 1914, Germany had colonies in Africa, the Far East and the Pacific, and the second largest fleet in the world – after the British Royal Navy.

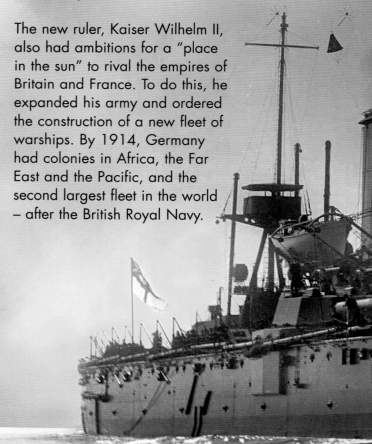

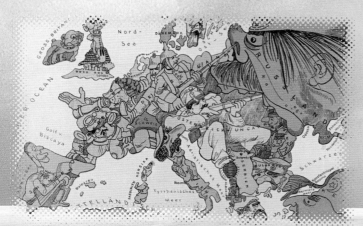

This 1914 German map of Europe shows Germany (blue) and Austria-Hungary (yellow) as determined soldiers, with weapons at the ready.

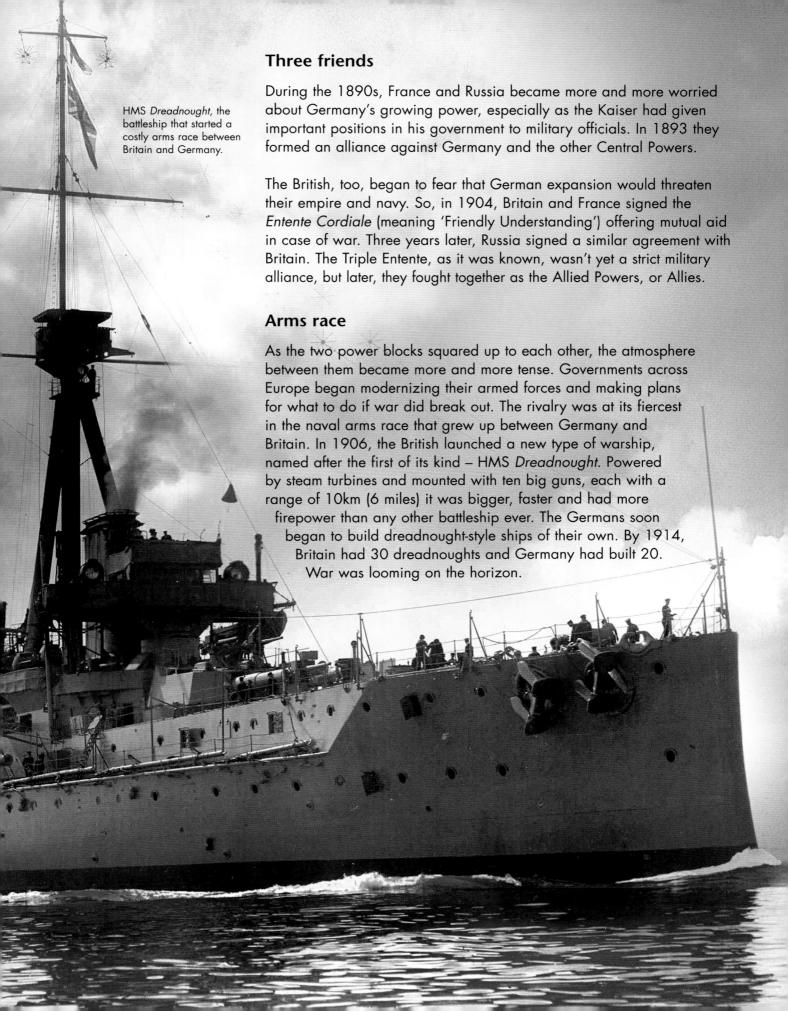

HMS *Dreadnought*, the battleship that started a costly arms race between Britain and Germany.

Three friends

During the 1890s, France and Russia became more and more worried about Germany's growing power, especially as the Kaiser had given important positions in his government to military officials. In 1893 they formed an alliance against Germany and the other Central Powers.

The British, too, began to fear that German expansion would threaten their empire and navy. So, in 1904, Britain and France signed the *Entente Cordiale* (meaning 'Friendly Understanding') offering mutual aid in case of war. Three years later, Russia signed a similar agreement with Britain. The Triple Entente, as it was known, wasn't yet a strict military alliance, but later, they fought together as the Allied Powers, or Allies.

Arms race

As the two power blocks squared up to each other, the atmosphere between them became more and more tense. Governments across Europe began modernizing their armed forces and making plans for what to do if war did break out. The rivalry was at its fiercest in the naval arms race that grew up between Germany and Britain. In 1906, the British launched a new type of warship, named after the first of its kind – HMS *Dreadnought*. Powered by steam turbines and mounted with ten big guns, each with a range of 10km (6 miles) it was bigger, faster and had more firepower than any other battleship ever. The Germans soon began to build dreadnought-style ships of their own. By 1914, Britain had 30 dreadnoughts and Germany had built 20. War was looming on the horizon.

ASSASSINATION AND CRISIS

On Sunday June 28, 1914, disaster struck in the Bosnian capital of Sarajevo. A nineteen-year-old student shot Archduke Franz Ferdinand, the heir to the Austro-Hungarian throne. The assassination provided the spark that ignited the First World War.

Balkan belligerents

The Balkan states of southeastern Europe had a long history of wars and ethnic tension, going right back to the time of the Roman empire. During the 18th and 19th centuries, they had been fought over by two powerful empires: the Ottoman Turks and the Austro-Hungarians. Bosnia and Serbia had been ruled by the Turks until 1878, when Bosnia was handed over to Austria-Hungary and Serbia was granted independence. Since then, Serbia had expanded its territory and was beginning to pose a threat to Austrian power in the region.

This map shows the Balkan states in 1914, sandwiched between the two great empires of Austria-Hungary and Ottoman Turkey.

Most Bosnians and Serbs were Slavic people. Many of them wanted to bring an end to Austro-Hungarian rule in Bosnia so that they could unite their two countries and form an independent Slavic nation. Passions ran high, and some revolutionaries were prepared to go to extreme lengths to achieve this goal.

Franz Ferdinand and his wife Sophie in Sarajevo, about to climb into their car. Minutes later they would be shot dead.

Suicidal assassins

When the heir to the Austro-Hungarian throne, Archduke Franz Ferdinand, announced an official visit to Sarajevo, a Serbian terrorist organization called the Black Hand decided it was time to strike. It recruited and trained three Bosnian student activists, and armed them with pistols, hand bombs and cyanide capsules. Their mission was to assassinate the Archduke, then to commit suicide so that the killing could not be linked to the Black Hand. The young Bosnians – Gavrilo Princip, Nedjelko Cabrinovic and Trifco Grabez – were all dying slowly of tuberculosis. Their lives seemed a small price to pay for what they believed to be a just cause.

Gavrilo Princip: the Bosnian teenager who unwittingly started the First World War. He received a twenty year sentence, but died in prison, of tuberculosis, on April 28, 1918.

Police seize one of the Bosnian assasins on June 28, 1914. For many years this picture was said to show the arrest of Gavrilo Princip, but it is now thought to be Nedjelko Cabrinovic.

Royal murder

When Franz Ferdinand and his wife Sophie arrived in Sarajevo, they were driven to a reception with the Governor of Bosnia. The streets were lined with well-wishers cheering the Archduke as he waved from an open-top car. But hidden among the crowds were the three assassins, and four accomplices, intent on murder. As the motorcade passed Nedjelko Cabrinovic, he hurled his bomb. It missed Franz Ferdinand's car, but hit the one behind, injuring its passengers and several onlookers. Chaos spread through the crowd, as the imperial party sped for the safety of the City Hall. For now, the plot had failed.

After the reception, the Archduke decided to visit those injured in the earlier attack. His driver took a wrong turn, right past Gavrilo Princip, who seized his chance. Grabbing his pistol, he fired at almost point-blank range, shooting Franz Ferdinand in the neck and Sophie in the abdomen. The driver raced back to the Governor's residence, but the Archduke and his wife died before they could receive medical help.

INTERNET LINK

For a link to a website where you can watch film footage of Franz Ferdinand in Sarajevo on the day he was assassinated, go to **www.usborne-quicklinks.com**

Taking the blame

Princip and Cabrinovic both swallowed their cyanide, but the poison failed and they were arrested, along with their accomplices. Under interrogation, they soon revealed that the Black Hand had orchestrated the assassination.

The Austrians insisted that the Serbian government should take responsibility for the Black Hand's actions. They issued them with a strict set of demands. When the Serbs failed to meet all these demands, Austria-Hungary, with German backing, declared war on Serbia on July 28. Tensions between the European powers now came to a head. The die was cast.

EUROPE IN ARMS

As news of the assassination spread across Europe, few people could have imagined the impact it would have. But when the Germans offered their unconditional support to Austria-Hungary, the complex web of European alliances came into play. What had started as a local crisis triggered a chain of events that sent Europe careering headlong into full-scale war.

Two British soldiers – nick-named 'Tommies' – board a train at London's Victoria Station, bound for France.

German forces moved swiftly to seize the Belgian capital, Brussels, in the first month of the war.

Domino effect

Within days of Austria's declaration of war on Serbia, Europe's military leaders put their war plans into action. On July 31, the Russians announced that they were moving their army into position, ready to help their Serbian allies against Austria-Hungary, if necessary. The Germans saw this as an act of aggression. So, on August 1, they declared war on Russia. The French, in turn, rallied their troops to support the Russians. This provoked the Germans to declare war on France on August 3.

16

The Schlieffen Plan

Germany was now at war with France to the west and Russia to the east. War on two fronts would mean splitting the army in two, weakening its effectiveness. But, back in 1899, the military commander Alfred von Schlieffen had anticipated this problem and had prepared a plan. His theory was that Russian troops would take at least six weeks to get ready to cross the German frontier, because their vast country had a very poor rail network. This would give the Germans plenty of time to defeat France, on the Western Front, before dealing with Russia, on the Eastern Front. On August 4, 1914, the German army put the Schlieffen Plan into action. They marched into Belgium, heading for Paris by the shortest, flattest route.

Britain enters the war

The Germans did not expect Britain, the world's greatest sea power, to join a European land war. But, by invading Belgium, they made a big mistake. Belgium was a neutral country, and Britain had a long-standing treaty to protect it. The German chancellor considered the agreement a mere "scrap of paper" – but the British took it more seriously. Belgium's ports provided a vital link between Britain and the rest of Europe. If the Germans captured them, it would severely harm British trade and security in the English Channel. Eleven hours after the invasion, Britain declared war on Germany.

A family affair

Europe was up in arms, but many people still believed that diplomatic talks could defuse the situation. The British king, George V, and Kaiser Willhelm II were both grandsons of Queen Victoria, and Tsar Nicholas II of Russia was married to one of her granddaughters. They hoped their family ties would make a war between their countries impossible. But, despite a flurry of telegrams from one cousin to another, it was too late to stop the military advance that had been set in motion.

Queen Victoria – the 'Grandmama of Europe' – sits at the heart of her extended family. Seated on the left is Kaiser Wilhelm II, behind him in a bowler hat is Tsar Nicholas II. Behind the Tsar is his uncle, the future Edward VII, father of George V.

17

PLANS UNRAVEL

As the fighting began, army commanders put into action war plans made years before. But neither the plans, nor the men's training, took into account the massive advances made in weapons technology during the previous two decades. By the end of the first month's fighting, it was clear that the war was not going to go according to plan. New weapons would mean a new kind of war.

This huge 'Big Bertha' siege gun could fire an 820kg (1,800 pounds) shell over 15km (9 miles).

Belgian soldiers defend a bridge against German troops. The Belgian army was far outnumbered, so could only hope to slow the German army's advance.

Big guns in Belgium

For the Schlieffen Plan to work, the German army chief of staff, Helmuth von Moltke, needed his troops to push through Belgium and on to Paris as quickly as possible. But the Belgians put up an unexpectedly stubborn resistance from their forts around the city of Liège. They inflicted heavy losses on the Germans and slowed their progress. But, eventually, Moltke's troops smashed through the forts, using their secret weapon – a massive siege cannon known as Big Bertha. After that, they swept through Belgium, terrorizing soldiers and civilians alike.

INTERNET LINK

For a link to a website where you can view an animated map of the German advance to Paris and the opening battles of the war, go to **www.usborne-quicklinks.com**

German troops enter French territory, pushing through woodland in the Argonne region.

Battling on the frontiers

As the Germans advanced through Belgium, a British force of about 100,000 men landed in France and clashed with the Germans near the Belgian town of Mons. At the same time, the French launched Plan XVII – their strategy to take back Alsace and Lorraine – with a series of offensives along the Franco-German frontier, that became known as the Battle of the Frontiers.

At this stage, the pace of the war was rapid and exhausting. Armies were constantly on the move across vast battlefields. It was the first time many of the soldiers had faced machine guns and chaotic battles were fought under a hail of bullets. The Allies were outnumbered and outgunned at every turn. The French, fighting in red and blue uniforms, made easy targets and suffered huge casualties. Forced to retreat, they abandoned their Plan XVII. Now they were fighting to save Paris itself.

Russian sacrifice

To the east, Russian forces moved quicker than the Germans had expected. On August 4, they invaded East Prussia (now northern Poland), where there was only a small German army. This forced Moltke to divert 100,000 troops away from France. On August 26, the Germans began their counterattack, driving the Russians into dense woodland near Tannenberg. There, in just four days, Russia suffered one of the most crushing defeats of the war, with around 60,000 casualties. The Germans captured some 92,000 Russian soldiers and 500 guns. After further defeats at the Masurian Lakes, the Russian army retreated from East Prussia for good.

Fighting for Paris

Despite the Russian diversion, the Germans had come within 40km (25 miles) of Paris. The French government fled, along with a million Parisians, leaving the rest to prepare for a siege. On September 3, the French commander-in-chief of the Allied troops, Joseph Joffre, ordered his men to take up a defensive position along the River Marne. Three days later, the Battle of the Marne began.

Strengthened by extra British troops and French reinforcements, transported from Paris in a fleet of taxis, the Allies now had the advantage. Their exhausted German opponents had marched more than 240km (150 miles) and were running out of supplies. By September 9, the battle had turned against them and they began to retreat. The Schlieffen Plan had failed, and Paris was saved.

Under French escort, some of the 29,000 German troops captured during the fighting on the Marne are marched into captivity.

Winter 1914

OVER BY CHRISTMAS?

During the opening months of the war, thousands of men throughout Europe enthusiastically volunteered to fight, confident that it would be a quick, clean contest, and that they would all be home for Christmas. But, by October 1914, armies on both sides stopped advancing as they were ordered to dig trenches all along the Western Front, the German frontier with Belgium and France. The fighting rapidly reached stalemate. As winter set in, soldiers realized they faced a long and bloody fight in the mud.

Excited French troops wave from a train as they leave Paris for the front, August 1914.

CARVING A NEW FRONTIER

With the German army in retreat after the Battle of the Marne, the ambitious Schlieffen Plan was in tatters. Desperate to turn the situation back to their advantage, Kaiser Wilhelm appointed General Erich von Falkenhayn as overall commander, in place of General von Moltke. But Moltke had one final order for his exhausted troops: to "fortify and defend" their positions above the River Aisne. This simple instruction would change the whole course of the war.

The ground where the Allies dug their first trenches was very wet and prone to flooding.

The line hardens

The German armies halted their retreat at the Chemin des Dames Ridge. They turned this 40km (25 miles) long wedge of high ground into a fortress, protected by a network of trenches, barbed wire and machine gun posts. When the British and French attacked the ridge on September 14, they were stopped dead in their tracks. Caught without shelter from the German guns, the Allies started digging their own defensive trenches. Amazingly, they would still be living in these crumbling earthworks four years later, fighting over much the same shell-scarred battlefield.

On the offensive

Frustrated by the hold-up at the Chemin des Dames Ridge, the Allies changed their tactics. The country to the north of it lay open. If the French could rush an army around the side, or flank, of Falkenhayn's troops, they would be able to cut the German supply lines and capture the ridge. But Falkenhayn had his own plans for the gap in the north. He ordered his generals to outflank the British and seize the Channel ports of Calais, Dunkirk and Boulogne, only 160km (100 miles) away. His soldiers could then march on Paris and snatch a stunning victory for their new commander.

As the Germans retreated to the Aisne, they blew up bridges behind them, making it difficult for the British and French to pursue them.

Plugging the gaps

Both sides scrambled north, in what became known as the Race to the Sea. They fought battles and dug trenches along the way, marking their progress across the Belgian region of Flanders. But the race ended in a frustrating draw, as the opposing armies arrived at the dark waters of the North Sea, before either could win an advantage. Falkenhayn's generals found what they thought was a weak point in the British-held territory, at the Belgian town of Ypres. There, in late October, they launched a desperate attack.

A taste of things to come

The Battle of Ypres was a bloody and disastrous introduction to trench fighting for all concerned. The British were outnumbered, outgunned, and ill-prepared, but they still managed to hold their ground. The German infantry suffered terrible casualties, losing whole battalions of young recruits as they charged across open fields to their deaths.

The fighting finally sputtered out at the end of November, when heavy rains turned the battlefield to mud, and ammunition supplies ran low. Still in Allied hands, Ypres would be the setting for years of bitter fighting and another two major battles. Already, at least 50,000 German and 24,000 British troops lay dead in Flanders fields.

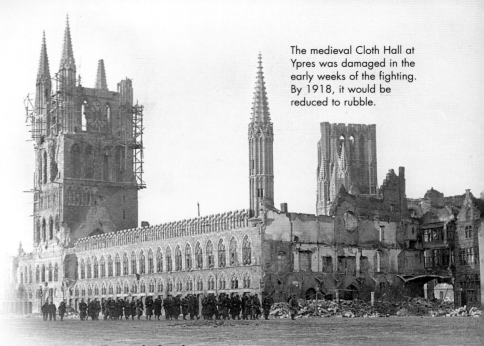

The medieval Cloth Hall at Ypres was damaged in the early weeks of the fighting. By 1918, it would be reduced to rubble.

Trench-lock

The fast-paced fighting of the previous months now ground to a standstill. Trenches stretched out from the Chemin des Dames ridge in a jagged scar, across northern Europe. This border between armies was known as the Western Front. It snaked 765km (475 miles) from the Belgian coast to the mountains of Switzerland. Millions of men guarded their dirt fortifications, with the industrial might of Europe's nations gearing up behind them. The long years of deadlock in the trenches had only just begun.

BATTLES
1. Mons (Aug. 1914)
2. Marne (Sept. 1914)
3. First Ypres (Oct. 1914)
4. Arras (Oct. 1914)
5. Neuve Chapelle (March 1915)
6. Second Ypres (May 1915)
7. Loos (Sept. 1915)

This map shows the main battlefields of the Western Front during the first year of fighting. By this time, most of the front line was scored with trenches.

FIRE, WIRE AND MUD

Commanders on both sides believed the war in the trenches would be short-lived. But, they were used to fighting in the open, with armies charging at each other across huge battlefields. The shelter of the trenches, combined with the destructive power of modern weapons, made it impossible for either side to break through in the old way. In the winter of 1914, whole armies ground to a halt. They would spend years locking horns in the mud.

Killing evolves

The tactics and weapons used in an attack hadn't changed much since the 19th century, but defending troops had a range of new and deadly tools at their disposal. Their rifles, machine guns and high explosive shells ripped any attacking infantry to shreds. This firepower could have destroyed the warring armies in less than a year, if it hadn't been for the shelter offered by the trenches.

This is a detail from *Over the top* by John Nash, an official war artist for the British government. The stark scene depicts the artist's own experience of war in the trenches.

INTERNET LINK

For a link to a website where you can play a game to defend a trench and choose the equipment you might need on different missions, go to
www.usborne-quicklinks.com

Steel brambles

The trenches may have been filthy, uncomfortable and dangerous places, but they did offer some protection from enemy fire. German military engineers took particular care designing their trenches. Their front line was a labyrinth of ditches, tunnels and deep shelters that protected soldiers from explosive shells. They were also quick to lay thick beds of razor-sharp barbed wire to protect their trenches. It was hard to cut by hand and exploding shells only lifted it off the ground and dropped it down in a tangled and impenetrable mess. So, for both sides, it was easy to defend a position, but almost impossible to attack it successfully.

Going over the top

But, even after the slaughter at Ypres, many generals were still convinced that by shelling enemy positions, then sending waves of attacking infantry, they would eventually break the enemy line and force a return to fighting in the open. However, millions of men would die testing this theory in the blood-soaked years to come. The order to go 'over the top' meant that soldiers had to scramble out of their trenches and charge straight into enemy fire.

Into the void

On the night before an infantry attack, thousands of soldiers gathered at the front. They could hear their own shells screaming overhead and crashing into enemy lines. If all went according to plan, the barrage would clear a path through the barbed wire and kill most of the defenders, but it rarely did. The open ground between the trench lines, known as no-man's-land, was a strip of broken, desolate earth, stripped bare of any vegetation by shellfire. It could be anything from shouting distance across, to 5km (3 miles) wide.

In most attacks, commanders lost sight of their men the moment they climbed up into the smoke and confusion of no-man's-land. The only way to give them new orders was by messenger, or by means of an experimental telephone system that used buried wires. But messengers were shot down as they sprinted back and forth, and high-explosive shells slamming into the ground cut the telephone wires. It could take hours for an officer to receive vital orders, while the situation around him was changing by the second.

In the first years of the war, soldiers were ordered not to run or zigzag as they crossed no-man's-land. Generals thought troops might get confused and panic if they didn't advance in orderly ranks. But this only made it easier for enemy machine gunners to mow them down in neat lines.

In this painting, French troops make the terrifying journey across no-man's-land, past tangles of barbed wire to attack enemy trenches.

GOING UP THE LINE

The Germans were the first to dig in, seizing any available high, dry ground. All along the Western Front, they held the best positions. The Allied soldiers had to dig wherever their advance ended, even where the earth was boggy or rock-hard. Their trenches were often shallow and easily flooded. But, wet or dry, every man sheltering in the dirt shared the same daily terrors.

INTERNET LINK

For a link to a website where you can explore a panoramic reconstruction of a trench system, go to www.usborne-quicklinks.com

First impressions

Just getting to the trenches was an ordeal in itself. New soldiers usually arrived by train at a rest area, located miles behind the front line. Then, they marched to the front at night, when there was less risk of being spotted by enemy gunners. Approaching the battle zone, they passed along shattered roads, through ruined villages and forests of splintered trees, until their path dipped and narrowed and they entered a communication trench. These long, twisting ditches were the arteries for all the supplies and fresh troops that fed into the trench network.

The combat zone

After months of shelling, some communication trenches were so torn and featureless that arriving soldiers needed guides to lead them. It was easy to get lost when all you could see was the night sky and bare mud walls. Frightened and disorientated, the men reached the reserve trenches first. There were usually one or two of these running in parallel to the front line and they were used as work areas and fallback positions in case of an attack. But the soldiers' final destination was the fire trench, bordering no-man's-land. Here they were greeted by an overwhelming stench of unburied corpses, gun smoke and open latrines – the pits that served as toilets.

Mud and rain meant the trenches needed constant maintenance. These British men taking a rest from digging are wrapped up in a variety of hats, scarves and furs, sent from home to keep them warm.

Mind your head

Soldiers quickly learned to keep their ears open and their heads down at all times. It was rare for a trench to be much deeper than head height. This only added to feelings of tension and claustrophobia, as thousands of soldiers died from head wounds. It was only late in 1915 that French troops were issued with steel helmets; the British didn't receive them until 1916. The army used the euphemistic term 'wastage' to describe the daily losses in the trenches.

Constant companions

There were other, ever-present hazards – rain and snow, plagues of vermin and disease. Thousands of soldiers died of exposure or lost their feet to a fungal infection known as trench foot. Body lice made the men itch and gave them fevers. Huge rats gorged themselves on the dead, and one German officer described flies so thick on the ground they looked like a cushion of blue velvet.

Soldiers had to manage with all this as best they could, as they lived in the fire trench for a week or two at a time. Then, they would spend another week in a support trench, before replacements came and they could go back to the reserve area for a week or two, before the cycle began again.

The lay of the land

People tend to think of trenches as being straight, but in fact they were made up of short, straight sections – called traverses – linked together at right angles. This meant that soldiers could dodge around a corner to shelter from bullets or shrapnel from shells, whatever angle they were coming from. Piles of sandbags formed a 'parapet' along the front of the trenches, to give cover from snipers. More sandbags at the back formed a 'parados' to protect the men from shells exploding behind them, and shots fired from the reserve trenches.

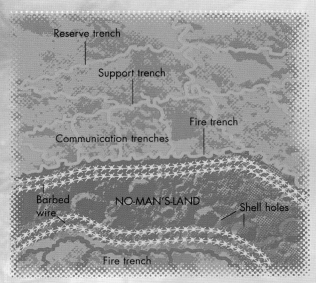

This diagram shows the typical layout of the trenches. By the end of the war, there were over 32,200km (20,000 miles) of these snaky systems carved out of the Western Front.

27

A STORM OF STEEL

The single biggest killer in the First World War was artillery fire. It churned up the ground, ripped men apart and buried them alive under mounds of earth. In the days leading up to a big infantry attack, artillery teams bombarded enemy positions with millions of high-explosive shells. As far away as London, people could hear the roar of the guns in northern France – the distant thunder of an industrialized war.

Making shells in a munitions factory was a hazardous job, as accidental explosions were a constant danger.

On the assembly line

For hundreds of years, warring armies had used artillery to fire cannonballs and other missiles. But, in the decades leading up to the First World War, scientists began combining advances in weapons technology with the manufacturing power of huge factories. Thousands of guns rolled off the production lines. And they were bigger, easier to fire and deadlier than ever.

INTERNET LINK

For a link to a website where you can find out more about all the weapons used in the war, and see pictures of many of them, go to **www.usborne-quicklinks.com**

Canadian soldiers loading a howitzer artillery gun. Such weapons were designed to fire a shell high into the air so it plunged down on a trench or fort with deadly, penetrating force.

A hundred ways to die

These artillery weapons were only part of the new and terrifying arsenal of killing machines. In the trenches, there were a hundred different ways to die. Hand grenades had been around for years, but new varieties were developed during the war. These were safer for the soldier throwing them, but they caused terrible injuries in cramped trenches. Both sides also used flame-throwers to send jets of fire into enemy positions.

Machine guns were also in use by this time, and their fire cut through attacking infantry like a scythe. In 1885, an American inventor, Hiram Maxim, had harnessed the energy released by a shooting bullet to load the next round in an instant. Belts of bullets fed into the gun so it could fire 500 rounds every minute. Bullets could maim and kill, but what soldiers feared far more was shrapnel and high-explosive shells. They were used in an attempt to destroy enemy trenches in advance of an infantry attack.

German soldiers on the edge of an Allied trench. Standing up to throw a grenade, as the man on the left is doing, exposed a soldier to terrible risk from enemy fire.

New ways of killing

Artillery shells were packed with recently invented explosives, like dynamite or TNT, and came in a fearful range of shapes and sizes. Shrapnel shells burst into hundreds of razor-sharp fragments before they hit the ground, slicing through flesh and bone. The shrapnel often picked up dirt before entering the body, causing fatal infections and blood poisoning. The effects of high-explosives were even more terrifying – they could rip a man to tiny pieces. Massive siege shells were designed not to explode until they'd smashed through a fort's stone and steel fortifications.

Perfect timing

Even with all the improvements in artillery, army gunners still had a difficult task. They had to fire test shots to find the right target. This gave trench defenders plenty of warning before raids. There were problems with faulty shells that didn't explode, known as duds, while poor communications sometimes resulted in barrages falling too late or too early to be of much use to the attackers. It would take years for gunners to achieve the perfect timing and accuracy needed to protect infantry as they attacked – a key tactic that would eventually help to unlock the Western Front.

GHOSTS, SHADOWS AND LIES

Life in the trenches could be a strange and bewildering experience. The heat and haze of battle sometimes played tricks with a soldier's eyes, making it hard to make out what was real or imaginary. Fantastic stories and superstitions were whispered among the troops, the eerie myths of a disturbing war.

A last goodbye

In sections of trench where there was heavy fighting, soldiers lived alongside the unburied bodies of dead friends and enemy fighters. In this hellish landscape of corpses and mud, soldiers regularly reported seeing ghosts of missing pals returning to see their old posts and comrades. Back at home, some families reported surprise visits from male relatives, apparently at the very moment when they had been killed on the battlefield.

Phantom warriors

Other ghosts got stuck into the fighting. After the Battle of Mons in August 1914, British troops were buzzing with stories of a lost platoon guided to safety by a friendly phantom. The idea that the spirit world was on their side must have appealed to the men. They had been outnumbered and outgunned, and some of the soldiers believed that they had only been saved by a troop of warrior angels, who appeared to fire flaming arrows at the Germans.

The myth was probably based on a ghost story, published in a newspaper in 1914. In it, the British army was aided by Saint George and a host of angels. The author of the tale, Arthur Machen, denied suggestions that it was based on real events, but many people refused to accept that it was all make-believe. Similar myths of ghostly patriots remained popular throughout the war.

ANGEL OF MONS

Valse

by PAUL PAREE.

This 1916 illustration of the Angel of Mons is from the cover of the sheet music for a waltz inspired by the legend.

The body factory

Myths had a powerful effect on soldiers' morale and on how they felt about the enemy. In 1917, British soldiers heard whispers about a secret, ghoulish factory where the Germans turned their war dead into explosives and fertilizer. The story was so powerful, that it helped to convince the Chinese to declare war on Germany in August 1917. It was only when the fighting was over that a British army officer admitted the story was a propaganda lie, to make the Germans sound like monsters.

INTERNET LINK
For a link to a website where you can read Arthur Machen's ghost story 'The Bowmen' in full, go to www.usborne-quicklinks.com

Albert's Angel

Soldiers marching off to war are always on the lookout for good or bad omens. Thousands of men passed through the town of Albert on their way to the front, gazing in amazement at the cathedral. A statue of the Virgin Mary holding the Christ Child topped the cathedral's tower. But because the tower offered commanding views of the battlefield, it was a prime target for enemy gunners. A shell had knocked the statue over, and for years it hung at a bizarre angle. Many soldiers believed that when the statue finally crashed to earth the fighting would end, and the side responsible would lose the war.

The statue of Mary hangs perilously from the cathedral tower in Albert. Eventually, she was toppled by British gunners in 1918, proving the myth to be false.

Cloud ships

High explosive shells could create amazing light effects and the gasses they produced may even have affected local weather. At Gallipoli, in August 1915, British survivors of one battle described how a whole battalion of 800 men had vanished inside a mysterious, glowing cloud that carried them away without a trace.

Several years passed before the myth was explained. A Turkish farmer was clearing some thick woodland a few miles from the battlefield when he discovered the bodies of hundreds of dead British soldiers, their bones strewn among the trees. The lost battalion had marched through the mist into wild country, where they had been ambushed by the enemy, and wiped out to the last man.

31

NORTH SEA RAIDERS

While opposing armies fought it out in the mud, British and German battleships prowled the waters of the North Sea. Most people expected a quick showdown between the two fleets in the grand tradition of previous wars. But the war at sea began with another tried and tested tactic: naval blockade.

A Royal Navy signalman on board a British warship. The position of his flags spell out different letters of the alphabet.

Stranglehold

The British navy set up a blockade around Europe the moment war was declared, searching merchant ships and confiscating cargos bound for Germany. German chemists invented substitutes for goods that would have been imported – explosives, fertilizers, even coffee. But food rationing still had to be introduced and people struggled to find enough to eat. German admirals were desperate to smash the blockade, but most of their fleet was trapped inside the North Sea by British warships. Only their submarines – known as *U-boats* – could slip past the patrols. So in February 1915 they ordered the U-boats to sink any ship sighted in British coastal waters.

Warring fleets

In the years leading up to the war, Britain and Germany had spared no expense improving and expanding their fleets. Their 'big gun' dreadnoughts were paraded at sea, symbols of naval might, supported by an armada of other warships. Battle cruisers were lighter and faster than dreadnoughts, but still packed a powerful punch. Smaller vessels, such as destroyers, patrolled coastal seas.

Flying the flag

Ships were fitted with wireless radio sets that could send long-distance sound signals. As they were easy to intercept, messages were usually sent in code. But, it could take up to ten minutes to decipher and rush a message to a captain. So in battle conditions the fleets still relied on traditional flag signals to communicate between ships. This system was fine in slow, close-quarter battles back in the days when warships were powered by sail. But modern navies could be strung out for miles across the ocean, almost hidden by smoke and spray. Communication foul-ups sometimes ended in disaster.

Battle of the Bight

The British fleet struck first, sending a small group of cruisers and destroyers to attack German patrols in the Heligoland Bight on August 28, 1914. They sank two torpedo boats and a destroyer, and then lured a pack of pursuing enemy cruisers into the North Sea. British warships steamed up to sink three of these cruisers, and over 700 German sailors lost their lives.

Ship to shore

On November 3, the German navy began to turn its guns on British coastal towns and Great Yarmouth was shelled. Then, on December 16, their warships attacked Scarborough, Hartlepool and Whitby. Whitby's clifftop abbey was left in ruins and 139 people were killed before the raiders slipped safely back to base. The raids outraged the country and embarrassed the Royal Navy, who saw itself as the nation's protector.

Message received

In January 1915, the British navy struck again. They had recovered three codebooks from wrecked and captured German ships and were able to use this incredible good luck to read intercepted radio signals. On the night of January 23, they decoded an enemy message describing a raid planned for the morning. When German warships crossed an area called Dogger Bank in the middle of the North Sea, the British were waiting for them – in force.

The North Sea, showing the major battle sites in the early stages of the war, British and German naval bases and the British towns that were subjected to naval bombardment.

Disaster at Dogger Bank

The Germans tried to run, but there was no escape from the long-range guns of the British ships. Four German warships were caught at Dogger Bank. One, the *Blücher*, was sunk, and another badly damaged. On the British side, HMS *Lion* had to be towed back to port, but only 15 sailors had been killed. The German fleet had lost over a thousand men. It was a clear win for the British, but the war at sea was only just beginning.

German sailors cling to the side of the warship *Blücher*, as it capsizes at Dogger Bank. Many of the men who ended up in the cold waters of the North Sea in January would have died from exposure.

33

YOUR COUNTRY NEEDS YOU

The European powers had spent the years leading up to the war expanding and modernizing their armed forces, but few were ready by the time the fighting broke out. As the death toll in the trenches mounted, thousands more soldiers were sent to the front. Some were battle-hardened professionals, but for many others this would be their first ever taste of armed conflict.

The design of this 1914 British recruitment poster of Lord Kitchener has been much imitated ever since.

The call-up

By 1914, many young men in Europe were required to serve a short period of military service, known as conscription. This meant that countries like Germany and France already had reserves of trained soldiers to call on when the war broke out. The German army was the most efficient in the world; it began the war with a force of 4,500,000 men, all fully equipped. In the first weeks of the war, the French called up reserve troops and fighters from their colonies in North Africa, raising a force of 4,017,000 men.

Friends and brothers

At the outbreak of the war, Britain didn't have conscription, and its army was far smaller than that of France. Lord Kitchener, Secretary of State for War, needed to raise a new army, so he quickly appealed for volunteers. He knew men would be more likely to sign up if they could train and fight alongside their friends, so he set up so-called 'Pals Battalions' – groups of men from the same city, village or workplace. He also relied heavily on colonial troops. Within just two months, a spectacular 761,000 men had answered the call.

Some men recruited in London underwent their training in the streets because there was a shortage of army barracks.

German reservists get ready to go to the front. Their children have borrowed their distinctive spiked helmets.

Suited and booted

Soldiers on both sides were equipped with much the same basic kit to take to the front, but their uniforms were more varied. In the late 19th century, the British army had replaced its traditional scarlet with a less conspicuous khaki brown. Germany and Russia soon opted for muted shades too. The French marched to war in red trousers, making them easy targets at the Battle of Marne. After that, they adopted a dull blue. Despite these changes, some troops held on to regional elements of dress.

These illustrations are from a German poster of Allied uniforms in 1914. Among them are a French Zouave (from Algeria) in baggy pants and a red fez, a British Highlander dressed in a kilt, a Sikh in his turban and a Russian Cossack wearing a tall astrakhan hat.

The gentle art of persuasion

Even where there was conscription, governments went to great lengths to encourage young men to volunteer. Propaganda posters, leaflets and newspaper articles were all designed to build patriotic feelings and public enthusiasm for the war. Some campaigns were targeted at women, suggesting that they should persuade, or shame, their menfolk into enlisting. Some men, known as conscientious objectors, refused to fight because it was against their moral or religious beliefs. But the pressure to sign up was immense – anyone not in uniform was branded a coward.

French

British

Russian

A DAY OF PEACE

The first winter in the trenches was brutally cold. Soldiers sat through snowstorms, frosts and flash floods. But, despite the fighting and the weather raging around them, some men were determined to celebrate Christmas Day – even if it meant stopping the war to do it.

Royal presents

People at home didn't want the troops to think they'd been forgotten. Princess Mary, the daughter of the British king, set up a Christmas fund for sailors and soldiers. People gave so generously that the fund was able to send everyone in British uniform a special gift. This became known as the Princess Mary Box. It was a brass box crammed with tobacco and chocolates.

The Kaiser sent his men pipes, cigars, and more festive presents: tiny Christmas trees. Decking a tree was an old tradition in Germany, but when British soldiers south of Ypres saw lights and strange shapes moving about in the opposite trench, they wondered if there was a night attack coming. It was only when they heard the carol singing across no-man's-land that they realized the Germans were just celebrating Christmas.

German soldiers on the Eastern Front sing carols around a Christmas tree. They are lucky to be well behind the front line. There was no truce on the Eastern Front. For most, Christmas was just like any other day of fighting in the trenches.

Meeting halfway

Slowly, and more out of curiosity than anything else, men began to peer out of the trenches. Soon, soldiers on both sides were stepping into no-man's-land. It didn't take long for the rival soldiers to strike up conversations. They suggested having a short cease-fire – a truce so they could come out and bury their dead. As the sun came up on Christmas Day, crowds of soldiers could be seen in the middle of the battlefield. Men came face-to-face with their enemies, most of them unarmed and eager to shake hands.

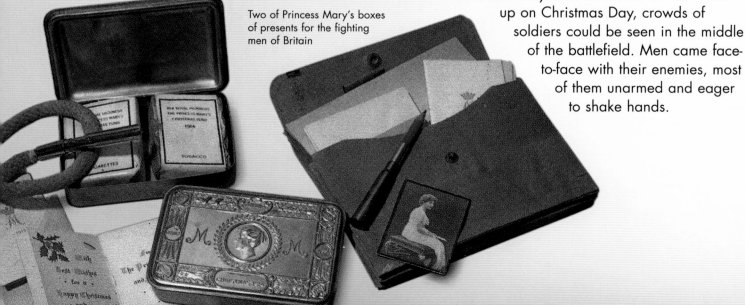

Two of Princess Mary's boxes of presents for the fighting men of Britain

A day in the open

The soldiers shared stories and traded tobacco or buttons from their uniforms. A man who had been a barber before the war offered haircuts to all comers for the price of a few cigarettes. In one section of the line, the two sides even played a friendly match of soccer.

But, as night fell, the men returned to their posts in the trenches. In most sections of the Western Front, the Christmas Truce lasted little more than a few hours. It was a pause in the battle, rather than a genuine peace. But it gave the soldiers an opportunity to get a glimpse of their enemy and to bury their dead comrades.

INTERNET LINK

For a link to a website where you can read eyewitness accounts of the Christmas Truce of 1914, go to
www.usborne-quicklinks.com

Live and let live

The generals on both sides were furious when they heard about the festive cease-fire. In the years that followed, army authorities made sure that such a truce would not happen again. The truce of 1914 involved thousands of men, mainly in the German and British trenches, but there were hundreds of smaller unofficial cease-fires at other times during the war. Soldiers would catapult messages between the trenches, agreeing not to fire their guns at certain times of the day or giving advance warning of artillery attacks. This was known as 'live and let live' and it usually only lasted a few days, until an officer realized what was happening and ordered his men to behave more aggressively.

United in adversity, British and German soldiers meet in no-man's-land on Christmas day, 1914. For a few short hours they exchanged cigarettes, food, even hats, and talked together.

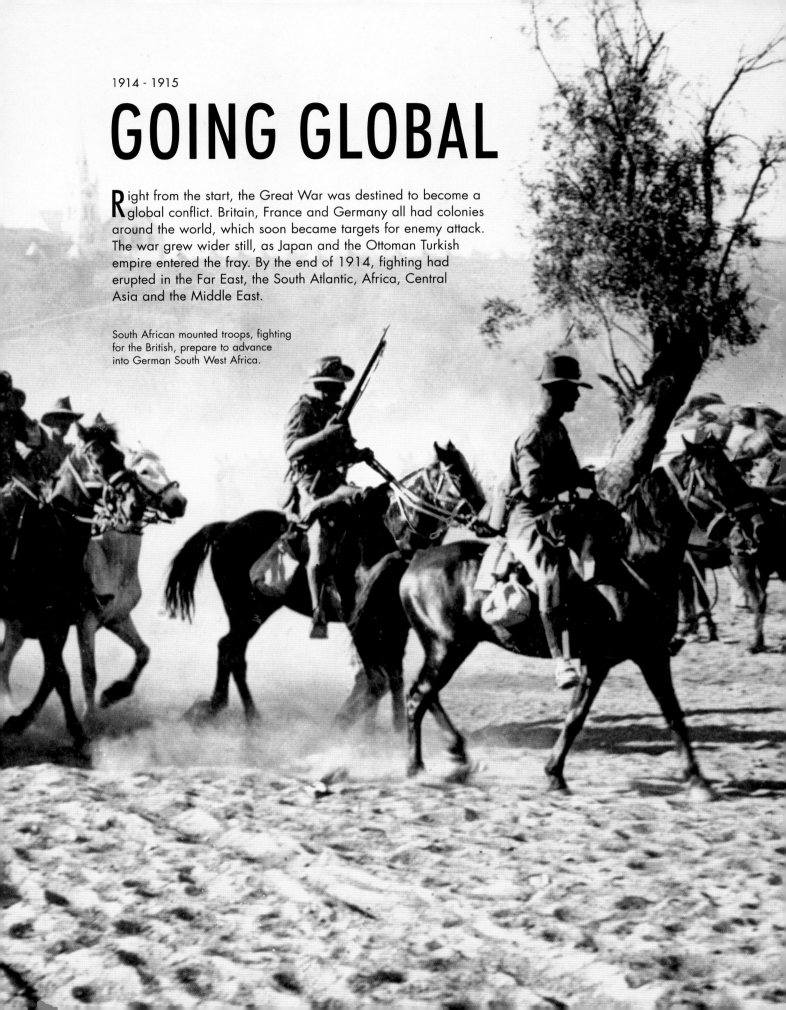

1914 - 1915

GOING GLOBAL

Right from the start, the Great War was destined to become a global conflict. Britain, France and Germany all had colonies around the world, which soon became targets for enemy attack. The war grew wider still, as Japan and the Ottoman Turkish empire entered the fray. By the end of 1914, fighting had erupted in the Far East, the South Atlantic, Africa, Central Asia and the Middle East.

South African mounted troops, fighting for the British, prepare to advance into German South West Africa.

CRUISER WARFARE

While fighting on the Western Front became concentrated on a small area on either side of the trenches, the war at sea ranged far and wide. The German navy only had a small fleet of cruisers outside the North Sea, but its commanders were talented and determined. They hoped an aggressive campaign against the Allies' ports, merchant ships and military vessels would weaken their economies and Britain's dominance of global waters.

Oriental offensive

The British decided to attack before the Germans had a chance to strike. Their first target was Germany's largest naval base outside Europe, the port of Tsingtao, on the Chinese coast. Here, the German fleet in the Far East, under Admiral Maximilian Graf von Spee, consisted of two large battle cruisers and three smaller ones. The British had a squadron of similar size in Hong Kong, but their ships were older and slower.

In 1902, the British had signed an alliance with Japan, to limit German expansion in the Pacific. Now they called on Japan to put the treaty into action. Seeing the war as a chance to gain land for their empire, the Japanese declared war on Germany on August 23, 1914. The Germans had a number of poorly defended island colonies in the Pacific. These were soon occupied by troops from Australia, New Zealand and Japan.

This lithograph shows Japanese soldiers taking part in a night time attack on the German naval base at Tsingtao.

Port in a storm

Tsingtao was heavily fortified and took longer to capture. At the start of September, Japanese ships began bombing the port, and sent 50,000 troops, joined by a small Anglo-Indian force, to attack by land. The defiant German force of just 3,000 marines held out for over two months until they were forced to surrender. Their defeat marked the end of Germany's empire in the Pacific.

Terror at sea

As soon as he heard that Japan was joining the Allies, Spee's fleet fled the Pacific for South America. Meanwhile, one of his captains, Karl von Müller, set off for India, which was part of the British empire. When he shelled Madras, one of India's key trading ports, he sent the financial markets in London into chaos. Müller went on to capture 23 merchant ships, then sank a Russian cruiser and a French destroyer. After two months prowling the oceans, his ship was finally sunk by an Australian ship that was escorting a convoy of troops from Australia and New Zealand to fight in Europe.

The surviving sailors of one of Spee's ships are picked up by British dreadnought HMS *Inflexible* after the Battle of the Falklands.

INTERNET LINK

For a link to a website with photographs of warships and maps showing the biggest naval battles of the First World War, go to www.usborne-quicklinks.com

Clash at Coronel

In late October, the Royal Navy intercepted a German radio message, which revealed that Admiral von Spee was on course for the coast of Chile. The nearest British fleet was on patrol off the southern tip of South America. Its commander, Vice-Admiral Sir Christopher Cradock, was ordered to deal with Spee.

The two fleets clashed near the Chilean port of Coronel, on November 1. The British force was outnumbered and outgunned by the Germans. As the sun went down, the British ships were silhouetted on the horizon, making them easy targets. Cradock's flagship, HMS *Good Hope*, and HMS *Monmouth* were sunk, and 1,570 sailors were killed. It was the first time Britain had been defeated at sea for over a century, and there was a public outcry. Desperate to save face, the British sent out two of their newest, most powerful dreadnoughts, *Invincible* and *Inflexible*, with the express purpose of finding Admiral von Spee's fleet and destroying it.

Fighting for the Falklands

The German High Command ordered Graf von Spee to return home. But with the British navy hot on his heels, he knew he would never make it. Instead he resolved to do, "as much mischief as I can, until my ammunition runs out, or until a foe far superior in power succeeds in catching me."

The Royal Navy had a radio communications station in the Falklands. Thinking it was undefended, Spee decided to attack. But this was exactly where *Invincible* and *Inflexible* were taking on fuel. The British counterattacked. Outgunned and low on ammunition, four German cruisers, including Spee's, were sunk. He went down with his ship, and his two sons were among the 2,200 German sailors who drowned. Germany's cruiser war was over.

AFRICAN ACTION

In 1914, most of Africa was divided into European colonies, so it wasn't long before the war spread there too. Over two million Africans served in the conflict, making great sacrifices for purely European causes.

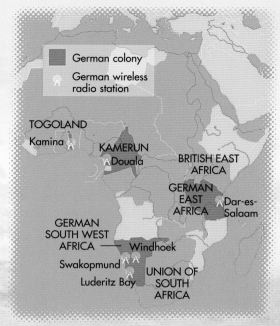

This map shows Germany's African colonies, shaded in red, and their six wireless radio stations.

Coastal targets

From the outset, the Allies' first aim was to capture Germany's African ports and wireless radio stations, to prevent supplies, troops or military orders from getting through. They quickly gained control of Togoland and the coast of Kamerun, but it was an easy start to what soon became a difficult, drawn-out campaign.

Southern rebels

As part of the British empire, the Union of South Africa joined the Allies, but not without a struggle. The country was divided between British and Dutch settlers (Boers) who had fought a bitter war in 1899-1902, ending in a British victory. The wounds of that defeat were still raw in the memories of many South African Boers. At the start of the war, the South African president, Louis Botha, sent troops to invade German South West Africa. Many Boers in the army refused to take part, and asked the Germans to help them retake South Africa. But the Germans couldn't spare any troops, as they were already vastly outnumbered defending their colony. Botha's war minister, General Jan Smuts, soon put down the Boer rebellion. By July 1915, he had forced Germany to surrender South West Africa.

Bees in the bush

In German East Africa, the British floundered when they came up against the talents of the charismatic German commander, Colonel Paul von Lettow-Vorbeck. Around 8,000 troops were shipped from India to try to seize the colony. In November 1914, they landed near Tanga, a German port north of Dar-es-Salaam. On the march through dense jungle to Tanga, the Indians were ambushed by von Lettow-Vorbeck's troops. His men were outnumbered, eight to one, but the Indians had no training in bush warfare and were easily overcome. Things got ugly when the fighting roused swarms of angry bees, forcing both sides to flee. Later, it became known as the Battle of the Bees.

British African troops from the Gold Coast wade across a river during the campaign in German East Africa.

Undefeated commander

Colonel von Lettow-Vorbeck became something of a legend among friends and enemies alike. After the Battle of the Bees, he invited the British commanders to his lodgings to compare notes over a bottle of brandy. He also arranged for the wounded Indian soldiers to be treated by his medics.

Without radio or naval links to Germany, von Lettow-Vorbeck's men became self-sufficient, growing their own food and raiding enemy stores for guns and ammunition. For the rest of the war, they used guerrilla tactics to play cat-and-mouse with the Allies. They lured them ever deeper into East Africa, but avoided direct combat as much as possible. He was the only military commander to last the entire war without suffering a single defeat.

Colonel von Lettow-Vorbeck (second from the right) enjoys a drink with friends at his lodgings in German East Africa.

The burden of war

Many Africans who volunteered for the army were taken on to work as porters. Africa had few roads or train lines, so equipment, supplies and even officers were all hauled across the continent on men's backs. Porters were given smaller rations than soldiers, and thousands died of malnutrition, exhaustion and disease. Hundreds of thousands of African civilians are estimated to have starved during the war, when harvests failed because the farmers had been marched off to war.

43

TURKEY ENTERS THE WAR

Just days before the outbreak of war, the Turkish government had signed an alliance with Germany, against Russia. For the first two months, the Turks remained neutral. Then, on October 29, their fleet joined two German warships in an attack on the Russian fleet in the Black Sea. From this point on, Turkey was officially in the war on the side of the Central Powers.

The 'sick man' and the Young Turks

In 1914, the Ottoman Turkish empire, ruled by Sultan Mehmed V, was a shadow of its former glory. It was nicknamed the 'sick man of Europe' because it had lost control of many of its former territories and its government was in debt. The Sultan's power was on the wane too. Since 1908, Turkey had effectively been run by a political party known as the Young Turks. Led by a politician named Enver Pasha, they had modernized the Turkish government and its armed forces. They hoped an alliance with Germany would enable them to win back their lost empire too.

Enver Pasha (on the right), leader of the Young Turks, meets his new ally, Kaiser Wilhelm.

INTERNET LINK

For a link to a website with loads of snapshots of everyday life in the Turkish capital, Constantinople, at the outbreak of the war, go to
www.usborne-quicklinks.com

Oilfield empires

Britain and Turkey both controlled territory around the Persian Gulf. Southern Persia (present-day Iran) had become especially valuable to the British since they had discovered oil there in 1909, and set up the Anglo-Persian Oil Company. It was the Royal Navy's main fuel supplier, and they couldn't afford to risk losing it. Now that the Turks had entered the war, British oil supplies in the Middle East were under threat.

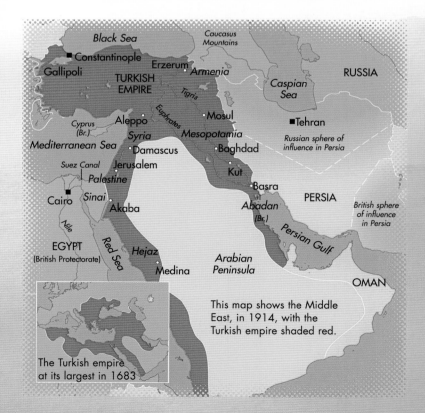

This map shows the Middle East, in 1914, with the Turkish empire shaded red.

The Turkish empire at its largest in 1683

Staff of the Anglo-Persian Oil Company construct one of the region's first oil derricks, in 1909.

Target Basra

The British had already sent Indian troops to guard the oil refinery on the British-held island of Abadan in the Persian Gulf, and the pipeline connecting it to the Persian oilfields. When Turkey declared war, the British government in India decided to invade Turkish Mesopotamia (now Iraq). If they could capture Basra and the surrounding area, they would be able to secure their oil supplies.

Indian troops advanced overland from Abadan into Mesopotamia. At the same time, British naval units sailed up the Euphrates to join them. The combined forces met only weak resistance from the Turks. Within a month, they had occupied Basra.

Indian machine gunners defend the Suez canal against attack from Turkish troops.

Suez

Humiliated by their defeat in Mesopotamia, the Turks were determined to strike back at the Allies. Officially, Egypt was still part of the Ottoman Turkish empire, but it had been under British control since the 1880s. Now the Turks wanted it back. On German advice, Enver Pasha decided to start by attacking the Suez Canal, which the British used to convoy essential supplies and troops from India and Australasia to Europe.

The Turkish army of 25,000 troops set out from Damascus, across the parched sands of the Sinai Desert. Tough soldiers, they were trained to march vast distances in extreme conditions, on very little food. They made the journey without losing a single man. But the Allies were waiting for them. Nine British warships were guarding the canal, and 30,000 British and Indian troops counterattacked with machine-gun fire from the opposite bank. The Turks suffered 1,200 casualties and retreated into the desert.

JIHAD AND GENOCIDE

Enver Pasha's determination to take back Turkey's old empire did not end with Egypt. While his soldiers were marching across the Sinai Desert, he sent more troops north, to the Caucasus Mountains. The region was home to people of many cultures and religions, whose territory had been fought over by Russia and Turkey throughout the last 200 years. Now this wild, mountainous land was to provide the backdrop for one of the biggest human tragedies of the war.

A holy war?

Islam was the official religion of the Ottoman Turkish empire. Two weeks after entering the war, the Sultan declared an Islamic holy war, or *jihad*, against the Allies. In fact, it had been the Kaiser's idea. He hoped that a jihad would inspire Muslims in India and Egypt to rise against the British empire, and knock them out of the war.

But the Sultan's call to holy war was largely ignored, even in Turkey. The Young Turks were driven more by political and territorial aims, than by religion. However, in the Caucasus region, Enver exploited local religious tensions, with horrific consequences.

Battling the elements

In December, 1914, Turkish troops invaded the Caucasus, aiming to ambush the Russians at Sarikamish. Since the Russian defeats at Tannenberg and the Masurian Lakes, much of the Russian army had been transferred to the Eastern Front in Poland, leaving only 60,000 men behind to face the Turks. When they heard that a Turkish army of nearly double that number was advancing rapidly, the Russians began to retreat.

Then the weather turned bad. Temperatures plummeted and blizzards left the Turks stranded. Many of them did not have proper coats, and some were even without boots. On December 29, the Russians launched a counterattack. This resulted in a catastrophic defeat for the Turks, whose ice-clogged artillery failed to fire. They lost over 75,000 men. As many as 30,000 of them are said to have frozen to death before they even met their enemy.

Constantinople – the political and religious heart of the Turkish empire

Exhaustion written on their weary faces, these Armenian people have been forced to trek from their homeland to Aleppo, in Syria.

Unholy massacre

The persecution did not end there. In June 1915, the Turkish government ordered the deportation of all Armenians to Aleppo, in Syria. Fired up with anti-Armenian and anti-Christian feeling, the Turkish army drove them out of their homes, seizing their possessions and raping the women. They were herded across the Syrian Desert, forced to make the 800km (500 miles) journey on foot, without shelter and with little food. Thousands died of exposure, starvation and disease on the way. Many who survived the journey suffered the same fate in squalid prison camps in Aleppo. Altogether, at least 800,000 Armenians died in what is now considered a brutal act of genocide.

Scapegoats

After the disaster, Enver Pasha looked around for someone to blame and he chose the Armenians. They were a Christian minority, living on both sides of the disputed territory. During the conflict, some Armenian soldiers serving in the Turkish army had gone over to the Russian side, hoping to drive out the Turks and declare Armenian independence. In the spring of 1915, all Armenians in the Turkish army were rounded up and sent to work camps, where most of them died.

A small number of the many thousands of Armenian children driven from their homes by the Turks

INTERNET LINK

For a link to a website where you can see photos of Armenian refugees taken by a German officer based in the Ottoman empire during the war, go to www.usborne-quicklinks.com

THE EASTERN FRONT

The Eastern Front was the longest battle zone of the war, stretching from the Baltic coast right down to the Black Sea. Fighting here were the three empires of Germany, Austria-Hungary and Russia. Battles took place on an epic scale, with grand sweeping offensives, covering hundreds of miles. This put a great strain on the countries involved, and none of them was able to achieve a clear victory.

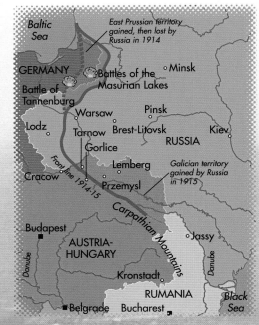

The Eastern Front during the early stages of the war. The green line shows the front line where most of the fighting took place.

An ailing empire

The Turkish empire was described as a sick man, but Austria-Hungary was in no fit state to fight a war either. Its vast, sprawling empire, was made up of people of many ethnic groups, including Hungarians, Czechs, Germans, Slavs and Serbs, many of them calling for independence. This meant that the empire was becoming more and more difficult to hold together. Parts of its army could not be trusted to stay loyal in the heat of battle.

Easy target?

As soon as Germany declared war, the Tsar's troops began preparing to invade Austria-Hungary's north eastern province of Galicia. The Russians knew that the Austro-Hungarians would be weak without the help of their allies, so they planned a lightning attack on the Austro-Hungarian frontier, while the Germans were still tied up in France.

Serbian onslaught

The Austro-Hungarians were not only concerned with Russia. Their first priority was to punish Serbia for the murder of Archduke Franz Ferdinand. Their military chief, Franz Conrad, believed the Russians would take 30 days to mobilize their troops. This would give them time to defeat Serbia – or so he thought.

Conrad placed some troops in Galicia, but sent the majority of his army into Serbia. They were told to expect resistance from both soldiers and civilians, and to show no mercy. In the opening days of the war, up to 4,000 Serbian civilians were killed. But their army fought back fiercely. By the end of December 1914, the Serbs had driven the Austro-Hungarians out of their country.

Fortress under fire

While most of the Austro-Hungarian army was fighting in Serbia, the Russians invaded Galicia. They won a crucial victory at Lemberg (now Lvov) in 1914, forcing the Austrians to retreat to the Carpathian Mountains. There, in September, the Russians besieged Przemysl, the fortress town where Conrad had his headquarters. In the spring of 1915, the 120,000 Austrian troops under siege surrendered. The Austrians continued to fight back, but they badly needed help from Germany.

INTERNET LINK

For a link to a website with maps, photographs and film footage of the war on the Eastern Front, go to
www.usborne-quicklinks.com

German troops march into the vast open fields of Galicia, which is now part of Poland.

A great retreat

The Germans could not allow Galicia to fall into Russian hands, as this might leave industrial areas in the east of Germany vulnerable to attack. So in spring 1915, their troops entered the region. Taken by surprise and low on ammunition, the Russian forces soon collapsed. In what became known as the Great Retreat, the Russians lost hundreds of thousands of men, and the Germans seized control of most of present-day Poland, Lithuania, Belarus, and later, the Ukraine.

After this drastic defeat, Tsar Nicholas sacked his uncle Grand Duke Nicholas, who had been in command of the Russian forces. He decided to do the job himself. This meant that the Tsar would be directly to blame for any military failures or unpopular strategies. It was an ill-judged decision that would later play a part in his downfall.

Communities in peril

Along the Eastern Front, especially in Galicia, the war brought much suffering to the population, which was a fragile patchwork of different racial and religious communities. No minority group was safe: Serbs, Slavs and Jews all suffered persecution at the hands of ransacking armies, occupying powers and old rivals.

From 1915, major cities on both sides were subjected to air attacks. This air raid warden, high above Paris, is sounding a siren to warn people to take shelter before an imminent attack.

1915

DEADLOCK

As the war dragged into a second year, soldiers and civilians had to adjust to the demands of a long-term conflict. Neither side could see a way to break the stalemate on the Western Front. Instead, commanders turned their attentions to other fronts, seeking new allies and using an array of deadly modern weapons, and desperate tactics to try to weaken their opponents.

A DEADLY MIST

After six months of savage fighting on the Western Front, Ypres was still in Allied hands. Allied soldiers occupied a bulge of land around the town which jutted deep into enemy lines. Here, German commanders used a terrifying new weapon to try to break the stalemate.

INTERNET LINK

For links to websites where you can watch an animated slideshow about gas attacks and see photographs of soldiers wearing different types of gas mask, go to www.usborne-quicklinks.com

A ghostly cloud

The bulge was known as the Ypres salient. It was heavily defended with trenches and artillery, and many believed the Germans would never break through. But, at dusk on April 22, 1915, French sentries north of Ypres noticed a ghostly, yellow-green cloud drifting across no-man's-land. They watched in horror as the cloud inched closer and their throats and eyes began to burn in pain. The Germans had opened 6,000 canisters of deadly chlorine gas. Heavier than air, the gas streamed into the Allied trenches, poisoning every hiding place. The French troops ran for cover, screaming and dying as they staggered away.

Drowning men

By releasing this gas, which they first used on the Eastern Front in January that year, the Germans had broken an international agreement. But they weren't the first to use chemical weapons in the war. French gunners had fired tear gas shells at the enemy the previous year. Tear gas caused coughing and sore eyes, but it didn't kill. Chlorine gas burned into a soldier's lungs and throat. The victims eventually 'drowned' on their own body fluids bubbling up from their damaged lungs. It was an agonizing way to die.

Until they developed more effective protection against gas, many soldiers had to improvise. These Scottish troops are using goggles and cotton masks.

A line of British soldiers, blinded in a gas attack, awaits medical attention. Each man clutches the shoulder of the man in front for support.

Forewarnings

German soldiers taken prisoner by the Allies had revealed the German plan to use gas, but these warnings were ignored. Some British generals thought gas couldn't be used as part of an organized attack, as it relied too much on the direction of the wind. But the new weapon had a devastating effect at Ypres. German infantry stormed through the 6km (4 miles) gap left in the line by the retreating French soldiers. By nightfall the Germans were only 3km (2 miles) from Ypres and had started digging in.

Fighting back

The German raiders wore cloth masks over their faces, to protect their eyes and filter gas out of the air they breathed. But the Allies quickly discovered how to make simple gas masks too. Chlorine dissolves in water, so if a soldier breathed though a wet cloth he was safe. Canadian and British troops wore rag masks over their faces and fought hard to defend their trenches.

This German soldier wears a more sophisticated gas mask than the ones on the opposite page. His horses have been provided with their own gas masks too.

The experiment fails

The Second Battle of Ypres, as it became known, raged on until the end of May. The Germans gained some ground, but they hadn't been prepared for the success of their attack. If they had had enough men they might have captured the whole salient and cracked the Western Front. But they ran out of troops and supplies before they could seize Ypres. The gas attack shocked the world, but Allied forces quickly began to use their own chemical weapons too. More effective gas masks were invented and soldiers gradually learned how to deal with this new horror. Gas just became one more hazard in a brutal and unrelenting war.

SETTLING IN

By the summer of 1915, there were four million soldiers eating, sleeping and dying in the trenches. Despite all its hardships, the men adapted quickly to their new life below the surface. The bulk of their time was spent preparing for attacks, taking turns at sentry duty – and digging. But they still tried to find a few minutes in the day when they could rest, joke and try to recreate some of the lost comforts of home.

In this cartoon from a postcard, French soldiers have set up a decoy for the enemy to shoot at while they play cards.

A nervous dawn

Armies work to timetables and routines, and trench duty was no exception. The men were awake before first light, preparing for *Stand-to*, the order to be ready with loaded weapons. Poor visibility at dawn and dusk made it hard to spot attacks, so soldiers climbed onto the firestep, a platform cut into the trench wall, to peer into no-man's-land. Some men called this the morning hate, when both sides exchanged a few warning shots and shouts. Others remarked on the beauty of the morning skies and the eerie quiet of no-man's-land.

A waiting game

In the daylight hours, it was too dangerous to move around in the open, so men cleaned their weapons, did their chores and tried to rest. If a soldier was a talented marksman, he might be chosen as a sniper, picking off enemy soldiers by aiming his rifle through a steel shutter in the parapet. But even a sniper's life was precarious – bullets could puncture steel plate, and every inch of the trenches was watched with periscopes and mirrors.

Forced to spend months away from home, soldiers found all kinds of ways to relieve the boredom and to keep morale up. These Canadian troops and their pantomime horse are rehearsing for a show.

Night raiding

Under the cover of darkness, soldiers slipped into no-man's-land to do things that were impossible in daylight, such as laying and repairing barbed wire. They kept total silence, muffling any tools with cloths and using hand signals to communicate. Units with special combat training went out on raids, to try to capture a prisoner who could tell them about the enemy's plans. Squads sent into no-man's-land, to recover their dead and wounded, could suddenly be lit up by flares and shot at by enemy machine gunners.

Creature comforts

In the reserve trenches, soldiers had more spare time. They held shooting contests, scavenged for weapons in old sections of the battlefield and wrote letters home. By cutting into the trench walls, they created small rooms called dugouts, furnished with beds, tables and chairs, and even electric lights and gramophone records. Postal services brought newspapers and food packages, as well as letters from home and, for the better-off soldiers, brandy and cigars. Even with all these distractions, many soldiers still found time to write and print their own unofficial front-line magazines, where they shared their experiences and poked fun at army life.

These French officers may be in a trench near the front line, but they are dining in style and even have a vase of flowers on the table.

INTERNET LINK

For a link to a website where you can find out more about life in the trenches, go to www.usborne-quicklinks.com

Fine dining

Officers and men served together in the trench, but behind the lines they went their separate ways. Privates (low-ranking soldiers) and junior officers enjoyed hot food and a bottle of wine in the rest areas, while senior officers could take rides on their horses or go off on shooting parties. Some generals lived almost like kings, sleeping in grand country houses and controlling their armies from way behind the lines. The French commander, General Joffre, even insisted on taking a two-hour lunch every afternoon. It's not surprising that some soldiers were suspicious of their commanders and the way they were directing the war.

A DANGEROUS VOYAGE

By May 1915, Germany's submarine blockade around Britain was causing a serious shortage of food and raw materials. U-boat crews had clear orders: sink anything that might be carrying troops or supplies to the enemy. But some captains of non-military ships thought they were safe from attack, and calmly set sail into dangerous waters.

The *Lusitania* leaves New York for the last time. Just a week later, the liner had been sunk.

An ocean greyhound

The British ocean liner *Lusitania* was one of the world's fastest and most elegant passenger ships. Her best cabins offered every luxury and she could carry almost 2,000 passengers and crew on her six-day Atlantic crossing.

On May 1, 1915, the ship left New York, bound for Liverpool. A few passengers were alarmed by announcements they'd read in the morning newspapers, paid for by the German Embassy, warning them not to sail into the submarine 'war zone' around Britain. But the ship's captain, William Turner, saw no cause for concern. He didn't believe the Germans would dare to attack an ocean liner as large and as famous as the *Lusitania*. And even with six of its 25 boilers shut down because of wartime coal shortages, he thought his ship could easily outpace a prowling U-boat.

Predator and prey

Five days into the voyage, Turner received a telegram from Royal Navy headquarters. U-boat *U-20* had just sunk two merchant ships, south of Ireland. On May 7, the *Lusitania* arrived in these same waters, lost in a thick fog. When the fog cleared, Turner turned ashore to fix his position by sighting a landmark. Little did he know, he was being watched through a U-boat periscope.

A German U-Boat from the First World War. These sinister weapons were so effective, they nearly starved Britain out of the war.

Torpedo away

Inside submarine *U-20*, Kapitan-leutnant Walther Schwieger couldn't believe his luck. He'd already spotted a 'forest of masts' on the horizon and realized a huge British ship was approaching. But the target was too far away and moving too quickly. Suddenly, the ship altered course and headed straight for the U-boat. Not hesitating for a second, Schwieger sent a torpedo hissing through the choppy sea.

Shock waves

The torpedo ripped into the liner's front cargo hold and exploded. Seconds later, another explosion, more powerful than the first, tore through the ship. The *Lusitania* rolled sideways, throwing passengers off their feet and sending lifeboats crashing into the waves. It took only 18 minutes for the mighty liner to sink to the bottom, with the loss of 1,198 lives.

Schwieger always said he was amazed that a single torpedo had destroyed the ship. He thought there would be time for the passengers to climb into lifeboats and escape before the liner sank. But his attack without warning sparked international fury and anti-German riots across Britain and the US. Most damaging of all, it led some leading American politicians to accuse the Germans of piracy, and to call for the United States to join the war.

Secret cargo

With over 120 American citizens drowned, US President Woodrow Wilson was forced to act. He sent the German government a series of strongly-worded protest notes, demanding an immediate end to submarine warfare. In response, the Germans tried to justify the sinking by accusing the British of transporting munitions inside passenger ships. The *Lusitania* had indeed been loaded with crates of bullets and shell parts, but there was no proof that these had caused the massive second explosion – as the Germans claimed. A recent theory suggests it might have been caused by an exploding boiler.

While diplomats argued, public opinion in America began to harden against Germany. All around the United States, people began to ask themselves how much longer they could avoid being drawn in to this destructive global war.

> ### INTERNET LINK
> For a link to a website with photographs and paintings of the *Lusitania*, and to read the stories of some of the victims and survivors of the sinking, go to **www.usborne-quicklinks.com**

The destruction of the *Lusitania* caused outrage around the world. This is the cover of a French book, which describes the sinking of the liner as a crime.

OUT OF THIN AIR

While fighting on land and sea raged on, generals looked skyward for fresh ways to attack the enemy. They ordered aircraft designers to make bigger and more powerful planes to carry bombs. And the Germans sent a formidable new invention lumbering across the skies. It was called the zeppelin.

Count Ferdinand von Zeppelin, who spent his entire fortune developing his airships

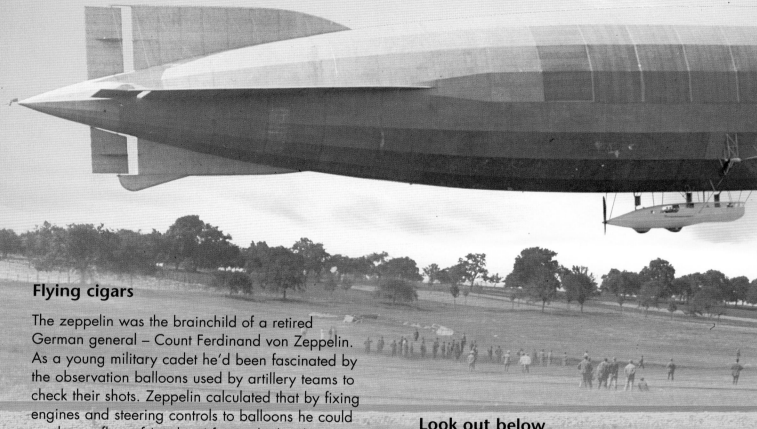

Flying cigars

The zeppelin was the brainchild of a retired German general – Count Ferdinand von Zeppelin. As a young military cadet he'd been fascinated by the observation balloons used by artillery teams to check their shots. Zeppelin calculated that by fixing engines and steering controls to balloons he could produce a fleet of 'airships' fit to rule the skies.

In the early 1900s, dozens of inventors were working on airship designs, but Zeppelin's was one of the best. His was tube-shaped and as long as a battleship. Instead of relying on a single balloon to lift it off the ground, it boasted over a dozen huge sacks of hydrogen gas inside a skeleton of metal hoops, covered in tough fabric. Three propellers moved it through the air and it was powerful enough to carry passengers – and high explosive bombs.

Look out below

The German navy began using zeppelins for reconnaissance patrols above the North Sea. Then, during the first months of the war, they were used to bomb the Belgian forts of Liège and Antwerp. At first, some German politicians had their doubts about using zeppelins as bombers because they were very expensive to build. But, in January 1915, the Kaiser gave the order for zeppelins to be sent to attack British towns.

Into thin air

On January 13, 1915, a pair of zeppelins bombed the east coast of England, killing four people. This was the first of over fifty air raids carried out over Britain that year. There were zeppelin raids on Paris too. This was partly in response to French air raids on German cities. Blackouts were enforced in many places, making it difficult for the zeppelin pilots to spot their targets. The menacing bulk and droning growl of the airship soon earned it a fearsome reputation, inspiring dread among the civilians cowering in the darkness below.

Taking the flak

Zeppelins cruised at very high altitudes, usually beyond the range of artillery gunners on the ground. But if an airship was hit, the shell passed straight through it. Leaking gas slowly, the zeppelin had plenty of time to limp home for repairs. Some pilots were so desperate to hit back at the airships, they flew to dangerous heights to attack them from above, with light bombs or grenades. But by early 1916, British fighter planes were armed with a new kind of 'incendiary' bullet that set fire to the gas in the airships, sending them up in flames.

Zeppelin *LZ77* takes off in Germany. It raided eastern England in 1915 and was shot down in France the following year.

INTERNET LINK

For a link to a website with facts, figures, photographs and diagrams of zeppelins or to find out what life was like during the air raids, go to www.usborne-quicklinks.com

---

British officials inspect the skeletal remains of zeppelin *L33*, which was shot down in September, 1916.

Angry giants

Next, Zeppelin built a new airship that could fly higher than the fighters, but the German military was already developing a new weapon – the Gotha bomber. In June 1917, a group of these huge planes swarmed over London, pounding the city and killing 162 people. Gothas were fast and well armed, but British designers quickly produced planes to fight back with even greater firepower. The zeppelins and heavy bombers were menacing symbols of the air war, but the air raids did little to affect the eventual outcome of the war.

59

THE HOME FRONT

With civilians living under the threat of
bombardment and dealing with shortages
caused by naval blockades, the First World War
had a greater impact on people's everyday lives
than any previous conflict. While the men were
away fighting, it was up to the people left behind
to keep the 'home front' running smoothly.

Women into work

Many women had worked before the war, but the
jobs available to them then were limited, and most
were expected to stay at home to look after the
family. In the early part of the war, women were
mainly involved in charity work or making
bandages, socks and balaclavas to send to the
trenches. But as more and more men left for the
front, women had to take their places.

The war created new jobs too, keeping the armed
forces supplied with munitions, food and
equipment. Governments used propaganda posters
to persuade women of all ages and classes that
it was their duty to work for the war. Millions
answered the call. They operated telephone
exchanges, drove buses, worked in agriculture and
even took on dangerous and heavy jobs such as
mining, shipbuilding and packing explosive shells.

The Germans came up with clever ways to get around
shortages on the home front. This poster asks people to
save their fruit stones and take them to government
collection points so the nut oil can be turned into fuel.

The politics of war

In most countries, rival political groups agreed to
put aside their differences to focus on winning the
war. Governments were reorganized so members
of different parties could work together in what is
called a coalition government. They brought in
tough measures to control industrial production
and wages, and to prevent workers from striking.

Before the war, most women weren't allowed to
take part in elections. In Britain, women known
as Suffragettes had spent decades fighting for the
right to vote. Their leader, Emmeline Pankhurst,
suspended the 'Votes for Women' campaign to
encourage women to support the war. Eventually
this would further their cause. In the General
Election of December 1918, British women over
30 were granted the vote for the first time, partly
in recognition of their wartime efforts.

> ### INTERNET LINK
> For links to websites where you can find
> out more about life on the Home Front
> and see more propaganda posters, go
> to **www.usborne-quicklinks.com**

These Welsh women are hauling clay to a factory where it will be
made into bricks.

Even with women replacing male farm workers, most countries experienced food shortages at some point. Everywhere, posters and leaflets advised people not to be wasteful. Everyone had to get used to waiting in line for food when it became available. Rationing was introduced in Germany, and later, in Britain too. But, as goods became scarce, prices rose faster than people's wages and many struggled to afford even the basics. Britain and France got over the problem by fixing prices, but in Germany, Austria-Hungary and Russia, the shortages were much worse and thousands of civilians suffered terrible poverty and malnutrition.

While everyone on the Home Front tried to keep business running as usual, they dreaded hearing the news of the death of a loved one. People anxiously scoured daily casualty lists, published in the newspapers, to find out whether anyone they knew was dead, missing or wounded. Official notices that men had been killed in action opened with the words, "It is my painful duty to inform you…" and were usually sent to the soldiers' relatives by telegram. For the millions of women and children who read these harrowing words, normal family life would never be the same.

Hard times and good times

Many people who lived in the combat zones were forced to flee their war-ravaged homes. Some were able to stay with relatives, but many had to escape their countries and take shelter in refugee camps. They were clothed, fed and given medical care by local charity workers, but their lodgings were often very basic.

Even for those who didn't face such traumatic upheaval, it was important to keep up morale. Paris was not far from the Western Front, so many soldiers visited the city on leave. To entertain the troops, many cafés, cabaret bars, cinemas and galleries stayed open throughout the war.

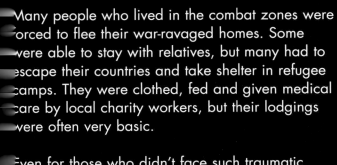

This munitions factory worker – or 'munitionette' as they were called – is checking and packing shells to send to the front.

GALLIPOLI

For the British and imperial forces, Gallipoli was the most disastrous campaign of 1915. Their plan had been to capture the Dardanelles Straits and the Gallipoli peninsula from Turkey, then to storm Constantinople. But the operation was doomed from the start, by poor leadership and bad planning. The men who served in Gallipoli endured appalling conditions as they fought a hopeless battle through nine bitter months.

This German cartoon shows Turkey as a man sweeping the Allies from his shore.

Churchill's plan

When the Turks entered the war, they blocked the Dardanelles Straits to all enemy ships. This cut off the Russians from their allies and trapped most of their fleet in the Black Sea. Already fully stretched by the war in Galicia and the Caucasus, they asked Britain for help.

Winston Churchill, the future British prime minister, was the First Lord of the Admiralty, in charge of the Royal Navy. He was convinced that if they could push through the Dardanelles, Allied naval forces would be able to capture Constantinople, forcing the Turks to surrender.

Deadly straits

Putting Churchill's plan into action wasn't going to be easy. The Dardanelles were laid with mines, and the cliffs overlooking the water were lined with guns and forts. In February 1915, the Allies bombarded the forts at the mouth of the straits, ready to steam in. On March 18, an Anglo-French armada of 16 battleships thrust into the narrow straits. A French ship and two British ones struck undetected mines and sank, and three more ships were badly damaged. The fleet was withdrawn and minesweepers were sent in to clear the way. But heavy shelling from the shore made this impossible. So, the British decided to send land forces to try to capture the Gallipoli Peninsula, instead.

Blood on the beaches

On April 25, 35,000 Allied troops went ashore at Cape Helles, and 17,000 men from the Australian and New Zealand Army Corps (Anzacs) landed on the west coast. Neither landing went to plan. The Anzacs landed in the wrong place: a narrow beach, hemmed in by steep hills (later known as Anzac Cove). Before they could clamber out of the cove, the Turks opened fire on them from trenches in the high ridges above. Further south, at Cape Helles, soldiers were shot down before they even reached the shore. The sea is said to have turned red with their blood.

The Allies had no choice but to push forward. But they didn't get far. The Turks, fighting to save their country, put up a strong resistance. Soon, both sides were digging in for trench warfare. In August, the Allies sent in reinforcements, landing at Suvla Bay, but they still failed to break the deadlock.

Flies, thirst and frostbite

It wasn't just enemy soldiers the men in Gallipoli were fighting. As spring turned to summer, the intense heat became almost unbearable, and drinking water grew scarce. The corpses rotting in no-man's-land, now buzzing with flies, began to reek. The flies contaminated the soldiers' food, infected their wounds and spread diseases. Dysentery raged through the trenches. Then the harsh winter set in. The numbers of sick soldiers soared, with men suffering from both frostbite and pneumonia.

INTERNET LINK

For a link to a website with eyewitness accounts and images of events at Gallipoli, go to www.usborne-quicklinks.com

Bayonets at the ready, Anzac troops scramble uphill to attack the Turkish front line.

The battlegrounds of Gallipoli. Shown here are the Allied landing zones and the deadly Dardanelles Straits.

Map labels

- Turkish minefield
- Turkish army position
- Allied landing point

Turkish 7th Division

Gallipoli

Gallipoli Peninsula

Suvla Bay

Turkish 19th Division

2nd British landing

Dardanelles Straits

Anzac Cove

Anzac landing

TURKISH EMPIRE

Turkish 9th Division

Cape Helles

1st British landing

BULGARIA
Black Sea
Constantinople
Gallipoli Peninsula
GREECE
TURKISH EMPIRE
Aegean Sea

Costly victory

In November, the Allies decided to withdraw their troops, and by January 9, 1916, the last of them had left. They had lost nearly 50,000 men, most from disease, and they had absolutely nothing to show for it. Churchill had already resigned as a result of the fiasco, and the British government was replaced by a new coalition, soon to be led by a new prime minister, David Lloyd George. The people of Constantinople celebrated their proud victory. But it had come at a terrible price: more than 87,000 Turks died defending Gallipoli and their remaining army was in tatters.

Antipodean pride

Gallipoli was the Anzacs' first major action of the war and they had fought with great determination. A third of those who took part in the landings died. Many Anzacs were British-born and proud to fight for Britain. But they returned home with a strong sense of their own distinct national identities. Gallipoli earned a special place in the history of Australia and New Zealand. Every year people remember their war dead on April 25, which is named Anzac Day.

WAR IN THE SNOW

While sun-scorched armies were slogging it out in Gallipoli, two more countries were gearing up to throw themselves into the line of fire. Italy and Bulgaria had been sitting on the sidelines since the start of the war. In 1915, the two countries finally declared their allegiances and entered the conflict on opposing sides.

Italian soldiers hoist a heavy field gun up a steep snow-bound cliff.

'Sacro egoismo'

When the war broke out, Italy declared its neutrality, although it was technically allied to the Central Powers. But the Italian prime minister, Antonio Salandra, secretly negotiated with both sides to see which would make him the better offer. He called this policy *sacro egoismo* (or 'sacred self-interest'). On April 26, 1915, Italy joined the Allied Powers. In return, they were promised control of Italian-speaking areas of Austria-Hungary and other territories, if the Allies won the war.

Uphill battles

The Italians declared war against Austria-Hungary (but not Germany) on May 23. They immediately launched attacks along the whole of the frontier, most of which ran through the Alps. The Austrians retreated a short way, but only to dig trenches on higher ground. This gave them a tactical advantage over their attackers. Bitter fighting took place along the Isonzo River on the eastern section of the Front. By the end of 1915, the Italians had fought four battles to try to take control of the river. But they suffered over 300,000 casualties and barely gained an inch of territory.

Soldiers on skis

The Alpine terrain of the Italian Front was possibly the toughest battleground of the whole war. Battling dizzying high altitudes, heavy snowfalls and frequent avalanches, the two armies dug trenches into the jagged peaks of the Alps. Both sides used specialist troops, trained in rock climbing and skiing. They had to develop ingenious engineering techniques to haul heavy artillery and supplies up the sheer rock faces and glaciers. During the war, around 650,000 soldiers lost their lives on the Italian Front. In the winter of 1915-16 alone, about 100,000 men died in avalanches.

> **INTERNET LINK**
> For a link to a website with a slide show exploring the dangerous and varied landscape of the Italian Front, go to **www.usborne-quicklinks.com**

Burdened with supplies, and equipped with skis, Italian soldiers weave their way up a precarious path along their Alpine frontier.

Bulgaria does a deal

Like Italy, the Bulgarian government chose the side that made the highest bid for their support. With recent successes in Galicia and the Dardanelles, the Central Powers seemed close to winning. So when they promised the Bulgarians control of southern Serbia, they jumped at it. The deal was sealed in September 1915. Within weeks, Bulgaria and Austria-Hungary began a mass assault on Serbia, on two fronts.

Retreat, but no surrender

Serbian troops had successfully fought off the Austro-Hungarian invasion at the start of the war, but the effort had left them exhausted. Hopelessly outnumbered and low on munitions, they begged their allies for support. On October 5, British and French forces landed at the Greek port of Salonika. But, with Bulgarian troops in force on the frontier, the Allies couldn't get through. Four days later, the Austrians took the Serb capital, Belgrade.

Fearing brutality at the hands of these occupying forces, the Serbian army, their king, Peter I, and thousands of civilians fled across the mountains to Albania. Most made the arduous journey on foot. King Peter survived, but over 94,000 soldiers and an unknown number of civilians died of cold and hunger on the way. As a result, Serbia suffered a higher casualty rate (as a percentage of the population) than any other country in the war.

About 155,000 Serbs made it safely to Albania, then sailed to refugee camps in Corfu. Still, they would not give in. As soon as they recovered their strength, 80,000 Serbian soldiers joined the Allies at Salonika, determined to liberate their country. They faced a difficult struggle. The armies on both sides dug trenches and settled in for a long, hard battle for control of southeast Europe.

This map shows the Balkans and the Italian Front on the Alpine border between Italy and Austria-Hungary.

This dramatic picture captures the instant a French soldier is shot. It is from a French movie about the Battle of Verdun, made in 1928 with actors who fought in the war and filmed on the sites where the battles took place.

1916 - 1917

THE BIG BATTLES

By the end of 1915, military commanders on both sides decided that the only way to break the stalemate in the trenches was to launch their biggest battles yet, in the year ahead. Allied Generals met at Chantilly, in France, where they planned simultaneous attacks on all fronts in the summer of 1916, with a major offensive on the Western Front near the Somme river. But the German high commander, General Falkenhayn, had plans of his own. He aimed to attack the French at Verdun in February. He hoped that this would "bleed France white" and force the Allies to surrender.

Neither of these grand schemes would go according to plan, but 1916 saw a series of huge battles, all relying on the same brutal tactic: slaughter on a vast scale.

THE MINCING MACHINE

In February 1916, a German army of a million men attacked the ancient French city of Verdun. Germany's commanders weren't trying to capture Allied territory or punch a hole in the Western Front. Instead, they were trying to draw the French forces into a long and bloody battle, to grind them down to the last man.

By the end of the siege of Verdun, the ancient fortress city was in ruins.

A numbers game

The German commander, General Erich von Falkenhayn, believed the war had to be won on the Western Front, and he was convinced that, if his troops could crush the French, the other Allies would be forced to make peace. Falkenhayn knew that French troops had strict orders never to give up land to the enemy, so he looked for a weak spot in their line – somewhere dangerous and difficult to defend. Sitting on a salient in the Western Front, Verdun was exposed to German guns on three sides. Since Roman times it had been protected by a ring of stone forts. But these were crumbling and neglected because the French thought they would be useless in modern war. For supplies, the city and its 200,000 defenders relied on a few shell-blasted roads, whereas the Germans had a rail depot just behind their line.

Falkenhayn made the Kaiser a chilling promise. For every dead German at Verdun, three Allied soldiers would be killed. The battle would blaze like a forest fire until the whole French army had been drawn in and consumed.

Closing in

The German attack began with a massive, thousand-gun artillery barrage. German troops surged forward as soon as the shelling lifted, using flamethrowers to drive any surviving defenders out of their trenches. The French fought bravely, but on the third day, the Germans were just a few miles from the city walls.

Road warriors

In desperation, French generals appointed a new commander, General Philippe Pétain, to save Verdun. He worked around the clock to improve his artillery, demanding bigger and better guns, and he used thousands of trucks to bring supplies into the city. They called the road La Voie Sacrée – the Sacred Way. Keeping it open became a patriotic mission for the French army.

INTERNET LINK

For a link to a website where you can take a virtual tour of modern-day Verdun, where the battlefields are still strewn with the debris of war, go to **www.usborne-quicklinks.com**

La Voie Sacrée, April 1916. By June, the road was flowing at full capacity, with 12,000 vehicles passing along it every day.

The tide turns

Through March, April and May, the Germans struggled to break French resistance. But their troops were torn to pieces by Pétain's artillery. Verdun was slowly turning into a death-trap for the attackers, with slaughter so shocking, soldiers compared it to a mincing machine. Pounded by millions of shells, the battlefield had become a featureless plain of churned mud and broken bodies. Fighting finally stopped in early December, with the French recapturing their lost ground. Both sides had suffered equally. Over a million men were dead, missing or wounded.

Falkenhayn had underestimated just how savage the fight for Verdun would be. The Kaiser was disappointed and, in August, he appointed two new, aggressive commanders to lead the German military: Field Marshal Paul von Hindenburg and General Erich von Ludendorff.

DREADNOUGHTS DUEL

After two years of small raids in the North Sea, the British and German fleets finally met head-on at the Battle of Jutland. In the largest steel-ship battle ever seen, there was an awesome display of firepower. But when the smoke cleared over the waves, both sides claimed a victory.

Beatty's flagship, HMS *Lion* (left) is hit by German shells and battle cruiser HMS *Queen Mary* is blown up at Jutland.

Sail out and fight

Battles always reflect the character of the commanders who plan and fight them and Jutland was no exception. In January 1916, Admiral Reinhard Scheer took charge of the German High Seas Fleet. Scheer thought his navy had been too timid in its attacks on the British Grand Fleet. So, he ordered his captains to be more aggressive and daring. In May 1916, he took the whole fleet out to sea, hunting for British patrols.

Jellicoe's choices

In the afternoon of May 30, 1916, British Royal Navy codebreakers passed an urgent message to their commander-in-chief, Admiral John Jellicoe. They had picked up Scheer's radio signals and decoded them using captured German codebooks. They knew exactly what Admiral Scheer was planning.

Jellicoe had to make a difficult decision fast. He desperately wanted to smash the rival fleet, but he had the heavy responsibility of maintaining British naval superiority in the North Sea. If he lost a dozen ships in a submarine attack or unlucky battle, the British sea blockade would collapse and Britain might even lose the war. Despite this, Jellicoe decided to fight.

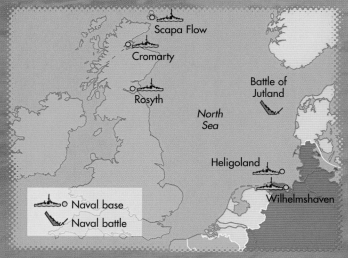

Scapa Flow

Cromarty

Rosyth

Battle of Jutland

North Sea

Heligoland

Wilhelmshaven

○ Naval base
Naval battle

This map shows the British and German naval bases in the North Sea, and the site of the Battle of Jutland.

INTERNET LINK

For links to websites where you can see a gallery of photographs of the Battle of Jutland, and listen to an account of the sinking of the HMS Indefatigable, go to **www.usborne-quicklinks.com**

Enemy sighted

Jellicoe set out with the Grand Fleet from the naval base at Scapa Flow, in Orkney, on 31 May. At the same time, a scouting party of six battle cruisers left the port of Rosyth, under the command of Admiral Beatty. When Beatty spotted two small German ships he gave chase. What he didn't know was that five enemy battle cruisers were waiting just over the horizon.

For the next hour, both sides battered each other with massive shells. Two of Beatty's battle cruisers were sunk and his own flagship was soon belching smoke and flames. But he didn't break off his attack until he sighted the High Seas Fleet rushing in his direction. He immediately turned his ships north, hoping to draw the Germans to Jellicoe's dreadnoughts.

Shortly before the Battle of Jutland, Jellicoe's fleet cruises the North Sea in a formation of six columns. For the battle itself, the British battleships would move into a single line to face their opponents.

Battling it out

The two fleets were hurtling at each other on a collision course. Jellicoe's armada was almost twice as powerful as Scheer's, with 28 dreadnoughts facing the Germans' 16. But tactics and luck would play a large part in the battle ahead.

With only two hours of daylight left, Jellicoe finally spotted the German dreadnoughts and gave the order to fire. But it was the startled Germans who had the first success, as their shells tore into the British battle cruiser HMS *Invincible*. Not wanting to push his luck, Scheer turned his entire fleet under cover of a thick smoke screen. He made a run back to port, thinking he could sneak past the British as they steamed to Heligoland. But the Grand Fleet intercepted his line of ships and scored several hits before Scheer turned again, leaving a 'suicide squad' of old battleships and torpedo ships to protect his rear.

Fearing a massive torpedo attack, which would inflict serious damage on his fleet, Jellicoe held his ships back. By the time he finally decided it was safe to give chase, the German dreadnoughts had slipped away.

Winners and losers

Scheer immediately declared a great German triumph. His fleet had sunk three Royal navy battle cruisers and 12 other ships, at the cost of a single battle cruiser and 10 other German ships. But it was a hollow victory. Jellicoe was criticized for being too cautious, but he had seen off the German fleet and protected his superiority in numbers. The British still ruled the North Sea.

DOOMED YOUTH

Boy Seaman John Cornwell was only 16 years old when he fought at Jutland. He won his country's highest medal for bravery – the Victoria Cross – and the British press called him a hero. But Cornwell was just one of thousands of young soldiers throughout Europe who risked their lives in the war. As many as 15% of all British and German troops were said to be younger than 19 years old.

John Cornwell won the Victoria Cross medal for his bravery.

One big adventure

Like most people at the time, Cornwell left school at 14. He was working as a delivery boy when the war started. His father went to France with the army but Cornwell had always dreamed of becoming a sailor. Going to sea must have seemed like a great adventure to him. He was only 15 years old when he presented himself at a navy recruitment office. To join the army you had to be 18 – 19 if you wanted to fight overseas – but the navy had a long tradition of recruiting younger boys.

When Cornwell finished his training, he joined a gun team onboard HMS *Chester* and within a few months he found himself in the thick of it, fighting at Jutland. An explosion killed the rest of his team and wounded Cornwell – but he stayed at his post beside the gun, fighting on. His ship returned to port and Cornwell was rushed to the hospital, where he died the following day. His sense of patriotic duty and self-sacrifice impressed the public, who turned out for his funeral procession in droves.

Proof of age

Many boys from poor families were tempted to volunteer by the army's promise of regular food and pay. Instead of seeking foreign adventure, they saw a chance to escape the misery of the slums. Recruitment officers didn't always ask for identification, so many boys simply lied about their age. One British 16-year-old tried to volunteer and made the mistake of saying he was 18. The officer smiled and told him to come back the following morning and see if he was 19.

The British army didn't introduce conscription until 1916, but during the last year of the war, many conscripts, like these boys, were very young.

Fighting to the death

For many young soldiers, the hardships of trench life were too much, no matter how physically tough they thought they were. One Australian lad, Jim Martin, signed up when his father was turned away for being too short. He was just 14 years old when he sailed for Gallipoli with the Australian army. Martin was big for his age and his farm job had made him strong. But he died of disease and exhaustion after weeks of hard fighting.

The war's horrors spared nobody, neither the brave nor the young. Boys fought and died alongside old soldiers, as countries sent their male populations into the furnace of war.

Classroom heroes

Germany had a huge, conscripted army and didn't actively recruit young boys until late in the war. But, even so, whole classes of them signed up in 1914 to prove their loyalty to the Kaiser. Thousands of young soldiers, aged between 16 and 20, died in the carnage of the First Battle of Ypres. The loss of so many young men shocked the German public. Mourning parents called the battle the Massacre of the Innocents.

INTERNET LINK

For a link to a website where you can read about the experiences of boy soldiers of the First World War, go to www.usborne-quicklinks.com

SKY FIGHTERS

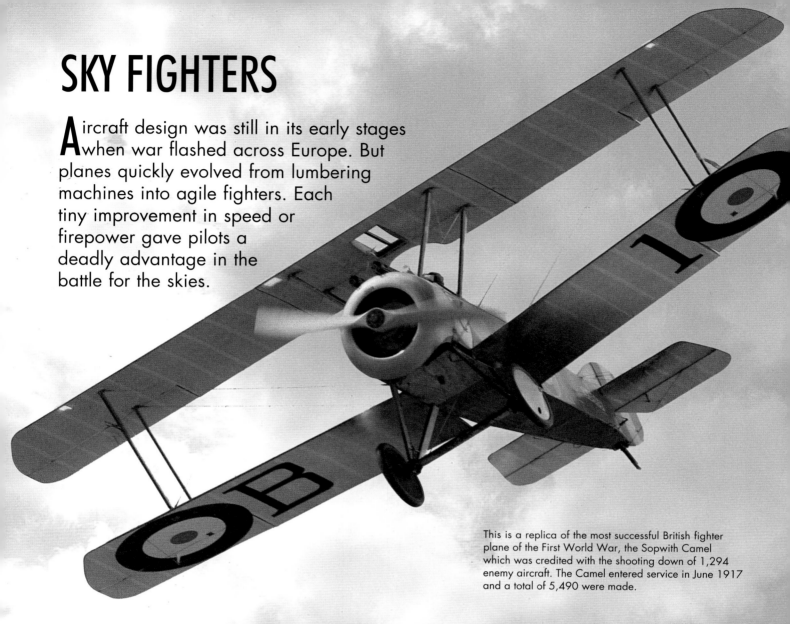

Aircraft design was still in its early stages when war flashed across Europe. But planes quickly evolved from lumbering machines into agile fighters. Each tiny improvement in speed or firepower gave pilots a deadly advantage in the battle for the skies.

This is a replica of the most successful British fighter plane of the First World War, the Sopwith Camel which was credited with the shooting down of 1,294 enemy aircraft. The Camel entered service in June 1917 and a total of 5,490 were made.

A problem with propellers

As soon as fighting started, both sides used unarmed scout planes to spy on enemy positions. When two rival pilots met in the sky, they simply waved or took potshots at each other with their pistols. Designers soon realized that a plane fitted with machine guns could win battles in the sky.

The best position for a gun was pointing straight ahead, but on most planes the propeller got in the way. In early 1915, an ingenious French pilot named Roland Garros got around this problem by fixing steel deflectors to his propeller blades. If a bullet hit a blade, it would bounce off the deflector towards its target. Garros shot down several enemy pilots before his plane was captured.

A Dutch designer

The Germans ordered the Dutch designer Anthony Fokker to examine and copy the deflectors. But he came up with something better – synchronization gear. This was a system of rods and levers that fired a machine gun only when there was a gap for the bullets to pass between the propeller blades. Fokker installed the gear in his Eindecker monoplane – a single-wing aircraft – to create the first proper fighter plane.

> ### INTERNET LINK
> For links to websites where you can find out more about the Red Baron and other flying aces of the First World War, and see photographs of different kinds of aircraft, go to **www.usborne-quicklinks.com**

Fokker fodder

Throughout the winter of 1915 the Allies were losing two or three planes a day to *Eindeckers*. British newspapers called this phase of the war the Fokker Scourge. Allied casualties were so great, British pilots jokingly described their Royal Flying Corps (RFC) as the Suicide Club. But during the Battle of Verdun, the Allies improved their tactics and their planes, and won back control of the skies. One French squadron, known as the Storks, even became famous for their fighter 'aces' – pilots who had shot down five or more enemy aircraft.

It wasn't until early 1917 that new machines once again gave the Germans the upper hand. In April of that year, the RFC lost 245 planes to German fighter pilots, among them the war's greatest ace – Manfred Baron von Richthofen – better known as the Red Baron.

The Germans built about 300 *Fokker Dr. I* triplanes like this modern replica. A triplane is a plane with three wings.

A flying circus

Richthofen was a skilled hunter and he used his knowledge of stalking and surprise to destroy 80 Allied aircraft. He earned his nickname after painting his plane blood red – a brazen coat of arms that terrified inexperienced pilots. Other German flyers followed the Baron's example, decorating their planes with bright paints. This led Allied soldiers to nickname them the Flying Circus.

This photograph of Manfred von Richthofen, the Red Baron, captures some of the young pilot's unswerving determination.

Ace of aces

Every country from Australia to Russia had its aces, usually presented as dashing daredevils in the popular press. The American Edward Rickenbacker notched up 26 kills in just a few, frenzied months of 1918. Frenchman Georges Guynemer became a newspaper celebrity with his 53 victories and was mobbed in the streets by his fans. But Richthofen's incredible record of 80 confirmed kills must earn him the title Ace of Aces.

Knights of the air

Although fighter pilots began flying in larger groups as the war progressed, most air combat came down to one-on-one shootouts known as dogfights. Planes sometimes broke apart as the pilots dived and climbed, and fire was always a risk. French and German pilots were equipped with parachutes, but British flyers weren't. Parachutes were considered too bulky and heavy and some generals thought pilots would be tempted to jump at the first sign of danger.

Safety in numbers

In the winter of 1917, the tide turned yet again in the air war, as German factories struggled to keep pace with Allied aircraft production. New planes such as the British *Sopwith Camel* had impressive power and agility compared to the German machines. Richthofen was chasing one of these fighters when he was shot down and killed in early 1918. His Flying Circus was soon outnumbered and decimated. By the end of the war, the Allies were the masters of the sky.

SLAUGHTER AND SACRIFICE

Hoping to divert German troops and supplies from the bloodbath at Verdun, British commanders launched a massive offensive on the Western Front, near the Somme river. After shelling the German trenches for seven days and nights, they expected a quick breakthrough. But the opening hours of the attack were the bloodiest of the entire war.

Moments before going over the top, soldiers attach bayonets to their rifles, ready to advance.

The Big Push

The German line at the Somme was guarded by trenches, miles of barbed wire and hundreds of concrete machine-gun posts. Underground bunkers protected soldiers from even the heaviest shells. But British generals were confident that nothing could stand in the way of what they called their Big Push. They thought that colossal firepower would be able to smash through any obstacle.

An opening barrage of two million shells ripped into the German trenches from above. Below ground, the British planted 21 huge mines, in tunnels they had been digging secretly for months. The mines were timed to explode the moment the barrage lifted. Then, the plan was to send over a wave of infantry to capture any survivors, and to clear the way for the cavalry to charge deep into German territory.

God and the cavalry

In charge of the offensive was Sir Douglas Haig, who had become Commander-in-Chief of the British forces in December 1915. A keen horseman, he believed cavalry still had an important part to play in the war. Few officers dared to disagree. Haig was a strong-willed and ambitious man who believed God was on his side. Even so, he expected heavy casualties at the Somme. But he thought it was a price worth paying for victory.

The blast of a massive underground mine, containing 20,400kg (45,000 pounds) of high explosive, detonated at 07:20, ten minutes before the first wave of British troops went over the top.

The walk-in

At 07:30 on July 1, the barrage lifted and whistles sounded along 40km (25 miles) of the Allied front – held by British troops to the north and a smaller French force to the south. The morning was hot and still, as thousands of soldiers obeyed the signal to step out into no-man's-land. They had been ordered to advance slowly, because their generals didn't trust them not to panic or stumble during the attack. So, they set off at a walk, expecting their opponents to be lying dead in their ruined trenches.

But the barrage had failed. Safe in their dugouts, the Germans heard the silence and guessed an attack was coming. They carried their machine guns to the surface and checked the barbed wire. It was still intact along much of the line.

Open Fire!

Thousands of soldiers died that morning, cut down by heavy machine-gun fire and shrapnel shells. The infantry broke on the German wire like a wave smashing into a cliff. Although some units made it through the wire and into the German trenches, they were soon dislodged by counterattacks. Only the French had some success, capturing a short section of the line in the south, where the German positions were weaker.

The cost

The Allies failed to make the breakthrough they had expected on the opening day of the battle. But, with the French still struggling at Verdun, they had to keep fighting at the Somme, in an attempt to wear out their opponents. The battle lasted until November, when rain flooded the battlefield. The Allies gained a few miles – but at a great cost.

More than a million men were killed or wounded in the Battle of the Somme. The Germans suffered the worst, with as many as 680,000 casualties. Around 125,000 men from Britain and its empire were killed, some 20,000 of them on the first day. Whole communities of young men – many from the Pals Battalions – simply vanished into the mud of no-man's-land, sending shock waves of loss and anger rippling through their hometowns.

INTERNET LINK

For a link to a website with photographs, art, movie footage and personal accounts of the Battle of the Somme, go to **www.usborne-quicklinks.com**

British infantry advance into no-man's-land through the tangled mess of barbed wire. This photograph comes from *The Battle of the Somme*, a movie made in 1916, which combined real footage of the battle with re-enactment scenes.

TRIALS AND TRAUMA

The trenches were a man-made hell where soldiers lived in constant fear for their lives. Some men found the pressure unbearable and went insane or ran away. But military courts had no sympathy for anyone breaking army rules and the punishments they used were often as brutal as the war itself.

A bad case of nerves

There were few things more terrifying than sitting through days of heavy shelling. The ground shook like an earthquake and the incessant roar of explosions made it impossible to rest. Around one in fifty British trench soldiers suffered from a complete physical and mental collapse, known as shell shock, at some point in the fighting. At the time of the war, doctors didn't know much about stress, depression or mental breakdown. They thought shell shock was caused by the air pressure from exploding bombs disturbing a soldier's brain.

Some shell shock victims trembled with convulsions and couldn't talk or think clearly. Others cowered at the slightest noise. Rest was the only cure, and thousands of men were sent home to specialist hospitals. The less fortunate were granted a few weeks leave, then ordered back to the Front. If the prospect of more shelling was too much to bear their only hope of escape was suicide, self-wounding or desertion.

Tickets home

There were thousands of cases of self-wounding during the war, as soldiers shot themselves in the foot or hacked off a thumb. If the wound was serious enough, a man could be sent home for good. But army doctors had strict orders to investigate all suspicious injuries and anyone caught could expect harsh treatment in a prison hospital swiftly followed by a military trial.

This dejected young British soldier, suffering from shell shock, has been taken prisoner by the Germans. He is wearing waders that were given to many men to keep them dry in flooded trenches.

Shot at dawn

Desertion, or going AWOL (Absent Without Leave) is one of the most serious crimes in any army. After a military trial that was often over in minutes, a dazed soldier could be sentenced to death by firing squad. Dozens of other crimes could warrant the death penalty, including self-wounding, cowardice or falling asleep on sentry duty. According to official claims, the British shot 346 soldiers, the French 133 and the Germans 48, but the real figures are probably much higher.

Dreaded punishments

For drunkenness and other petty crimes, offenders were usually given extra work duties or a short period behind bars. But British soldiers who misbehaved in this way could suffer 'Field Punishment No.1' – being strapped or shackled to a post for several hours. Soldiers hated this torture. It humiliated and terrified the victim, as he couldn't run for cover if a stray enemy shell came over.

Two American soldiers have been made to wear signs on their backs – denouncing them as a 'straggler' and a 'deserter' – to humiliate them in front of their comrades.

Brothers in arms

However dreadful they were, the threat of punishments only partly explains why so many men put up with the trenches. Most soldiers showed incredible resilience and determination to do their duty. They stayed because they believed in what they were doing – or because they didn't want to let down their friends.

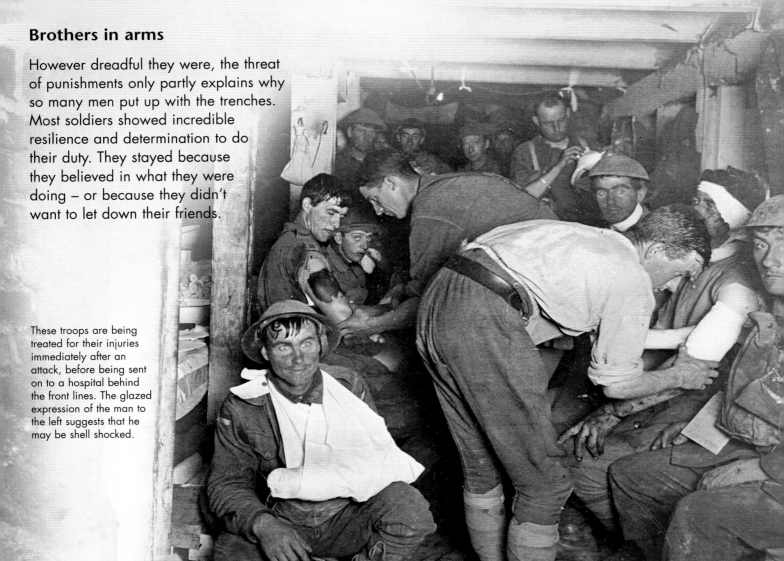

These troops are being treated for their injuries immediately after an attack, before being sent on to a hospital behind the front lines. The glazed expression of the man to the left suggests that he may be shell shocked.

WOMEN IN UNIFORM

It was not only on the home front that women played a vital part in the war. From the start of the conflict, they volunteered their services in hospitals, nursing sick and wounded soldiers. Some got even closer to the action as ambulance drivers and stretcher bearers, providing immediate medical care on the front line. But as the war went on, women were called upon to join the uniformed ranks of the armed forces too. Most worked behind the front lines, but a few women actually fought on the battlefield.

This British poster was designed to urge women to join the Women's Royal Naval Service, known as the Wrens.

Nurses under fire

Most hospitals were safe behind the front lines, but even there they were subject to enemy attacks. Every day, nurses had to cope with the harrowing sight of dead and mauled bodies, and to give their traumatized patients comfort and reassurance, as well as medical treatment. Closer to the fighting, many women showed amazing courage, risking their lives to drive ambulances and give First Aid, often under enemy fire.

One of the most famous nurses of the First World War was a British woman named Edith Cavell. She worked in a Red Cross hospital in German-occupied Brussels. Although she treated refugees and soldiers of all nationalities, she also secretly helped hundreds of Allied soldiers in her care to escape from behind enemy lines. When the Germans discovered what she had been doing, they arrested her and executed her by firing squad.

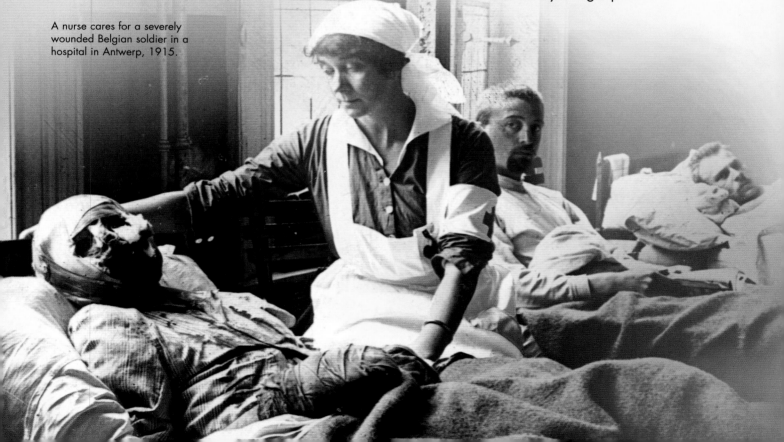

A nurse cares for a severely wounded Belgian soldier in a hospital in Antwerp, 1915.

These four mechanics of the Women's Royal Air Force are working on the fuselage of a fighter plane.

Supporting roles

All armed forces rely on the support of large numbers of non-combat staff, known as auxiliaries. They include cooks, clerks, engineers, telephone operators and dispatch riders. By 1917, many of the men performing these tasks were needed to make up the numbers on the front lines, so women were encouraged to take their places.

Warrior women

Most countries tried to protect their women from the dangers of battle, but the small Serbian army suffered such heavy losses that it had to take on female soldiers. One of them was a British woman named Flora Sandes. She had gone to Serbia as a nurse, but took up arms when the country was invaded. In Russia and Germany, a few women were so eager to fight, they pretended to be men.

INTERNET LINK

For links to websites where you can read extracts from nurses' own accounts of working on the front line, and find out more about the experiences of women in the armed forces during the First World War, go to www.usborne-quicklinks.com

Russian amazons

By mid-1917, the Russian army was in crisis, as thousands of men had deserted the ranks. A woman named Maria Bochkareva persuaded the government to let her set up a women's unit – the so-called 'Battalion of Death' – partly to shame the men into fighting again. The 2,000 strong battalion was involved in heavy fighting, and within just three months, there were only 250 left.

Shaven-headed women soldiers of the Russian 'Battalion of Death' stand to attention in their uniforms, 1917.

SHOCK TACTICS

With the Germans concentrating all their efforts on the Western Front, the maverick Russian general, Alexei Brusilov, launched a major assault against Austria-Hungary. The Brusilov Offensive, as it became known, was arguably Russia's most successful operation in the entire war. Much of Brusilov's success was down to his development of a radical new style of fighting: shock tactics.

A punishing attack

Allied commanders had planned to launch a summer offensive along the whole of the Eastern Front, at the same time as their push at the Somme. The Russians would attack the Germans to the north and the Austro-Hungarians to the south. But the Austro-Hungarian commander, General Conrad, had other plans. On May 15, he launched what he called a 'punishment expedition' in northern Italy. Conrad's troops soon broke through the Italian front line, and the Italians appealed to Russia for help.

Brusilov's plan

General Brusilov was in charge of Russian operations along the southern section of the Eastern Front, on the Austro-Hungarian frontier. In order to divert Conrad's troops away from Italy, he brought forward his part of the summer offensive. He also hoped he might be able to take back territory the Russians had lost in Galicia the year before.

Brusilov believed the best tactic was to take the enemy by surprise. He planned to attack on a wide front, digging tunnels, or saps, as close as possible to the Austro-Hungarian trenches without being detected. Then, specialized units of soldiers – 'shock troops' – would stage lightning attacks, blowing open holes in the Austro-Hungarian front line for the rest of the Russian army to advance through.

General Brusilov studies a map during the offensive that was named after him.

A surprising success

The attack began as dawn broke, on June 4. The Austro-Hungarians were taken completely by surprise, just as Brusilov had planned. His troops broke through enemy lines with ease, taking thousands of prisoners, as their opponents were stunned into surrender. To fight off the Russians, Conrad was forced to shut down operations on the Italian Front.

In July, Russian forces on the northern part of the Eastern Front also went on the offensive. But they were soon stopped in their tracks by fresh German troops, sent to reinforce their allies. In the south, Brusilov battled on successfully until September. By then, his troops had recaptured a belt of territory almost 100km (60 miles) wide. Around 600,000 Austro-Hungarians were killed or wounded.

Russian shock troops advance during the Brusilov Offensive, summer 1916. The Russians had spent the winter training new recruits and building up stocks of munitions. But, strengthening their army led to great hardship among the people back home.

Rumania's short war

The neutral Rumanian government watched all this with keen interest. Believing the Austro-Hungarians were all but defeated, they decided to throw in their lot with the Allies. Their main motive was to win Transylvania, an Austro-Hungarian province that was home to around three million ethnic Rumanians. On August 27, Rumanian troops invaded Austria-Hungary, through the Transylvanian Alps. It was an unwise move. German, Austro-Hungarian and Bulgarian troops soon forced them to retreat. On December 6, the Central Powers captured the Rumanian capital, Bucharest.

Passing glory

By mid-September, Brusilov's forces had advanced as far as the Carpathians. But they ground to a halt when they got beyond the reach of supplies or reserve troops. They were sent south to help the Rumanians in their failing campaign. By the end of the year, all the territory Brusilov had won was back in enemy hands. Russian troops had succeeded in bringing the Austro-Hungarian force to its knees, but they ended the year exhausted and demoralized.

This map shows the front line on the southern part of the Eastern Front during 1916.

83

SECRETS AND SPIES

Knowledge is power. Knowing what your enemy plans to do next, while keeping your own intentions secret, can mean the difference between victory and defeat. Throughout the war, both sides used spies to keep watch on each other, and took careful measures to prevent valuable information from falling into the wrong hands.

A Belgian firing squad takes aim during the execution of a captured German agent, October 1914.

Staking out the opposition

Even before the war, British agents in Germany had been busy collecting information. Their main focus was shipbuilding and arms supplies in the naval bases, but they also gathered road maps and train timetables – any 'intelligence' that might be useful in a military campaign. Meanwhile, German spies were doing the same thing in Britain. What neither country realized was that many of their agents were themselves under surveillance, from the very people they were spying on. As soon as war was declared, all suspected spies in enemy territory were swiftly rounded up and imprisoned.

INTERNET LINK

For links to websites where you can find out more about First World War espionage, and find out how to make invisible ink go to www.usborne-quicklinks.com

Homeland security

In Germany, all foreigners – merchant seamen and even a few tourists – were taken prisoner.
In Britain, all Germans and Austro-Hungarians, including many who had lived there most of their lives, were classed as 'enemy aliens' and sent to internment camps for the rest of the war. With anti-German feeling running high, the British royal family changed their name, from the German-sounding Saxe-Coburg, to Windsor.

Governments brought in new laws limiting ownership of anything that might be used to contact the enemy. This included telephones, telegraph equipment, flag-poles and even pigeons. People were told to report anything suspicious. In the so-called 'spy mania' that followed, police investigated thousands of suspected spies, but very few turned out to be real.

Censors and code breakers

Throughout the war, governments on both sides, censored newspaper reports of the conflict. This helped to keep public opinion on their side, and prevented information from being published that might be of use to the other side. Postal services were censored too. Secret service officers opened and read all suspicious letters, intercepting messages to and from enemy agents, leading to the arrest of several spies.

In the trenches and out at sea, military orders had to be passed on by telephone or telegram. Spies could easily tap into lines or pick up wireless transmissions, so messages were usually sent in code. Unfortunately for the Germans, the Allies got hold of three of their naval codebooks, early in the war. From then on, British code breakers, based in Room 40 of the Admiralty headquarters, were able to intercept and decode most German naval signals. This gave them a huge advantage, particularly during the Battle of Jutland.

Spy tactics

Spies developed some ingenious ways of smuggling messages out of enemy territory. These included writing in invisible ink and concealing notes in hollowed-out coat buttons and glass eyes. Despite these tricks, many of the people involved in wartime espionage were untrained civilians, and they often got caught.

"If you could only send me some money, I could get my brother, who is in the navy, to give me all the navy movements..." This message, from a German spy in Britain, was written on sheet music in invisible ink. It was intercepted in the post by British intelligence.

Femme fatale

The most infamous spy of the war was a Dutch woman named Margareta Zelle. Part Javanese, she reinvented herself as an oriental princess and exotic dancer under the stage name of Mata Hari. During the war, her act was a huge hit with soldiers on leave, and she had a string of love affairs with military officers.

German agents paid her to gather information. But later she offered to work as a spy for the French too. This made her a double agent. When the Germans captured a French agent, Mata Hari was held to blame. She was arrested in Paris and shot at dawn on October 13, 1917.

Mata Hari, in full costume, performs the dance that made her the darling of the troops.

DESERT WARS

A romantic hero: Thomas Edward Lawrence in traditional Arab dress

At the start of the war, the British had brought troops to the Middle East to defend their oil supplies. But they soon made plans to push further into Turkish territories. After Gallipoli, British commanders decided that the only way to topple the Turks was to provoke their Arab subjects to revolt.

Stirring a revolt

Under the Young Turks, Arabs were treated as second-class citizens, and many had begun to talk of throwing off Turkish rule. In October 1914, the British High Commissioner in Egypt began negotiating with the Arab leader, Sherif Hussein of Mecca. He offered to supply money and arms for a revolt against the Turks, and promised that the Arabs would be left to rule their own lands after the war. In Cairo, the British set up the Arab Bureau, whose staff liaised with Arab leaders to build support for the revolt. Among them was an idealistic young intelligence officer named T.E. Lawrence – who later became famous as Lawrence of Arabia.

Meanwhile, British and Indian forces were advancing up the Tigris river into Mesopotamia. They had already captured Basra, Kurna and Kut, and in May 1915, they began to push north, toward Baghdad, the regional capital.

British under siege

In November 1915, British and Indian troops were close to Baghdad when they met tough Turkish resistance. Half their 8,500 men were killed or wounded and they retreated to Kut. But the Turks surrounded the city and held it under siege.

British forces tried to sail up the Tigris to rescue their beleaguered comrades, but heavy floods blocked their way. In March 1916, Lawrence undertook a secret mission, to attempt to pay the Turkish generals to end the siege. But they weren't interested. After 147 days under siege, with men dying like flies from sickness and starvation, the British finally surrendered on April 29.

Lawrence of Arabia

Before the war, Lawrence had learned Arabic and grown familiar with local customs, while studying archaeology in the Middle East. At the Arab Bureau, he gathered information about the Turks' military strategies, their strengths and weaknesses. With help from Lawrence and the Arab Bureau, Sherif Hussein finally took up arms against the Turks in June 1916. Within three months, Arab forces had captured Mecca, Jedda and Taif, and were advancing north.

Guerrilla tactics

In October, Lawrence joined Hussein's son Emir Feisal, in charge of part of the Arab army. He decided to adopt Arab dress. This irritated his British commanders, but it helped him to gain acceptance among his fellow fighters. It was practical too, as the head-cloth gave protection against the searing sun, wind and sand.

The Turkish army far outnumbered Arab forces, so Lawrence advised Feisal to use guerrilla tactics against them. They carried out night raids on Turkish camps, and mined bridges and train lines to sabotage their communications and supplies. This forced the Turks to divert large numbers of troops away from the fighting elsewhere, including Mesopotamia.

A change of fortunes

The British saw their chance to renew their campaign in Mesopotamia. So they sent in reinforcements, heavy artillery and a new commander, Sir Stanley Maude. He made rapid progress, retaking Kut in February 1917, and capturing Baghdad on March 11. With much of Mesopotamia now in Allied hands and the Arabs in revolt, the Turks looked close to defeat.

British troops march triumphantly into Baghdad, past a large crowd of local onlookers.

INTERNET LINK

For a link to a website where you can find out more about Lawrence of Arabia and the Arabs' guerrilla tactics, go to **www.usborne-quicklinks.com**

This photograph, taken by Lawrence from the back of a camel, shows Emir Feisal (second from the right, dressed in white) leading his guerrilla forces through the desert.

Two anti-tsarist Russian soldiers ride through Petrograd on the running board of a motor car, March 1917. One of them has attached a red flag to his bayonet.

CRISIS AND RESOLUTION

By 1917, three years of fighting had taken their toll on soldiers and civilians on both sides, and many began to demand an end to the conflict. In Russia, the people overthrew the government and pulled out of the war. But, while Russia was in turmoil, the Allies gained a strong new member, as the US finally joined the war. By spring of 1918, both Allied and German commanders were determined to bring the war to a climax, by launching one last big push on the Western Front. Eventually, the Central Powers were forced to admit defeat. The war finally ended on November 11, 1918.

RIOTS AND REBELS

After several years of war, soldiers and civilians were pushed to the limits of their endurance. Facing food shortages at home and slaughter on the battlefields, some people took to the streets to demand change. Their protests sparked riots, mutinies – even revolution.

Trouble in Dublin

Ireland was part of the United Kingdom, but Irish nationalists wanted more control over their own affairs. In 1914, the British government had agreed that Ireland could set up their own parliament, but the deal was postponed by the outbreak of war. The nationalists agreed to wait, and thousands of them enlisted to fight for the British army.

But a rebel group called the Irish Republican Brotherhood saw the war as the perfect opportunity to claim total independence. On April 24, 1916, just over a thousand rebels took control of central Dublin, in what became known as the Easter Rising. After five days of bloody street battles with British soldiers, the republicans surrendered. Ireland remained in turmoil, and the soldiers who'd gone to fight for Britain would return after the war to a divided and unsettled land.

In central Dublin during the Easter Rising, British troops take cover behind a makeshift street barricade made from pieces of furniture.

French troops resting, by Christopher Nevinson. The French soldiers in this painting have stopped by the roadside on their way to the front. They look tired and despondent, as though all fighting spirit has left them.

Breaking ranks

By the start of 1917, the French army was exhausted and demoralized. Soldiers complained that the government didn't understand the miseries of the trenches. They wanted better food, more leave and an end to the large-scale offensives that cost thousands of lives. Some infantrymen started to 'baa' and bleat whenever they saw an officer – like lambs being led to the slaughterhouse.

In April 1917, the French commander, Robert Nivelle, launched a massive assault on the Western Front. He promised a quick breakthrough and an end to the war, but his offensive failed and the resulting casualties were shocking. Feeling betrayed, around half of the French army mutinied against their commanders by refusing to attack. The mutiny lasted for three months. Remarkably, the Germans failed to take advantage of the situation because they had no idea what was going on. In August, the French brought in a new commander, Philippe Pétain. He ended the crisis by offering better conditions for his men, helping to raise their morale.

INTERNET LINK

For a link to a website with photographs, articles, posters and rebel songs from the Easter Rising, or to explore the luxurious lifestyle of the Russian royal family through an online scrapbook, go to **www.usborne-quicklinks.com**

Give us bread

Long before the war, many Russians had been unhappy with the tsars, who had the power to rule the country as they pleased. In 1905, factory workers in the capital city, St. Petersburg, protested against Tsar Nicholas II. This sparked strikes and riots in other towns, and he was forced to set up a parliament to rule with him. But he made sure it had very little power, and most Russians still had no say in the way their country was run.

The war caused terrible food shortages. Many Russians, who were already living in dire poverty, began to starve. People blamed the Tsar for their suffering and for the carnage at the front. They took to the streets, demanding more food, democratic elections and an end to the war. In March 1917, riots broke out in St. Petersburg – which had been renamed Petrograd at the start of the war, to sound less German. The Tsar ordered the soldiers of the city garrison to crush them, but they mutinied and joined the rioters instead. The Tsar abdicated on March 15, and new government took charge. But the riots were only the beginning of a greater revolution that would explode across Russia later that year.

Rough treatment

The most serious British mutiny was at a tough training camp in France. When a soldier was unfairly arrested at the camp in September 1917, thousands of troops turned on the military police and chased them into town. Two days of rioting followed, until soldiers armed with wooden clubs put an end to the protest. To prevent news of the unrest reaching the enemy, the whole incident was declared top secret and covered up by the British government.

A mutinous Russian army officer distributes anti-tsarist newspapers to an eager mob in a Moscow street, February 1917.

PEACE, BREAD AND LAND

Tsar Nicholas' downfall came when he lost the loyalty of his army. But, instead of learning from the Tsar's failure, the new government was determined to keep fighting the war. This unpopular decision brought anger and resentment, still felt by many soldiers and civilians, back to the surface. Recent history was about to repeat itself.

Similar to the British poster of Kitchener, this Russian revolutionary poster urges peasants to join a workers' cooperative.

A losing battle

In June 1917, the head of the government, Alexander Kerensky, appointed General Brusilov to lead a new offensive against Austria-Hungary. Brusilov launched the attack on June 18, sending shock troops ahead of regular forces. Things began well for Brusilov until German troops launched a strong counterattack. Within three weeks, the Russian army was in retreat and in total disarray, as even its commanding officers turned against the government.

INTERNET LINK

For a link to a website with pictures and more information on the Russian Revolution, Lenin and the Bolshevik leaders, go to www.usborne-quicklinks.com

Storming the Winter Palace. This re-enactment was staged in 1921, to celebrate the anniversary of the 1917 revolution.

Power to the people

While the Russian army was suffering at the hands of German forces, at home the government came under attack from a political party called the Bolsheviks. They urged people to overthrow the government and take control for themselves. They called on peasant farmers to seize the land from their landlords, industrial workers to take control of the factories and soldiers to abandon their posts.

Storming the palace

On October 24, 1917, Bolshevik troops surrounded the Winter Palace in Petrograd, the seat of the new government. The building was defended by a small number of soldiers who remained loyal to Kerensky. But they put up little resistence as the revolutionaries stormed the palace, arrested Kerensky's government and seized power. Two days later, the Bolsheviks declared their leader, Lenin, head of the new government.

End of the line

Meanwhile, Tsar Nicholas and his family were taken prisoner and hidden in the remote Siberian city of Yekaterinburg. When their captors heard reports that anti-Bolshevik troops were approaching the area, they worried that they might be attacked and the Tsar set free. So the Boshevik guards lined up their royal prisoners and shot them dead.

Tsar Nicholas II poses in the snow with his children and nephews, around the time of his abdication in March 1917.

In October 1917, Lenin delivers a rousing revolutionary speech to a crowd of soldiers and workers.

Lenin's promise

The Bolshevik Revolution had been quick and fairly bloodless, but that didn't mean that everyone in Russia supported the new regime. To unite the people behind him, Lenin promised "peace, bread and land" for all, and called on European nations to end the war. He didn't expect the Allies or the Central Powers to agree to a cease-fire, but he hoped that their refusal might help to provoke revolution in other countries. To his dismay, the Germans offered to make peace, on the condition that they could take control of much of European Russia. When the Bolsheviks refused, German troops attacked, forcing them back to the negotiating table.

From war to civil war

On March 3, 1918, Lenin's foreign minister, Leon Trotsky, finally signed the peace treaty between Russia and the Central Powers at the Polish city of Brest-Litovsk. The treaty forced the Bolsheviks to hand over much of western Russia to the Germans, costing the country a third of its population, half its industries and almost all of its coal reserves. Many Russian patriots were furious at what they saw as a shameful peace. With Allied support, anti-Bolsheviks took up arms against the Bolsheviks. Russia's part in the First World War was over, but the country was now plunged into a civil war that would last for nearly three years.

WAKING THE GIANT

In the face of Allied and American outrage after the sinking of the *Lusitania*, the Germans had scaled down their U-boat attacks. But from February 1917, they began torpedoing all ships bound for Allied ports without warning. This was the turning point for the American president, Woodrow Wilson, who had struggled for years to keep his country out of the war.

U-boat aggression

German navy commanders promised the Kaiser that their U-boats could starve Britain into submission within five months. But the ruthless sinking of merchant and passenger ships infuriated Wilson, who believed the oceans should be the "free highways" of the world. After the sinking of the *Lusitania*, he had warned the Germans that America wouldn't tolerate any further loss of life at sea.

On February 26, a journalist named Floyd Gibbons reported a torpedo attack on a British passenger ship, *Laconia*, off the west coast of Ireland. Gibbons had survived the sinking, but three Americans died in the icy Atlantic waters. When his article was published, it provoked a debate across the USA – how much longer could the country keep out of the war?

Diplomatic skulduggery

Wilson had other reasons to be furious about Germany's actions. In January 1917, the German foreign secretary, Arthur Zimmermann, had sent a coded telegram to his ambassador in Mexico. Zimmermann ordered the ambassador to make a secret pact with the Mexican and Japanese governments, in case America entered the war. Germany promised the Mexicans "generous financial support" and control of Texas, New Mexico and Arizona if they would join the Central Powers.

Zimmermann's telegram ranks as one of the most explosive documents in history. It was intercepted by British code breakers at Room 40, who presented US officials with a copy in February. The following month, the story broke in newspapers around the world.

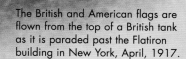

The British and American flags are flown from the top of a British tank as it is paraded past the Flatiron building in New York, April, 1917.

94

A change of heart

The President was a peace-loving man, who had used the campaign slogan "he kept us out of the war" to win the 1916 election. But the U-boat threat to American ships and civilians, combined with Germany's shadowy approaches to Mexico, were too much for him. In early April, he asked the US Congress to declare war. On April 6, Wilson announced to the world that the United States was at war with the Central Powers.

This painting, by Edmund Tarbell, depicts President Woodrow Wilson in a scholarly pose at his desk.

Peacemaker

Wilson was anxious to persuade his critics that his intention in joining the war was "to make the world safe for democracy" – not to make territorial gains. He put together a secret panel of scholars and soldiers – known as 'The Inquiry' – to report on the European situation. Using their findings, Wilson started drafting a plan for a League of Nations, which would promote lasting peace, democracy and free international trade. In January 1918, Wilson set out this ambitious vision in a speech that became known as the Fourteen Points.

Countdown

Wilson's aim might have been world peace but first he had to help smash the Central Powers. At the beginning of 1917, the US army was only 100,000 strong, but after a huge recruitment drive, and the introduction of conscription (the draft), it would land over two million men in Europe before the end of the war. Fleets shipping troops across the Atlantic were protected by naval convoys so Germany's U-boats were powerless to stop them.

While America geared itself up for a massive military expedition, Allied leaders celebrated the promise of a fresh army fighting on their side. In November, the British prime minister, Lloyd George suggested the formation of a new Supreme War Council, with a seat for each Allied nation – including the United States. Help was on its way.

This recruitment poster copies the famous Kitchener poster of 1914.

INTERNET LINK

For links to websites where you can read the Zimmerman telegram and find out more about President Wilson, go to **www.usborne-quicklinks.com**

American commander John Pershing (far left) inspects a battalion of African-American troops. Around 200,000 black Americans served in the war, but they were segregated from their white comrades, and few saw active combat.

DROWNING IN MUD

While they waited for the US troops to come to their aid, British generals came up with a plan to break the U-boat stranglehold by capturing German ports along the Belgian coast. It resulted in a disastrous battle that was one of the most heartbreaking of the war.

Stuck in the mud at Passchendaele, two horses are struggling to drag a water cart out of the quagmire and back onto the wooden track.

Third time lucky

The British commander, Sir Douglas Haig, believed the German army was exhausted after the Battle of the Somme. So he calculated that a quick strike through Flanders would break their line, opening the way for his cavalry troops to occupy the U-boat ports of Ostend and Zeebrugge.

Haig's faith in his plan wasn't shared by the British prime minister, David Lloyd George. He argued that it would be wiser to wait for the US army to arrive. But Haig insisted it was vital to keep up the pressure on the Western Front. So, on July 31, Allied troops launched the infamous Third Battle of Ypres, which has become known as Passchendaele.

No place for fighting

The Passchendaele Ridge, near Ypres was a stretch of high ground held by the Germans, surrounded by low, open plains. It was well defended: fresh battalions waited miles behind the line and hundreds of bombproof machine gun nests and artillery posts overlooked no-man's-land. They even had stores of mustard gas ready to release.

Haig decided to shell the ridge for ten solid days before sending his men over the top. But the area around it was a marsh, already churned up by years of shelling. Haig's barrage turned it into a muddy slime. Then it started to rain.

INTERNET LINK

For links to websites where you can see photographs and read eyewitness accounts of Passchendaele, go to
www.usborne-quicklinks.com

Mud warriors

Weather experts had warned Haig about the high rainfall in Flanders, but the rain in the summer of 1917 was the worst for 30 years. Shell craters in no-man's-land filled with water and the only way to make progress across the quagmire was to creep over duckboards – wooden slats, tied together. Wounded or exhausted men often slipped into the mud and disappeared. Tens of thousands of them still lie buried there today.

The creeping barrage

But Haig pressed on with the battle, ordering his soldiers to attack under the protection of a new artillery tactic, known as a creeping barrage. This relied on gunners to shell the ground immediately ahead of charging infantry. As the men advanced, the gunners adjusted their range to keep shells landing just before them. If all went to plan, the infantry would be supported up to their target – which they would hold until reinforcements arrived. But, in the chaos of battle, creeping barrages were notoriously difficult to control.

Australian soldiers walk across a duckboard track over the blasted Passchendaele battlefield, in this picture taken by the Australian photographer, Frank Hurley.

Young lions

By October, courageous British and Australian troops had made some inroads into the enemy line using the creeping barrage tactic. But the suffering of the men – and the thousands of horse teams used to pull artillery pieces – was appalling. With no hope of a breakthrough, Haig still resisted calls to stop the fighting. It was a decision that baffled even his closest supporters.

There is a famous remark made by two German generals. Some historians have used it to argue that the lives of British soldiers were squandered by their commanders. One of them claimed that the British fought like lions. "True," the other replied, "but they are lions led by donkeys." Haig always stubbornly refused to allow heavy casualty figures to change his objectives. He triumphed in the end, but the infantry paid a terrible price.

On November 6, Canadian soldiers finally captured the village of Passchendaele and Haig agreed to end the battle. But the U-boat bases had escaped attack. Only five months later, the Germans would retake every inch of the ground they had lost.

"I died in hell -
(They called it
Passchendaele)."

War poet, Siegfried Sassoon

BACKS TO THE WALL

With Russia out of the war, the Germans had a million combat-ready soldiers to move to the Western Front. Before the US troops could arrive in strength, the German commanders decided to launch what they called their Spring Offensive. This meant throwing everything they had into a series of desperate battles.

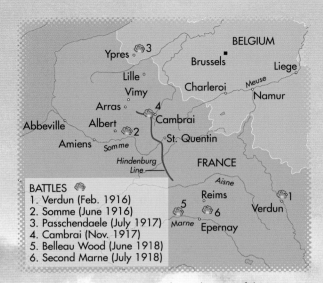

BATTLES
1. Verdun (Feb. 1916)
2. Somme (June 1916)
3. Passchendaele (July 1917)
4. Cambrai (Nov. 1917)
5. Belleau Wood (June 1918)
6. Second Marne (July 1918)

This map of the Western Front shows the sites of the main battles of the second half of the war and the Hindenburg Line – a vast network of trenches and concrete dug-outs.

Lightning strikes

The Germans had spent the latter part of 1917 planning the offensive and training their men in new fighting skills. Just before dawn on March 21, they began shelling the Allied lines with a 'devil's orchestra' of roaring guns, as one soldier described it. The barrage lasted for five hours. Before the defenders could recover, groups of German infantry started appearing out of the morning fog.

These were storm troopers, elite soldiers armed with light machine guns, flamethrowers and grenades. They looked for weak points in defensive positions and forced their way deep into the Allies' trench system, always advancing. Allied soldiers soon found themselves cut off from each other and outflanked by waves of regular German troops following the first assault force.

> **INTERNET LINK**
> For a link to a website where you can view an animated map of the German Spring Offensive of 1918, go to **www.usborne-quicklinks.com**

A new commander

The Allied line buckled along an 80km (50 miles) front, forcing them to retreat. As the Germans pushed closer to Paris and threatened the Channel ports, Allied politicians decided the troops needed decisive leadership to deal with the crisis. So, they appointed a French general, Ferdinand Foch, as overall commander to coordinate the actions of all the Allied forces on the Western Front.

To the last man

By April, the British were fighting for their lives against ferocious German attacks. Sir Douglas Haig sent his soldiers what became known as his 'Backs to the Wall' order: "Every position must be held to the last man...With our backs to the wall, and believing in the justice of our cause, each one of us must fight on to the end." Haig was asking his men for one last, heroic effort – and it worked. The British fought with all the skill and toughness they had gained in three years of trench fighting.

Under General Foch's overall command, French, American, British and Italian troops fought to victory at the Second Battle of the Marne in July. The Spring Offensive faltered, and the Germans went into retreat. They had captured land, enemy guns and thousands of prisoners, but they had advanced too quickly. They had no artillery support, and few supplies.

Running on empty

Britain was getting through the U-boat blockade by organizing their merchant ships into convoys protected by destroyer escorts. But the Royal Navy's blockade against Germany was stronger than ever. There were food shortages in German cities and the army didn't have enough meat or fresh produce to feed their men. German troops were so hungry they stopped their attacks to loot Allied dugouts and food tents, gorging themselves on fresh bread, eggs and wine.

Dark days

On August 8, the Allies broke through the German line at Amiens, prompting General Ludendorff to describe it as a "black day" for his army. By September his troops were retreating to the Hindenburg Line – the defensive position they had held the year before. Exhausted and malnourished, thousands of them fell prey to a deadly flu virus. It could kill a man overnight, and would sweep around the world later that year. But disease was only one of the dangers they faced. The Allies were preparing another massive attack of their own.

Past the body of a French soldier, German troops advance through smoke and fire during the Spring Offensive.

DEATH THROES

The failure of the Spring Offensive broke the fighting spirit of the German army. Most soldiers were tired of the war. Their families were starving and men who had been home returned to the front with stories of strikes and mutinies. Allied troops drew closer, but the Kaiser refused to surrender.

American 'doughboys' in action during the Battle of Belleau Wood, June 1918

Ready and willing

The arrival of the American Expeditionary Force, commanded by General 'Black Jack' Pershing, dealt a crushing blow to German morale. The fresh-faced American soldiers landing in France were nicknamed 'doughboys' by the local people, probably because they looked so plump and healthy. Most of them had no battle experience, but they fought like tigers. Any doubts about the quality and bravery of these new troops were settled in June 1918, at the Battle of Belleau Wood.

Floyd Gibbons – the reporter who had survived a run-in with a U-boat – was once again in the thick of it. He was following US Marines in a charge across open fields when they were caught in heavy machine-gun fire. Gibbons was hit three times and lost an eye as he tried to save an injured soldier. More than 5,700 Marines were wounded or killed in the battle.

Allied power

It wasn't just the arrival of the doughboys that depressed German soldiers. The Allies had a constant supply of food, guns and ammunition, whereas German shops and factories were running out of goods. Allied planes ruled the skies and their ships prowled the seas. On land, they enjoyed yet another advantage, which had proved a formidable weapon in November 1917, at the Battle of Cambrai: the tank.

Ironsides

Apart from a few experimental prototypes and captured vehicles, the Germans had no tanks of their own. They trained their gunners to target them on the battlefield, but they could never stop them all. Tanks carried machine guns and light artillery pieces. They climbed hills, forded streams and cleared paths through wire for attacking infantry. The Allies were preparing for an assault on the Hindenburg Line, and tanks would play a vital role.

Closing in

On September 12, an all-American force stormed and captured German trenches close to Verdun. The Allied war machine was at last in a position to strike at the Hindenburg Line. On September 26, a combined force of French, British and American armies attacked. They used heavy artillery to break up the wire and concrete fortifications, and sent tanks equipped with metal cribs or bundles of roped logs, known as fascines, to fill any deep ditches.

After four days of savage battle, the heart of the Hindenburg Line was torn open. British troops and soldiers from the British colonies advanced through. Overwhelmed, the Germans began to retreat, fighting their pursuers every step of the way.

Kaiser Wilhelm studies battle plans with his two military commanders, Field Marshal Hindenburg (left) and General Ludendorff (right).

Biting the bullet

Germany's proud military commanders, Hindenburg and Ludendorff, finally accepted that the war was lost. With rebellious soldiers and civilians marching in the streets demanding a new government, even the Kaiser agreed that it was time to negotiate for peace with the Allies, without the disgrace of having to surrender. In October, he sent officials to propose a cease-fire, or armistice.

But, even with his empire crumbling around him, the Kaiser still thought Germany could end the war without losing too much power or territory. He wouldn't listen to any suggestions that he might be forced to give up his position as supreme ruler. But he was unaware of the disaster that was overtaking his country. Germany was facing nothing less than total ruin.

British troops march alongside tanks as they lumber toward the Hindenburg Line, September 1918. On top of the tanks are 'cribs' – cages to be dropped into trenches, enabling tanks to roll over the top.

ARMAGEDDON

While the Germans were losing control of the Western Front, the Turks came under pressure in the Middle East. The Arabs continued their guerrilla war in Hejaz, and the British decided to invade Palestine and Syria. If they succeeded, they hoped this would be enough to knock the Turks out of the war for good.

Pushing into Palestine

In July 1917, the Arabs scored one of their most important victories by capturing the Red Sea port of Akaba. Throughout 1916, British forces, made up of Australian cavalry and camel-mounted troops, and Indian infantry, had advanced from Egypt across the Sinai Desert. Now they could use Akaba as a supply depot for an invasion of Palestine.

The British brought in a vigorous new commander, Edmund Allenby, to put their plan into action. He was under strict instruction to take the Palestinian capital, Jerusalem, by Christmas. In October, he overwhelmed the Turkish garrison at Gaza with an artillery assault, and used a massive cavalry charge to beat them into a retreat. On December 9, 1917, Allenby marched into Jerusalem. The holy city fell to the Allies two weeks ahead of schedule.

Waving the white flag. The mayor of Jerusalem (with a stick) surrenders to two British sergeants.

Double deals

From the outset of war in the Middle East, the British government had promised Arab leaders that they could rule their own lands independently after the war. But, unknown to the Arabs, they also made a secret pact with the French – the Sykes-Picot Agreement – to divide the region into areas that would be either French or British-run.

To muddy the waters still further, a powerful group of Jews from around the world, known as Zionists, had designs on Palestine too. They had long been campaigning to create a Jewish homeland there, where they could settle. As Allenby approached Jerusalem, the British foreign secretary, Arthur Balfour, wrote to Lord Rothschild, a leading Zionist, to declare his support. These dealings were at odds with the Arab cause, and when Lawrence found out, he was furious.

General Allenby makes his formal entry to Jerusalem. He marches behind the British governor of the city.

The road to Damascus

Lawrence and Feisal felt bitterly betrayed by the British government, but they continued to fight beside Allenby's troops. Blowing up the Hejaz train line, the Arabs prevented Turkish troops in Medina from moving north. This gave Allenby the edge he needed to launch the final big battle of his campaign. Fought near Megiddo (the site of the Biblical battle of Armageddon) in September 1918, it was a decisive victory for the Allies. Now, the road to Damascus, the Syrian capital, was wide open.

On October 1, the Arabs stormed Damascus and set up their own government, with Emir Feisal at the head. But, just two days later, Allenby caught up with them and announced that Syria would not be run by the Arabs, but by the French. Outraged, Lawrence immediately headed back to England to continue his campaign for Arab independence. Now his battles would be with Allied politicians.

Cavalry troops played a key role in the war in the Middle East. Here, Australian Light Horse regiments are advancing on Damascus. Sitting at the wayside are Turkish troops taken prisoner after the Battle of Megiddo.

A colossus falls

When the Russians pulled out of the war, Enver Pasha had sent troops to the Russian border, to regain territory the Turks had lost in the Caucasus. But this diverted their already depleted manpower away from Mesopotamia, where British troops advanced up the Tigris to take Mosul. When Allenby moved north through Syria, and seized Aleppo, the exhausted Turks finally gave in. On October 30, they signed an armistice and control over Turkish territory in the Middle East was split between the Allies. The colossal Ottoman empire – that had dominated the Middle East and the eastern Mediterranean for four centuries – had come to an end.

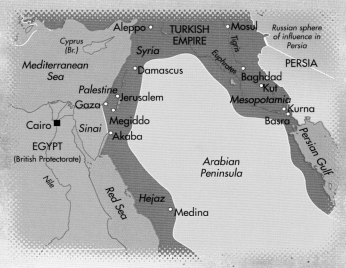

The Middle East in 1918

THE TIME FOR PEACE

With the German army retreating from France, and Turkey out of the war, the other Central Powers collapsed like a house of cards. They had staked everything on a brutal war of expansion. Defeat would cost them their empires.

A sinking ship

On September 15, 1918, an Allied force of French, Serbian, British, Greek and Italian troops, all based in Salonika, launched a daring assault against the rocky Bulgarian frontier. Thinking the war was lost, thousands of Bulgarian troops deserted. On September 28, their government signed a peace deal with the Allies.

Breaking strain

Many of the ethnic groups and member states that made up the Austro-Hungarian empire had long been demanding independence. The young emperor, Karl I, was desperate to save his fragile empire. In October 1918, he offered the member states more control over the way they were governed, but it was too little, too late. By the end of the month, Poland had claimed independence and Czech and Serb groups had broken away to form the new nations of Czechoslovakia and The Kingdom of Serbs, Croats and Slovenes – later renamed Yugoslavia. On November 1, Hungary, too, split from Austria.

The armistice between Germany and the Allies was signed in this train carriage. The negotiations were led by the Supreme Allied Commander, Ferdinand Foch (second on the right).

A final battle

As Karl's empire disintegrated, the Italians launched a furious attack against his army in the south of Austria. In the Battle of Vittorio Veneto they smashed their way into the country, capturing men and guns until the Austrians begged for peace on November 3. The emperor was forced to abandon his throne a few weeks later. The empire that had played a key role in starting the war, vanished forever from the map.

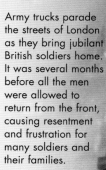

Army trucks parade the streets of London as they bring jubilant British soldiers home. It was several months before all the men were allowed to return from the front, causing resentment and frustration for many soldiers and their families.

Karl I succeeded his great uncle, Franz Josef I, to the Austro-Hungarian throne in the winter of 1916. Many of his people mistrusted him because his wife was Italian. He is pictured here, with his family, living in Switzerland after the war.

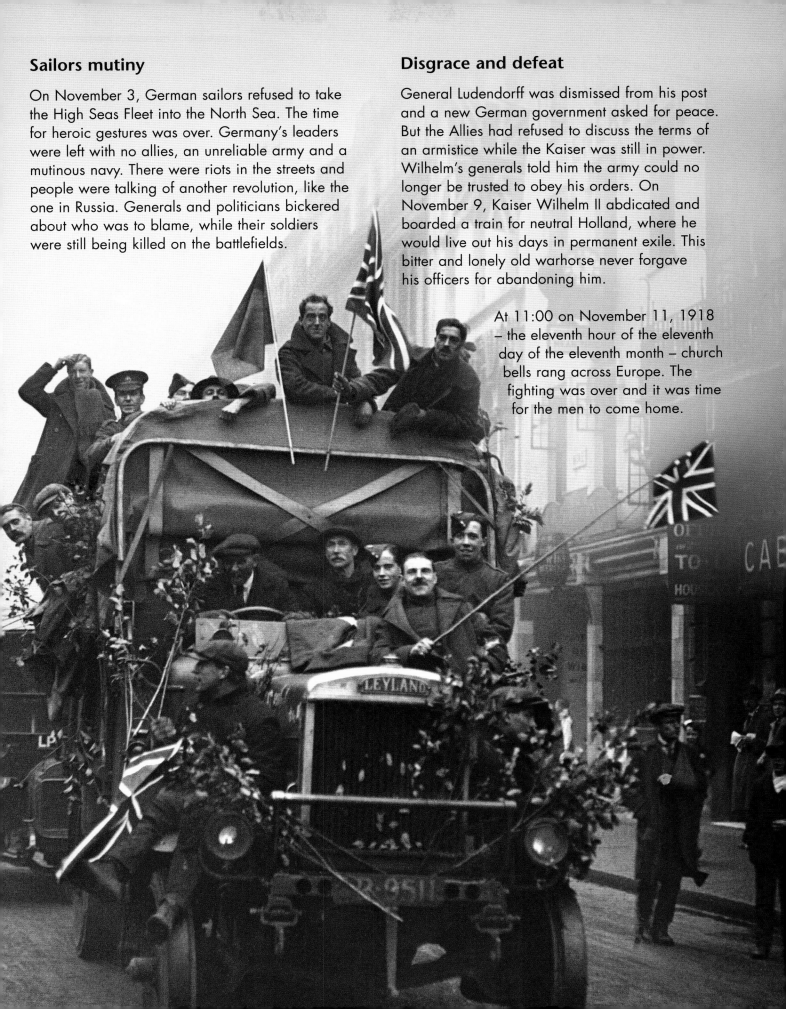

Sailors mutiny

On November 3, German sailors refused to take the High Seas Fleet into the North Sea. The time for heroic gestures was over. Germany's leaders were left with no allies, an unreliable army and a mutinous navy. There were riots in the streets and people were talking of another revolution, like the one in Russia. Generals and politicians bickered about who was to blame, while their soldiers were still being killed on the battlefields.

Disgrace and defeat

General Ludendorff was dismissed from his post and a new German government asked for peace. But the Allies had refused to discuss the terms of an armistice while the Kaiser was still in power. Wilhelm's generals told him the army could no longer be trusted to obey his orders. On November 9, Kaiser Wilhelm II abdicated and boarded a train for neutral Holland, where he would live out his days in permanent exile. This bitter and lonely old warhorse never forgave his officers for abandoning him.

At 11:00 on November 11, 1918 – the eleventh hour of the eleventh day of the eleventh month – church bells rang across Europe. The fighting was over and it was time for the men to come home.

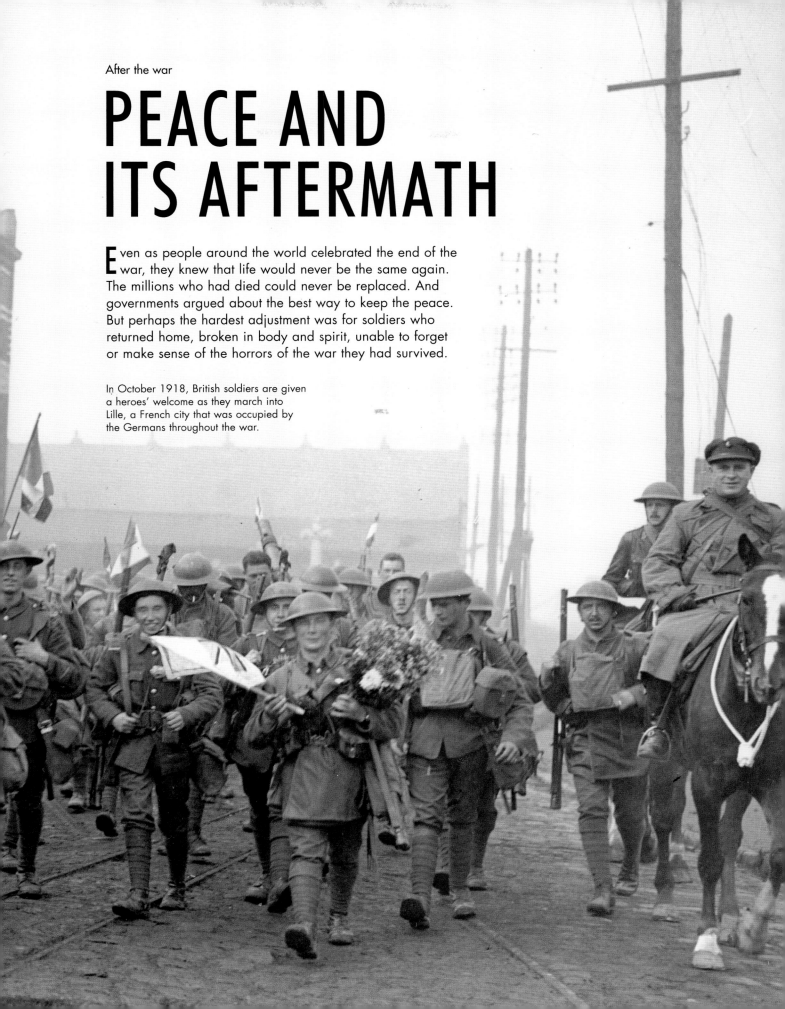

PEACE AND ITS AFTERMATH

Even as people around the world celebrated the end of the war, they knew that life would never be the same again. The millions who had died could never be replaced. And governments argued about the best way to keep the peace. But perhaps the hardest adjustment was for soldiers who returned home, broken in body and spirit, unable to forget or make sense of the horrors of the war they had survived.

In October 1918, British soldiers are given a heroes' welcome as they march into Lille, a French city that was occupied by the Germans throughout the war.

COMING TO TERMS

The armistice of November 1918 brought the fighting to an end. In January 1919, the Allied leaders invited diplomats from 32 nations to meet in Paris, to thrash out the international agreements that would be needed to keep the peace. But many of them disagreed about the terms, and the leaders of the defeated nations weren't even consulted. It was never going to be possible to please everyone.

The Treaty of Versailles

The peace talks were led by the prime ministers of Britain and France, David Lloyd George and Georges Clemenceau, and US President Woodrow Wilson. All three wanted to stop Germany from starting another war, but they disagreed about the best way to do it. Clemenceau and Lloyd George wanted to punish the Germans, but Wilson was more interested in setting up agreements that would prevent future wars. In the end, the three leaders reached an uneasy compromise set out in the Treaty of Versailles – so-called because it was signed at the Palace of Versailles, outside Paris.

The League of Nations

One of the first things agreed at the conference was Wilson's plan to set up a League of Nations. This would be a diplomatic organization in which international disputes could be discussed and resolved peacefully. It was to have limited success, partly because its members disagreed on how it should be run.

Punishing Germany

To limit the Germans' power to start another war, the treaty forced them to make huge cuts in the size of their military forces, and to hand over their colonies overseas. They even had to give up territories in Europe too. These included Polish, French and Danish lands conquered during the 18th and 19th centuries, as well as parts of France, Belgium and Russia that the Germans had occupied during the war.

INTERNET LINK

For a link to a website where you can find out how people from different countries reacted to the Treaty of Versailles, go to www.usborne-quicklinks.com

Germans take to the streets of Berlin to protest against losing the territories of Danzig and Posen after the Treaty of Versailles.

War guilt

Perhaps the most controversial part of the treaty was the 'war guilt' clause, which stated that Germany was to blame for starting the war. To compensate for the damage done during the fighting, the Allies ordered Germany to pay them huge sums of money. These payments – known as 'reparations' – were eventually set at £6,600,000,000 – a sum so big, the Germans estimated it would take until 1984 to pay it off.

Reactions in Germany

Although German politicians weren't invited to the Paris conference, they were summoned to Versailles to sign the treaty. They were shocked by how harsh the terms were, and at first they refused to sign. The German people bitterly resented the war guilt clause, as they felt they had only played a part in starting the war. Many staged street protests, but they had no choice but to accept it.

On June 28, 1919, the Germans reluctantly signed the Treaty of Versailles. Exactly five years after the assassination of Archduke Franz Ferdinand that had started it all, the First World War was officially over.

David Lloyd George (left), Georges Clemenceau (middle) and Woodrow Wilson – nicknamed the 'Big Three' – at the Paris peace conference in 1919.

REDRAWING THE MAP

With the Treaty of Versailles settled, further treaties were negotiated, to divide up lands held by Austria-Hungary, the Turkish empire and Bulgaria. Much of the map of the world was redrawn, as territories changed hands, national boundaries shifted and new countries were created. It wasn't a peaceful process, and has continued to cause unrest, and even armed conflict, in some of these regions ever since.

The day allotted for turning over territory to Rumania saw unrest in Hungary, as people tried, unsuccessfully, to resist the changes imposed on them.

New beginnings

When Austria-Hungary broke up, at the end of the war, the new countries of Czechoslovakia and Yugoslavia came into existence. Poland, which hadn't existed as an independent country since 1795, was put back on the map too.

To the north, Finland, Estonia, Latvia and Lithuania had been part of Russia until they were handed over to Germany under the Brest-Litovsk Treaty. The post-war treaties now recognized all these new countries as independent states, and set their official borders.

This map shows the new boundaries of Europe in 1924. Local disputes over territories meant that several revisions were made to the treaties of 1919.

Drawing the lines

As well as giving the new nations a chance to rule themselves, many of the changes in Europe were designed to reduce the power of the defeated nations. Austria, Hungary and Bulgaria were reduced to a fraction of their former size and deprived of many of their industrial resources, as much of their land was handed over to the surrounding countries. The Allied leaders hoped Czechoslovakia would provide a barrier between Austria and Germany, and that Yugoslavia would be big and powerful enough to bring peace and stability to the Balkans.

With the demands of so many countries to meet, the representatives of Britain, France, Italy and the USA often found it easier to make decisions without consulting the leaders of the smaller nations affected. This caused angry resentment in eastern Europe. People suddenly found themselves separated from their families by the new country borders and lumped together with people from different ethnic groups, whose language and culture they didn't share. So, right from the start, there were tensions, and sometimes violence.

Emir Feisal (front) and his Arab delegation, including Lawrence of Arabia (right of Feisal), at the Paris Peace Conference in 1919.

Broken promises

The former Turkish Ottoman empire was broken up too. The northern part was supposed to become the independent nation of Turkey, but Allied troops continued to occupy the region long after the treaties had been signed. Outraged, Turkish nationalists, led by General Mustafa Kemal, fought against the terms of the treaties. They drove out the occupying forces and eventually declared the independent Republic of Turkey in 1923.

During the war, the Allies had promised Arab leaders control of the Middle East. But they went back on their word, carving up most of the region into 'mandates' – states run by Britain and France, under the watch of the League of Nations. Half of Palestine was set aside as a homeland for Jewish people from around the world. But all this was met with armed resistance, so new treaties were brought in, during the 1920s, to give Arab leaders more control. The region has been troubled ever since.

This map shows the national boundaries in the Middle East in 1924. It also shows which mandates were run by France, and which were controlled by Britain.

INTERNET LINK

For links to websites where you can see maps and cartoons of the post-war treaties, and explore an interactive timeline of events in the Middle East since the war, go to www.usborne-quicklinks.com

THE GLORY AND THE PITY

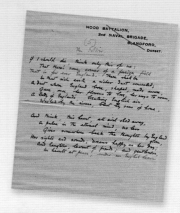

Rupert Brooke's original notes of *The Soldier* written on army writing paper

While politicians argued in Paris, soldiers prepared themselves to return home from the front, uncertain how they would explain their experiences to their families. Some turned to poetry, written by soldiers in the trenches, to make sense of the suffering and destruction they had seen. Many of these poems are so powerful, that they are still widely read today.

Warrior poets

Poetry was taken very seriously at the time of the war, as people believed it was the best way to express powerful feelings and beliefs – including love of your country. As they explored what it meant to fight and die for their homeland, some writers looked back to Greek and Roman poets for inspiration. These ancient poets had often argued that death in battle was the ultimate heroism.

England's finest

Rupert Brooke was a talented young poet fascinated by the idea of risking his life for his country. His poem *The Soldier* made him an instant literary star with its patriotic language:

A soldier takes advantage of a quiet moment to do some writing.

> *If I should die, think only this of me:*
> *That there's some corner of a foreign field*
> *Which is for ever England. There shall be*
> *In that rich earth a richer dust concealed;*
> *A dust whom England bore...*

Brooke's words seemed to capture a spirit of duty and willing self-sacrifice that gripped many soldiers at the opening of the war. He never fought, but he did die for his country. He enlisted and sailed for Gallipoli in March 1915. During the voyage he was bitten by a mosquito and died of blood poisoning. Brooke was buried on a Greek island, the home of the ancient warrior poets he so admired.

Broken hearts and minds

Men from across Europe and around the world went to war with visions of glory and heroism on the battlefield, but most were shocked by what they discovered in the trenches. Soldiers from every side expressed similar feelings of pain, loss and despair. Some even used their writing to demand an end to the conflict.

In 1917, a British poet and army officer, Siegfried Sassoon, wrote a letter to British newspapers describing the war as evil and unjust. Sassoon could have been shot, but the army decided he must be suffering from shell shock and sent him to a hospital in Scotland. Sassoon's poetry was well known by this time, and lots of his fellow patients asked him for help with their writing. Among them was a gentle young officer called Wilfred Owen, who would later become one of the most famous poets of the First World War.

> **INTERNET LINK**
> For a link to a website where you can read more poems by First World War poets, and find out more about their lives, go to
> **www.usborne-quicklinks.com**

A doomed poet

Owen was a shy and quiet man whose nerves had been shattered by months of hard fighting. He hated the war, but returned to the trenches in 1918 because he felt it was his duty to describe what was happening there. Owen wasn't interested in patriotism. His poetry was concerned with the hearts and minds of common soldiers.

War poet, Wilfred Owen

In *Dulce et Decorum Est*, Owen mocks the idea of proud warriors enjoying noble deaths. The title is a quote from a Roman writer, and translates as: it is sweet and right to die for your country. The poem describes a group of soldiers stumbling to reach a rest area:

Bent double, like old beggars under sacks,
Knock-kneed, coughing like hags, we cursed through
*   sludge,*
Till on the haunting flares we turned our backs
And towards our distant rest began to trudge.

When the men are suddenly gassed, Owen shows the reader a man dying from the gas. His pain and suffering are far from glorious:

If you could hear, at every jolt, the blood
Come gargling from the froth-corrupted lungs,
Obscene as cancer, bitter as the cud
Of vile, incurable sores on innocent tongues, —
My friend, you would not tell with such high zest
To children ardent for some desperate glory,
The old Lie: Dulce et decorum est
Pro patria mori.

Wilfred Owen was killed on November 4, 1918, just one week before the war ended. Church bells were ringing to celebrate Armistice Day when his parents received a telegram announcing his death. His poems are a chilling reminder of the suffering and pity of war.

A CHANGED WORLD

As soldiers returned home, many people were anxious to put the heartache and hardship of the war behind them, and get on with their lives. The cost of the war meant that governments faced massive debts, and everyone had to adjust to a future without the millions of men who had died. Life in the 1920s was going to be tough, but people wanted a reason to be cheerful again.

These children are using bundles of worthless German money as building blocks. Other people used the banknotes as fire lighters for their stoves.

Back to work?

During the war, agriculture and industry had expanded to meet the needs of the armed forces. This meant that many workers, including thousands of women, earned better wages and enjoyed greater social freedom than ever before. Soldiers returning home from the front were promised they could come back to work. But, as wartime industries were dismantled, there weren't so many jobs to go around. Women were expected to give up their jobs and go back home. For those left to support their families on a small war widow's pension, this was especially difficult. Government help for ex-servicemen left unemployed or disabled was little better. Many were forced onto the streets, and had to scrape a living by busking or selling trinkets. It was hardly the heroes' welcome they had expected to come home to.

INTERNET LINK

For a link to a website where you can read about the highs and lows of life during the Roaring Twenties, go to www.usborne-quicklinks.com

Worthless money

With many Germans already at starvation point as a result of the wartime blockades, the post-war reparations kept much of the population in poverty. The German government had no goods to trade with, so they simply printed more money to pay the Allies. This was a complete disaster. The more money they printed, the less it was worth. This is known as hyperinflation. By 1923, it was so bad that people suddenly found their life savings weren't even worth enough to buy a loaf of bread.

These people in Berlin are so poor, they are waiting in a bread line for free bread from the government, 1923.

Making good

Gradually, life became more prosperous, especially in America. Lessons learned from wartime industry – such as more efficient methods of mass-production – helped businesses to grow. Consumer goods such as radios, refrigerators and cars became cheaper and more widely available. Even in countries still struggling to recover from the war, young people wanted to have fun. Jazz music, dance halls, cinemas and revealing new women's clothes were all the rage, and the Hollywood movie industry boomed. This period became known as the Roaring Twenties.

As their lives improved, many people had more leisure time than ever before. This British car advertisement from 1930 shows a family on an outing in the countryside.

International rescue

The people of Europe soon gained from America's growing prosperity. In 1923, the US government arranged massive loans for Germany to help businesses and fund war reparations to the Allies. Money flowed into Europe, boosting industry and creating jobs. This took people out of unemployment and helped them to repair war damage. People began to feel things were getting better.

Boom and bust

In 1929, the US stock market, based on Wall Street in New York, crashed. Millions of people lost their investments; banks closed down; companies folded and people lost their jobs. Families all across America abandoned their homes and went in search of work. As the American government called in their loans, the world fell into a financial depression, which would cause years of high unemployment and hardship.

SOLDIERS' STORIES

Like the war poets, many novelists, playwrights and journalists came home from the war feeling it was their duty to write about their experiences. Some were so disturbed by the fighting, that it changed the way they looked at the world. They had to find new ways of writing to describe the terrible things they had seen.

In the field

One of the few novels published by a soldier during the war was *Le Feu* (*Under Fire*) by the French writer Henri Barbusse. Describing the war as a senseless and horrific ordeal, it caused outrage in France when it appeared in bookstores, in 1916. Barbusse had been a patriot, and volunteered to fight. But he was so shocked by the confusion and misery he saw on the battlefield he became a pacifist.

INTERNET LINK

For a link to a website where you can find out more about literature and journalism from the First World War, or to see the trailer for the 1930 movie version of All Quiet on the Western Front, go to www.usborne-quicklinks.com

This letter, from a chaplain serving on the Western Front, gives a vivid picture of the difficulties of trench warfare.

Letters home

During the war, newspapers had been so heavily censored and laden with propaganda, that many people didn't trust them. Letters from the front were censored too – sensitive details were cut or blacked out – but they gave readers a better sense of the mood in the trenches. After the war, some soldiers and nurses published their wartime letters and diaries for a public hungry to find out what it had really been like at the front.

Warrior writers

Different writers who had taken part in the fighting had very different responses to the war. Two British books – Edmund Blunden's *Undertones of War* and Robert Graves's *Goodbye to All That* – presented the conflict as a hellish but necessary duty. But the German writer Ernst Jünger took a very different tone. In his book *In Stahlgewittern* (*In Storms of Steel*) he praised the soldier's noble way of life and the excitement of battle. Another German, Erich Maria Remarque, produced a powerful anti-war book, *Im Westen Nichts Neues* (*All Quiet on the Western Front*). It followed a group of young volunteers through their nightmare in the trenches and their difficulties adjusting to life after the war.

A scene from the 1930 movie version of *All Quiet on the Western Front*

New directions

Some writers believed a whole generation had been cheated into fighting in the war and were then destroyed by it. One of them was the American Ernest Hemingway. He had been wounded in Italy, driving an ambulance behind the trenches. While living in Paris in the 1920s, he wrote about his wartime experiences in his book, *A Farewell to Arms*. In it, he explained that – for him – "words, such as glory, honor, courage" had lost their old meaning. To describe the world after the war, he had to come up with a new style of writing, using stark and brutal prose, which struck a chord with many war-weary readers.

Haunting memories

Many writers who had served during the war were haunted by the memories of the fighting. The sights and sounds of battle could suddenly resurface in their books – even those set in other worlds and times. J.R.R. Tolkien fought at Verdun and the Somme. In *The Lord of the Rings*, he described a swampy wasteland called the Dead Marshes. The bodies of slain warriors lay hidden in its murky waters, like the dead soldiers of a First World War no-man's-land, lost in their thousands in the mud.

The Harvest of Battle, by Christopher Nevinson. The flooded, muddy battlefield in this painting resembles Tolkien's description of the Dead Marshes in *The Lord of the Rings*.

VISIONS OF WAR

Many artists had served as soldiers during the war. Some governments even employed official war artists, photographers and film-makers to keep a visual record of the action. But some of the most powerful images of the war were produced after the fighting had ended.

The lonely dead

Taking pictures in the trenches was difficult and dangerous, and there were strict limits on where photographers were allowed to take their cameras. So there are very few pictures that show the intensity of battle. Many images of dead soldiers were censored or destroyed – in respect for their families and to keep morale strong at home. Those that were printed in newspapers usually showed lonely corpses in no-man's-land or one or two bodies sprawled in a trench. Looking at these pictures, it's hard to believe that thousands of men died every day of the war.

Charlie Chaplin as a soldier in the trenches, in his 1918 movie, *Shoulder Arms*. He carries an unusual kit, which includes a mouse trap, a cheese-grater and a tin bath.

INTERNET LINK

For links to websites where you can find out more about art, photography and movies of the First World War, go to **www.usborne-quicklinks.com**

John Singer Sargent's painting *Gassed*, shows British troops injured and blinded after a gas attack.

Photo stories

Some photographers were determined to show the terror and thrill of battle, even if they had to bend the truth to do it. The Australian, Frank Hurley, blended images of explosions, men and planes into a single photo. Critics attacked these 'collages' and called Hurley a fake, but his pictures are still among the most powerful of the war.

Crisis and comedy

Cinematography was a new art at the start of the 20th century, but this didn't stop the British filming their 'big push' at the Somme. Combining real footage of infantry leaving the trenches with staged action scenes, *The Battle of the Somme* was a massive hit when it was released in August 1916. But it showed few of the true horrors of the war.

Charlie Chaplin's *Shoulder Arms* took a more comic approach to the fighting. Playing an awkward American soldier, Chaplin disguised himself as a tree to spy behind enemy lines and ended the conflict by kidnapping the Kaiser.

A detail from *Skat Players* by Otto Dix. This shocking painting and collage depicts three crippled and mutilated ex-soldiers, playing cards.

War hungry

Otto Dix was a German painter who had volunteered to fight in the trenches, hungry for adventure. He won medals for his bravery, but the war sickened and haunted him. As Germany pieced itself together after the Armistice, Dix began painting the maimed ex-servicemen he saw begging on the streets. To many people they were an unwelcome reminder of the past, but Dix was determined that people should not be allowed to ignore their continued suffering.

LEST WE FORGET

As many as 21 million men, women and children lost their lives in the First World War. No previous conflict in history had caused so many casualties. Throughout the war, people worked to make sure the dead were treated with respect – even when the fighting made this difficult. But, when peace came, nations across the world made more lasting memorials to those who had died.

A German painting of a soldier's grave, in a poppy field in Flanders, 1919

Killed in action

The sheer numbers killed meant that it just wasn't possible for most countries to transport their dead back, to be buried at home. Many of the men who died in battle had to be buried hastily at night, just behind the front line. Where possible, these graves were given simple markers, and armies tried to keep a record of who was buried where, but many bodies were simply never found.

Set in stone

In Britain, France and Germany, almost every family lost at least one member. Grieving relatives needed to feel that their loved ones had not been forgotten. So, after the war, land close to the battlefields was set aside for cemeteries.

Many survivors felt that no one grave should look more important than any another, regardless of the rank, race or religion of the dead person. So each was marked by a simple headstone that recorded a name and a date. Back at home, many cities and local communities around the world set up their own war memorials in the years after the war, carved with lists of names of all those who had died.

A crowd looks on as a British general stands in front of a war memorial he has just unveiled in central London, October 1925.

We will remember them

In the years following the war, November 11, the anniversary of the Armistice, was set aside as a day of remembrance. Many people were struck by the beautiful red poppies that began to cover the battlefields of Flanders, once the fighting had stopped. The poppy quickly became a powerful symbol of the First World War dead.

Now, on November 11 every year, people wear poppies and lay wreaths at war memorials all around the world, to remember those who have died in all wars, not just the First World War.

THE SECOND WORLD WAR

In the twenty years between the wars, the science of warfare advanced at an unprecedented rate. During the First World War, vast armies bled each other white at Verdun, the Somme and on the Eastern Front, but neither side was able to achieve a clear breakthrough. In the Second World War, superior weaponry and tactics ensured that most of the great battles ended in decisive victories. Aside from Stalingrad, they were also won with far fewer casualties. This didn't mean that fewer people died in the Second World War. Millions of innocent people lost their lives during the course of the war — in the famines that came in the wake of the fighting, in Nazi death camps, and during bombing raids which both sides inflicted on the enemy civilian populations. In fact, far more civilians died than those engaged in the actual fighting.

Americans soldiers land at Omaha Beach, Normandy,
France, as part of the Normandy Landings, June 6, 1944.

THE WORLD AT WAR

The Second World War was the most catastrophic conflict in history. Every continent on Earth was drawn into its fiery cauldron. Fought between two opposing alliances, known as the Allies and the Axis, the war began on September 1, 1939, when Germany invaded Poland. It ended six years and a day later with the official surrender of Germany's ally Japan on September 2, 1945. In that time, as many as 50 million men and women may have been killed.

Hitler in full cry, during a Nazi Party rally on the eve of the war

Allied powers

Under Axis control

Neutral countries

By the autumn of 1942, Germany and her Axis allies controlled all the territory shown here in red. Also marked are the captial cities of the major Allied and Axis powers, and the sites and dates of major battles.

FINLAND

NORWAY

SWEDEN

SOVIET UNION

Leningrad 1941-44

Moscow 1941

DENMARK

Kursk 1943

Stalingrad 1942-43

IRELAND

Battle of Britain 1940

BRITAIN

NETHERLANDS

POLAND

Berlin 1945

Warsaw Uprising 1944

London

BELGIUM

Normandy Landings 1944

Battle of the Bulge 1944

GREATER GERMANY

SLOVAKIA

RUMANIA

Paris

FRANCE

SWITZERLAND

HUNGARY

ITALY

YUGOSLAVIA

BULGARIA

SPAIN

Rome

GREECE

TURKEY

Territory under Allied control

El Alamein 1942

SAUDI ARABIA

EGYPT

These German soldiers are marching in a victory parade following the conquest of Poland in 1939. The distinctive march is called the goose step, and was kept for special ceremonial occasions.

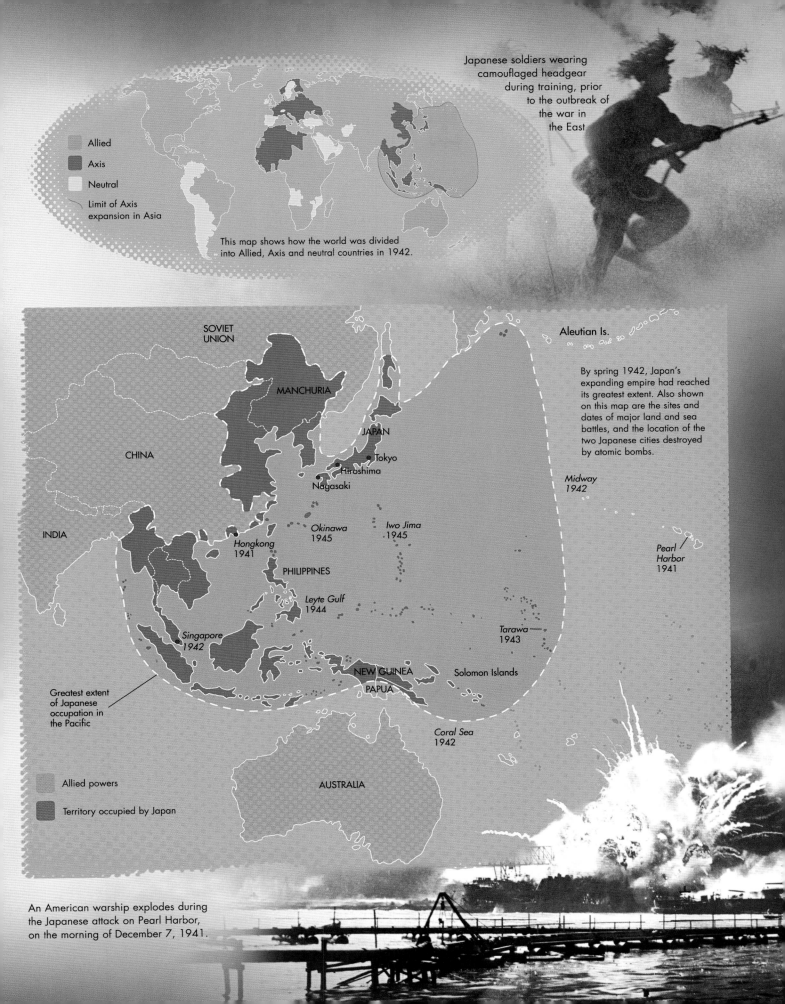

Allied

Axis

Neutral

Limit of Axis
expansion in Asia

This map shows how the world was divided
into Allied, Axis and neutral countries in 1942.

Japanese soldiers wearing
camouflaged headgear
during training, prior
to the outbreak of
the war in
the East

SOVIET
UNION

Aleutian Is.

MANCHURIA

By spring 1942, Japan's
expanding empire had reached
its greatest extent. Also shown
on this map are the sites and
dates of major land and sea
battles, and the location of the
two Japanese cities destroyed
by atomic bombs.

CHINA

JAPAN

Tokyo

Hiroshima

Nagasaki

Midway
1942

INDIA

Okinawa
1945

Iwo Jima
1945

Pearl
Harbor
1941

Hongkong
1941

PHILIPPINES

Leyte Gulf
1944

Singapore
1942

Tarawa
1943

Greatest extent
of Japanese
occupation in
the Pacific

NEW GUINEA

Solomon Islands

PAPUA

Coral Sea
1942

Allied powers

Territory occupied by Japan

AUSTRALIA

An American warship explodes during
the Japanese attack on Pearl Harbor,
on the morning of December 7, 1941.

THE RISE OF THE DICTATORS

The years after the First World War saw the rise of a new kind of political leader – the 20th century dictator. History is full of tyrants and monsters, but their powers were limited by the technology of their times. These new dictators used radio communication and broadcasts, to control every aspect of people's lives. Their whims and fancies destroyed millions of lives.

Mussolini, in full flow, addresses his fellow Italians in a New Year's Day speech in 1935.

A troubled world

The First World War left over 20 million dead, and dramatically redrew the map of Europe. Great empires and dynasties had fallen, and in the sullen peace that followed the victors nursed their wounds and the defeated yearned for revenge. Only America had done well out of the war, emerging as the world's most powerful nation.

Italian pioneer

The first great dictator to emerge from the ashes of war was a former teacher and journalist named Benito Mussolini – known to his people as *Il Duce* (meaning 'the leader'). Italy hadn't done well out of the war – although it had been on the winning side – and in the early 1920s, the country was crippled by strikes, street fighting between extremist political groups and general disorder. Mussolini, leader of the right-wing Fascist party, swept to power in 1922, promising to bring order and pride back to Italy. With tight control over the media and violent suppression of all opposition, he gave Italians the illusion that their country had become a thriving success. But his economic policies failed badly and he began to look abroad for a solution. Italy, he declared, should have a new Roman empire.

126

Hitler, on the eve of his seizure of power, uses his hypnotic gaze to full effect.

Hitler enters the stage

Germany had lost the war and her economy was in ruins. The worldwide Great Depression brought further misery to a country already suffering from massive unemployment after a decade of raging inflation.

Adolf Hitler, a former soldier and failed artist, offered the German people a clear solution to their problems. If they voted for him and his racist and ultra-right-wing Nazi Party, they would make the country great again and destroy the causes of Germany's misfortune. These Hitler named as Jews and communists. He came to power in 1933 and immediately began a process that would plunge the world into war and bring total ruin to his country.

INTERNET LINK
For a link to a website where you can explore the lives of Hitler, Stalin and Mussolini, go to
www.usborne-quicklinks.com

Japan's military leaders

Japan had been on the winning side in the First World War, but it too was suffering from serious economic problems as a result of the Great Depression. The military became increasingly involved in Japanese politics. They believed the solution to Japan's problems was to expand her empire – not only close to home in China, but over the whole of the Pacific, especially in territory controlled by fading colonial powers such as Britain, France and Holland.

Japan produced no individual dictator like Hitler or Mussolini, but the power of the military created an atmosphere just as oppressive as any dictatorship. "If there are any opposed to the 'Imperial Way' (Japanese expansion)," declared war minister General Ariki in 1933, "we shall give them an injection with a bullet and bayonet."

Foreign Minister Yosuke Matsuoka was one of many pre-war Japanese politicians who believed Japan should expand its empire.

The red czar

In Russia, the First World War had led directly to a communist revolution, and the country had been renamed the Soviet Union. When Lenin, the leader of the revolution, died in 1924, he was replaced by a wily Georgian named Joseph Stalin.

This photograph of Joseph Stalin shows some of the steely determination which allowed him to dominate the Soviet Union for three decades.

Stalin introduced vast changes in the Soviet Union, pushing through reforms that transformed the backward country into a powerful industrial nation. But he also had millions of people imprisoned and executed, including many officers of the Russian army – which became known as the Red Army.

The Russian communist rulers had much in common with the Nazis and Fascists – in their regulation of newspapers, radio and cinema; their suppression of all opposition; and their total control over people's lives.

THE FRAGILE DEMOCRACIES

Such was the dreadful cost of the First World War that even most of its victors seemed like losers. France and Britain had begun the 20th century as the world's greatest powers. But in defending themselves against Germany to maintain that position, they had paid a terrible price. The United States, who had prospered in the war, retreated from the world stage. As the dictators waxed in power, the democracies waned before their eyes.

An anxious crowd mills around Wall Street, on the day of the 'Wall Street Crash'.

The empires strike back

In the 19th century, Britain, France and other European nations had built up large empires in Africa and Asia, which they controlled and exploited. The colonies were both markets for the goods of the occupying country, and suppliers of cheap raw materials. But, by the 1930s, many of them were costing more to rule than they were making. And many of the local people had begun protesting against occupation, and demanding independence.

All fall down

When, in 1929, the US stock market failed, this triggered a serious economic slump, resulting in widespread unemployment, poverty and starvation. Imports to US factories and shops were seriously reduced, and overseas loans from American banks were recalled. The *Great Depression*, as it was known, affected countries throughout the world, from Britain to Japan.

Unwanted responsibilities

After the First World War, the United States emerged as the wealthiest and most powerful nation on Earth. American banks lent vast sums of money to the war-ravaged countries of Europe, while countries all over the world exported materials and goods to American factories and shops.

But many American citizens did not want their country to be involved in foreign entanglements – especially in another overseas war. This policy, called Isolationism, would later turn out to be unrealistic for America – and would have been disastrous for the rest of the world.

Fear of war

Because the First World War had caused such carnage, the victorious countries were determined to prevent another war from happening, especially as the new generation of bomber aircraft and poison gas would be able to cause terrible destruction to cities. During the 1930s, many people actively campaigned for peace. Politicians such as Winston Churchill, who talked of standing up to the dictators and preparing for war, were unpopular.

The League of Nations

The League of Nations, a forerunner of the United Nations, was made up of countries that pledged to settle their disputes without resorting to war. Member nations could show their disapproval of other countries by enforcing economic sanctions. But the League had two major flaws: the United States never joined, and there was no armed force to back up its decisions. Japan, Germany and Italy were all members, but they all left when their aggressive foreign policies were condemned by the League.

The Maginot Line

In case of war, the French hoped to defend their border against Germany with the Maginot Line – a string of underground forts, 140km (87 mile) long, built during the 1930s at a cost of $200 million. It was a formidable obstacle, but when war came, Hitler's armies simply avoided it, sweeping into France through Luxembourg and Belgium.

INTERNET LINK
For a link to a website where you can see more photographs of the Great Depression, go to
www.usborne-quicklinks.com

Unemployed Americans in Brooklyn, New York, queue for free food, during the Great Depression.

HITLER'S GERMANY

When the Nazis came to power in 1933, the British ambassador to Berlin, Sir Horace Rumbold, commented, "Many of us... have a feeling that we are living in a country where fantastic hooligans and eccentrics have got the upper hand." Only the Soviet Union could rival their sinister lunacy. But there was method in their madness. Hitler put his country back to work, and by 1939 Germany had become the most powerful nation in Europe.

The Nazis organized massive rallies, like this one at Nuremberg.

Here, Hitler surveys ranks of German soldiers before starting to speak.

Nazi propaganda

Once in power, the Nazis set about transforming their country into a reflection of their own crooked image. Radio, cinema, newspapers and magazines pumped out an endless stream of Nazi propaganda. Rallies and torchlit parades were held to reinforce their message – which could be summed up by three main points, made plain in Hitler's political testament, *Mein Kampf*.

✠ The Jews were the enemy of mankind, and should be destroyed.

✠ Communism too, should be eradicated.

✠ The Aryan race (people of pure Germanic blood), led by Hitler, should conquer and enslave the Slavs of Eastern Europe and Russia.

Back to work

The Nazis solved Germany's unemployment problem with ambitious public construction projects – grand new government buildings and a motorway system were built. Women were forced out of jobs and replaced by men. New jobs were created in armaments factories and in the armed forces. By 1939 Germany was a prosperous and formidably-armed country.

INTERNET LINK
For a link to a website where you can play a game to go undercover in 1930s Germany, go to
www.usborne-quicklinks.com

Race hate

At the very heart of Nazi policy was a deeply-felt hatred of Jews. As soon as the Nazis came to power, Jews were expelled from government and university jobs. Jewish shops were attacked, and Jews were bullied and humiliated in the streets. Many left. Others could not afford to go, or just hoped things would get better. But their future was bleak. Germans were also taught to despise other racial groups, such as the Slavs, Gypsies and Negroes. The Nazis called them *untermensch*, which meant 'sub-human' in German.

A Hitler Youth drum and bugle corps plays a fanfare during the beginning of a Nazi ceremony. Hitler believed that German boys should be prepared for war from an early age.

Snaring the young

Along with their corrosive anti-Semitism, perhaps the most disturbing thing about the Nazis was the way they tried to corrupt the minds of German children. Nazi ideas, especially on race, were taught as part of the school curriculum. Young boys joined an organization called the Hitler Youth, where they learned how to be soldiers. Young girls joined the League of German Maidens where they were taught that their greatest role in life was to provide boys for Hitler's armies.

Here is a question from a school mathematics textbook, used during the Nazi era: *"A bomber on takeoff carries 12 dozen bombs each weighing 10 kilos. The aircraft makes for Warsaw, the heart of international Jewry. It bombs the town. On takeoff, with all bombs on board and a fuel tank containing 1500 kilos of fuel, the aircraft weighs 8 tonnes. When it returns from the crusade there are still 230 kilos of fuel left. What is the weight of the aircraft when empty?"*

THE ROAD TO WAR

The 1930s were a dark and difficult decade. As the world struggled to recover from the Depression, Japan, Italy and Germany seized territory from other nations. The League of Nations, founded to prevent further wars, made feeble protests. But the dictators grew bolder. Would *anything* they did provoke retaliation?

1931

Japan invades the Chinese region of Manchuria, hoping to expand her empire in Asia. The League of Nations protests, but without success.

October 1935-May 1936

Italy invades Ethiopia from her nearby colonies of Eritrea and Somaliland. Barefooted tribesmen lose an eight-month battle against Italian forces, who use poison gas and bombers against them. The League of Nations protests, and imposes sanctions. But these are ineffective and are soon lifted.

British Prime Minister Neville Chamberlain with Hitler, September 1938

March 1936

German troops march into the Rhineland – the border region between Germany and France. According to the terms of the Treaty of Versailles, at the end of the First World War, this was supposed to be free of military forces.

July 1936-1939

General Francisco Franco leads a rebellion against Spain's left-wing government. Italy and Germany send arms and men to help him. In 1939, Franco wins and Spain becomes a fascist state. The bombing of Spanish towns by German aircraft increases the desire for peace in France and Britain.

October-November 1936

Germany, Italy and Japan discuss the formation of an anti-communist alliance, known as the Rome-Berlin-Tokyo Axis – later known as the 'Axis' powers.

1937-1938

Japanese forces seize the main ports of China. The Japanese army commits atrocities in the city of Nanjing – a deliberate warning to China not to resist.

March 1938

German troops enter Austria, and unite the country with Germany. Known as the *Anschluss*, this had also been forbidden by the Versailles Treaty.

August-September 1938

Hitler claims the Sudetenland, an area of Czechoslovakia where people speak German, should be part of Germany. The British and French prime ministers fly to Munich for crisis talks. Their countries are ill-prepared for war. There is also a feeling that Germany had been badly treated after the First World War and had grounds for complaint.

This results in a policy of 'appeasement' – giving in to German demands. The British and French allow Germany to take over Sudetenland. Hitler declares, "I have no more territorial demands to make in Europe." But it is a blatant lie.

March 1939

German troops seize western Czechoslovakia, and occupy Prague. The British and French realize appeasement has failed. Hitler's next obvious target, Poland, is offered military help. Rapid rearmament and conscription begins.

Summer 1939

As Hitler prepares Germany for the invasion of Poland, Britain, France and the Soviet Union have half-hearted discussions about an alliance against Germany.

August 1939

In a move which astonishes the world, sworn enemies Nazi Germany and Soviet Russia announce they have signed a non-aggression pact – promising not to attack each other. A secret clause divides Poland between them.

In Germany, military commanders are worried Hitler is set to take a disastrous gamble and commit their country to a war it cannot win. Hitler reassures them that after the conquest of Poland, Britain and France will be anxious to make peace with Germany.

INTERNET LINK
For a link to a website where you can
see film footage of conflicts around
the world in the 1930s, go to
www.usborne-quicklinks.com

German troops march through
the gates of Hradschin Castle,
Prague, during the occupation
of the Czech capital in 1938.

Residents of Warsaw get their first look at the German invaders, as motorcycle troops trundle over tramlines in the Polish capital on October 1, 1939. The occupation would last over four years and almost all the city would be destroyed.

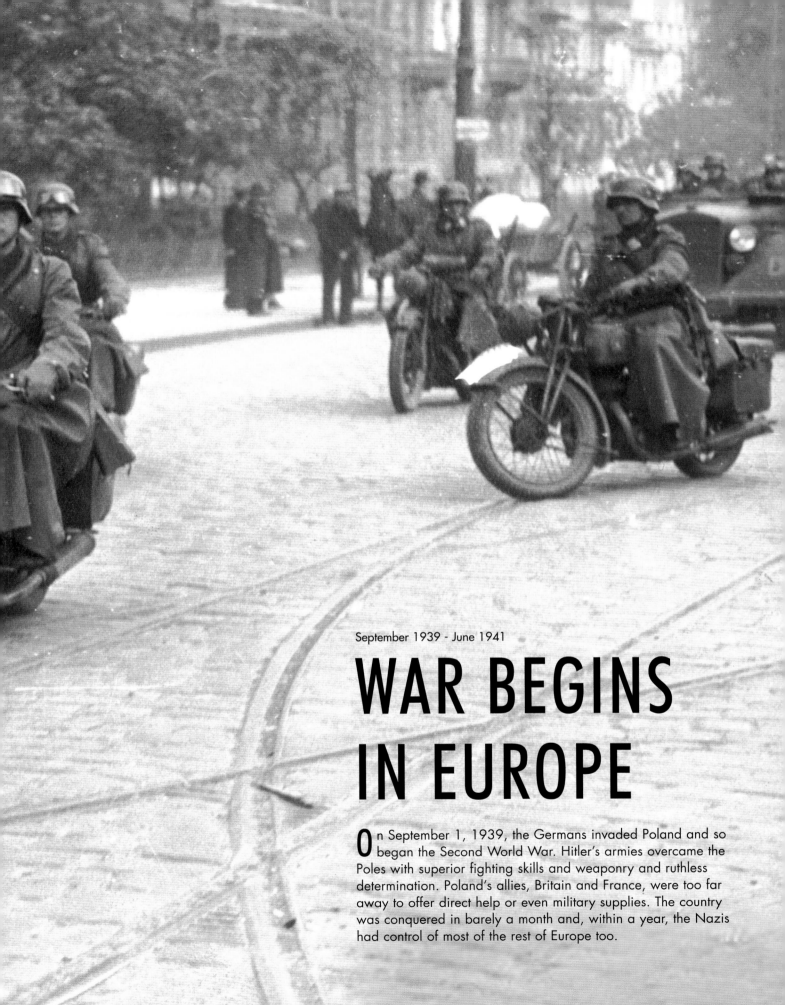

September 1939 - June 1941

WAR BEGINS IN EUROPE

On September 1, 1939, the Germans invaded Poland and so began the Second World War. Hitler's armies overcame the Poles with superior fighting skills and weaponry and ruthless determination. Poland's allies, Britain and France, were too far away to offer direct help or even military supplies. The country was conquered in barely a month and, within a year, the Nazis had control of most of the rest of Europe too.

WAR BREAKS OUT

The Second World War began in the hours before the dawn of September 1, 1939, when Nazi troops and aircraft flooded over Germany's eastern border and into Poland. This prompted Poland's allies Britain and France to declare war on Germany on September 3. Within two years the war would turn from a European to a global conflict, which lasted until September 2, 1945.

INTERNET LINK
For a link to a website where you can watch archive footage of Germany's invasion of Poland, go to www.usborne-quicklinks.com

German SS troops seek shelter behind a tank, during the invasion of the Baltic port of Danzig. If you look carefully, you can see the SS 'death's head' insignia on the tank.

A new way of fighting

The first week of September saw a succession of beautiful late summer days – perfect for the German army to try its new tactic of *Blitzkrieg* – meaning *lightning war*. First, squadrons of bombers flew deep into Poland, destroying air bases, fuel and ammunition dumps, railway stations and military headquarters. Then, dive bombers screamed down to machine-gun and bomb Polish front line troops. Tanks and troop-carrying vehicles probed the Polish lines for weak spots, bursting through to attack strong points from behind. Large numbers of foot soldiers followed, to mop up any remaining resistance. The idea of *Blitzkrieg* was not a new one, but the Germans were the first to try it.

Dirty tricks

The invasion of Poland started with a bizarre charade known as 'Operation Canned Goods' – staged by Germany to justify the attack. SS soldiers executed 12 ordinary criminals dressed in Polish army uniforms, and placed the bodies around a German radio station near the Polish border. Then they announced that the Poles had attacked the radio station. Journalists and press photographers were called in to record the grisly hoax.

Polish cavalry units like this one were unsuited to fight German tanks and aircraft.

136

The fate of Poland

Poland lost control of the war in the first two or three days. Although the Poles had a larger army than the Germans, they had fewer tanks and aircraft. The Polish front line quickly crumbled. Thousands of fleeing civilians clogged the roads away from the fighting, preventing reinforcements from coming forward. Polish troops were no match for their powerful opponents. The Polish capital Warsaw was heavily bombed, causing further panic and disruption. Within a week, the German army had reached the outskirts of Warsaw. The city held out for over two weeks, but finally surrendered on September 27.

Trouble from the East

On September 17, when most of the fighting was over, Poland was also invaded by Soviet troops. They swiftly occupied land that had secretly been given to the Soviet Union during negotiations for the Nazi-Soviet Pact.

"Close your hearts to pity"

The Nazis saw the Poles as subhuman – fit only for slavery. On the eve of the attack, Hitler told his generals: "Close your hearts to pity. Act brutally. Whatever we find in the shape of an upper class in Poland is to be liquidated…" Close behind came squads of SS *Einsatzgruppen* (special forces), with orders to find and kill Jews, and anyone – priests, teachers, aristocrats – who might organize resistance. 'House cleaning' was how the Nazis described this.

The worms turn

Hitler knew his attack on Poland carried the risk of war with France and Britain, but he was full of contempt for them. "They are little worms," he said. "I saw them at Munich. I'll cook them a stew they'll choke on." But the worms turned. Britain and France declared war on September 3. Germany now had two powerful enemies on its western border.

THE FALL OF WESTERN EUROPE

After his whirlwind success in Poland, Hitler hoped the French and British would be eager to make peace. But he was to be disappointed. During the winter months, fighting almost came to a standstill. The Germans called this phase of the war *Sitzkrieg*; the British called it the *Bore War*. It was the calm before the storm. When winter passed, the war began in earnest. Once again, *Blitzkrieg* proved very successful for the Germans.

German troops, heading for the English Channel, storm through a village in the first days of their invasion of France.

Slow start

At the start of the war, there was a sudden change of pace in France and Britain. People began to carry gas masks wherever they went, in case the German air force dropped gas bombs. Children were evacuated from cities, and sent to live in the country. But after a few weeks, when nothing happened, there was a sense of anticlimax. Fighting began again in the Spring of 1940, and brought a series of brilliant German victories.

The war heats up

On April 9, Nazi troops invaded Norway and Denmark. The Norwegians resisted the invaders until June 9. The Danes surrendered within hours. These further Nazi triumphs forced British Prime Minister Neville Chamberlain to resign. He was replaced by Winston Churchill, a famously staunch opponent of Hitler's. On May 10, German armies invaded Western Europe, and troops poured into Belgium and Holland. Within four days, Holland surrendered. Belgium was overrun by May 28. On May 13 the Germans unleashed a massive *Blitzkrieg* offensive in the French Ardennes region on France's Belgian border. Fresh from their recent triumphs in Poland, German tanks and soldiers, under General Heinz Guderian, reached the English Channel in a week.

INTERNET LINK

For a link to a website where you can watch a movie that gives you a glimpse of what it was like to be at the Dunkirk evacuation, go to **www.usborne-quicklinks.com**

A small miracle

Guderian's forces cut the Allied armies in two. Those stranded to the north were caught in a narrow pocket around the French port of Dunkirk. In an extraordinary few days, a fleet of 900 British ferries, sailing boats and navy vessels, helped by the French navy, rescued over 200,000 British troops and around 110,000 French, Dutch and Belgian troops.

The map of Europe in summer 1940

- Axis powers
- Areas under Axis control
- Allied nations
- Neutral nations

In less than a year, German armies conquered Poland, Norway, Denmark, Holland, Belgium and France. But Britain remained undefeated.

These British troops on the beach at Dunkirk, are surrounded by abandoned equipment and dead and wounded comrades. They had only their rifles to defend themselves from constant air attack by German dive bombers.

On to Paris

As the British withdrew from the continent, the German army pressed on to Paris. The French capital fell on June 14, a month after the invasion. A week later, France surrendered. Hitler was ecstatic. In the First World War, a million Germans had died in four years, trying to defeat France. Now Germany had succeeded in less than six weeks, at a cost of a mere 27,000 lives.

National humiliation

With characteristic spitefulness, Hitler ordered the French surrender to be signed in the same railway carriage that the French had used to accept the German surrender in the First World War. France was now divided into two. The north and west was occupied by the Germans. The south was ruled by the Vichy government – French politicians who collaborated with the Germans. The victory over France was Hitler's greatest military triumph. But although the future held further success, the tide would slowly turn against him.

Here, a week after the surrender, Hitler makes a dawn tour of Paris.

THE BATTLE FOR BRITAIN

By the late summer of 1940, most of Europe was in German hands. A plan was swiftly hatched to sweep away Hitler's final enemy: Britain. Codenamed *Operation Sealion*, the aim was for the German air force – the *Luftwaffe* – to win control of the skies over the English Channel. Then, an army invasion could be safely launched from the French coast, with no fear of air attack. A date was set for September 15, but first the RAF – the Royal Air Force – had to be defeated.

British *Spitfire* fighter planes such as this one were tremendously effective against German bombers and fighters.

Cat and mouse

The Battle of Britain began on July 10, when the *Luftwaffe* began attacking convoy ships in the Channel. The idea was to draw British planes into battle, and destroy them. The commander-in-chief, Hermann Goering, boasted he could defeat the RAF in just four days. But, in the fierce fighting that followed, the *Luftwaffe* lost 600 planes – twice as many as the RAF. So Goering changed tactics; this time it was very effective. British airfields were targeted, with heavy losses of both planes and men.

The *Spitfire* was one of the most admired fighter planes of the war because of its advanced design, which made it especially easy to fly.

INTERNET LINK
For a link to a website where you can find out how Londoners coped during the Blitz, go to **www.usborne-quicklinks.com**

The *Messerschmitt ME 109*, Germany's principal fighter aircraft during the war.

The Blitz

Just as the *Luftwaffe* was beginning to look like winning, the RAF bombed Berlin. An enraged Hitler immediately ordered Goering to bomb London. On September 7, a thousand German bombers and fighters attacked the British capital, killing about 500 people. The raids continued – but they gave the RAF time to repair its airfields and rebuild its strength.

Soon the *Luftwaffe* was seriously losing ground, and was forced to switch from daytime attacks to night raids. Although these were far trickier, their planes were less likely to be shot down. During the 'Blitz' – which lasted until May 16, 1941 – London and other cities were bombed almost nightly. But the British remained unconquered and Hitler was forced to admit defeat – for the first time since the war began.

St. Thomas's Hospital, close to the Houses of Parliament, was heavily damaged during the Blitz.

A long way from home

In their battle with the RAF, the German air force was struggling against several vital disadvantages. Their planes could only stay a short time over England before fuel ran low and they had to return home. RAF fighter planes such as the *Spitfire* and *Hurricane* could outfly many of the *Luftwaffe* fighters and bombers. By the time war broke out, the British had a useful radar system, which enabled them to detect incoming German planes, and spared RAF pilots the need to fly unnecessary, exhausting patrols.

The final losses in the Battle of Britain were 1,700 German planes, and 900 British planes. The RAF had 1,500 fighter pilots, drawn from Britain, the Commonwealth, Poland and Czechoslovakia. Over 400 of them died during the fighting, but their contribution had been crucial. At the height of battle, Winston Churchill famously described their achievement: "Never in the field of human conflict was so much owed by so many to so few."

GERMANY INVADES EASTERN EUROPE

With his enemies in Western Europe defeated, and Britain bloodied, Hitler began to plan the invasion of Russia. But, before he could, a series of crises in Eastern Europe demanded his attention. The most vexing of these was caused by Germany's own ally, Italy.

Italy joins the war

Although they were Axis allies, Mussolini did not commit his country to Hitler's war in Europe until he was sure the Germans would win. In the final stages of Hitler's campaign in Western Europe, Italy invaded France from the south.

With France defeated, Italian troops invaded the small colony of British Somaliland, which they managed to take in August 1940. This was their one success of the entire war – although it was seized back by the British within a year. In September they launched an invasion of British-occupied Egypt, from their colony of Libya, only to have their tanks run out of fuel 100km (60 miles) over the border. The British responded with retaliatory attacks on Libya. A disastrous invasion of Greece followed in October. The Italians were expelled within weeks, and lost half their battleships at Taranto.

German troops prepare to board transport planes to take them to Crete, in June 1941.

A powerful friend

Mussolini had desperately wanted to show the world that his Fascist Italy could be just as successful as Nazi Germany. He talked boastfully of "a new Roman empire" and referred to the Mediterranean Sea as "an Italian lake". Now, Hitler had to rescue his ally. German troops, rested and confident after their recent victories, flooded into Libya to save it from the British. The following spring, Greece was invaded again, together with Yugoslavia. Yugoslavia fell in little more than a week, but it would prove to be far easier to overrun than to hold on to. Hundreds of thousands of Yugoslavian soldiers disappeared into the mountains and forests, to harass the occupying German army for the rest of the war.

Mediterranean victories

The Germans took the Greek mainland within a month. Then, in a final military masterstroke, they invaded Crete. Hitler was determined that his one supply of oil, the Ploesti oilfields in Rumania, should be safe from British airbases in Greece and Crete.

In the first fully airborne invasion in history, 20,000 German soldiers parachuted onto the island or landed by glider. Facing them were over 40,000 Allied troops – from Britain, Greece, Crete, Australia and New Zealand. Although over 7,000 Germans were killed, their opponents were poorly equipped and worn out from fighting in Greece. The Germans captured the island within 10 days; it was to be one of Hitler's last great victories.

INTERNET LINK
For a link to a website where you can watch a slide show of Germany's invasion of Greece, go to www.usborne-quicklinks.com

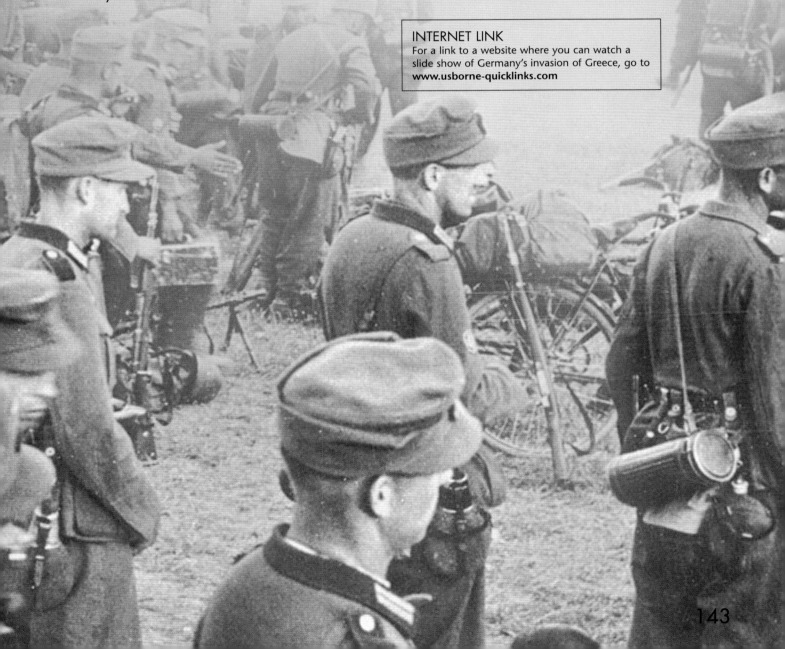

June 1941 - May 1942

EUROPEAN WAR TO WORLD WAR

Intoxicated by his own success, Hitler began to believe he could do anything if he willed it. On June 22, 1941, his armies poured into the Soviet Union. Stunning victories followed and, by early December, German soldiers were within 15 miles (20 km) of Moscow. This was the moment Japan chose to attack the world's greatest industrial power, the United States. Hearing the news, Germany, too, declared war on the United States.

Amid the wreckage of their own aircraft, ground crew on Ford Island Naval Air Station, Pearl Harbor, watch as another American ship is destroyed in the surprise Japanese attack of December 7, 1941.

OPERATION BARBAROSSA

On the dawn of June 22, 1941, the greatest invasion in the history of the world began. It was codenamed *Operation Barbarossa*. Three million German troops, and thousands of tanks and planes, poured over the Soviet border. They intended to conquer the world's largest country by the end of the summer. And they nearly did.

Confidence man

Hitler was so confident of success, he bragged to his generals: "We have only to kick in the door, and the whole rotten structure will come crashing down." On that June day three German army groups – North, Central and South – struck out for Leningrad (now St. Petersburg), Moscow and the Ukraine.

The German armies moved forward rapidly – employing the *Blitzkrieg* tactics that had won them easy victories in Poland and France. Soviet troops were totally disorganized. Stalin himself was so stunned by the attack, he spent 11 days in almost complete isolation, barely believing his former ally had betrayed him so ruthlessly.

Mistaken welcome

In some parts of the Soviet Union, especially Latvia, Estonia, Lithuania and the Ukraine, the Germans were welcomed as liberators. Many people there hated the tyrannous communist rule of Joseph Stalin. But this warm welcome soon changed to hostility and resistance. The Nazis regarded the people of the Soviet Union as slaves, and behaved towards them with great arrogance and brutality.

INTERNET LINK
For a link to a website where you can read eyewitness accounts of *Operation Barbarossa*, go to
www.usborne-quicklinks.com

The arrows on this map show the routes of German troops into the Soviet Union during *Operation Barbarossa*.

Leningrad and Moscow besieged

The war was not won by the end of the summer, but Leningrad was beseiged and, by early October, German soldiers had reached the suburbs of Moscow. They were so close, they could see the Kremlin's famous golden domes. But the first snow of winter had fallen, and autumn rain had turned roads to slush. Hitler had been so confident of a speedy victory, his soldiers had not been supplied with warm clothing, or winter equipment. Supplies were running out too, and men were weary from four months' fighting.

Some Soviet citizens, like these Ukrainian women, initially greeted the Nazis as 'liberators' – but they quickly changed their minds.

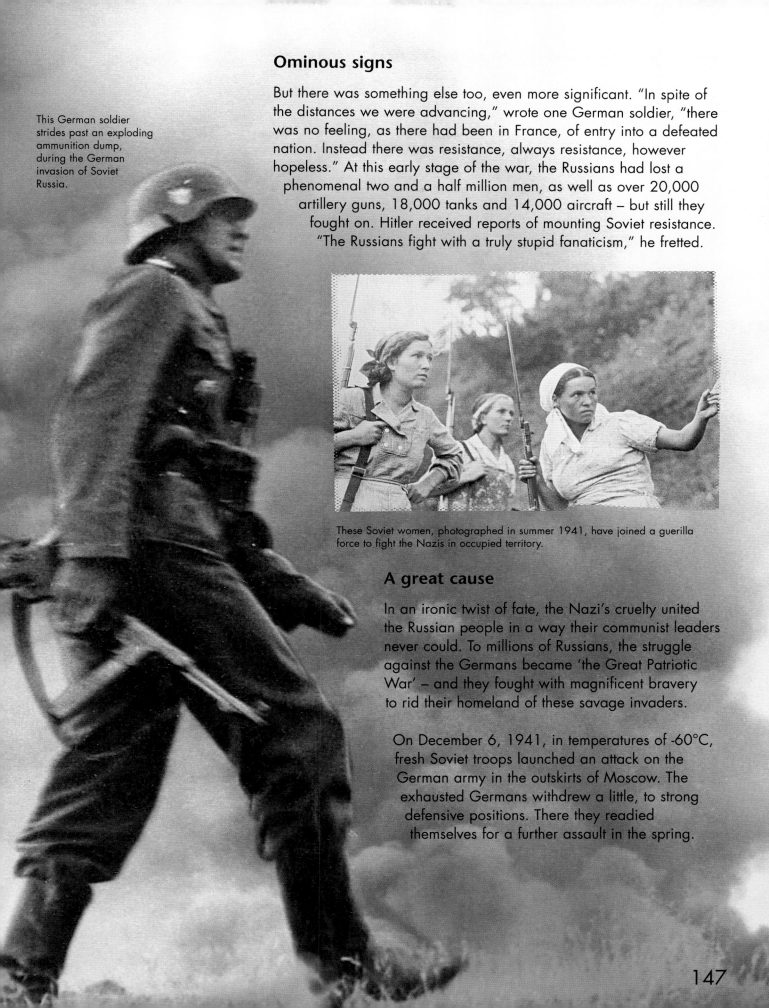

Ominous signs

But there was something else too, even more significant. "In spite of the distances we were advancing," wrote one German soldier, "there was no feeling, as there had been in France, of entry into a defeated nation. Instead there was resistance, always resistance, however hopeless." At this early stage of the war, the Russians had lost a phenomenal two and a half million men, as well as over 20,000 artillery guns, 18,000 tanks and 14,000 aircraft – but still they fought on. Hitler received reports of mounting Soviet resistance. "The Russians fight with a truly stupid fanaticism," he fretted.

This German soldier strides past an exploding ammunition dump, during the German invasion of Soviet Russia.

These Soviet women, photographed in summer 1941, have joined a guerilla force to fight the Nazis in occupied territory.

A great cause

In an ironic twist of fate, the Nazi's cruelty united the Russian people in a way their communist leaders never could. To millions of Russians, the struggle against the Germans became 'the Great Patriotic War' – and they fought with magnificent bravery to rid their homeland of these savage invaders.

On December 6, 1941, in temperatures of -60°C, fresh Soviet troops launched an attack on the German army in the outskirts of Moscow. The exhausted Germans withdrew a little, to strong defensive positions. There they readied themselves for a further assault in the spring.

147

THE SIEGE OF LENINGRAD

During the summer of 1941, the German army advanced deep into Soviet Russia. By mid-July Army Group North had made 800km (500 miles) in three weeks. Its target was Leningrad, the beautiful, historic city now called St. Petersburg. Hitler declared that the city would, "fall like a leaf." By early September, Leningrad's three million inhabitants were surrounded, and occupation seemed only days away.

A Red Army machine-gunner defends the outskirts of Leningrad during the three-year siege.

Changing plans

As the Germans approached, Leningrad prepared to fight to the end. Over 160km (100 miles) of anti-tank ditches were built, and buildings were booby-trapped. But, just as the Nazis reached the gates of the city, there was a sudden change of plan. Many of the troops were sent south, to take part in an assault on Moscow. So instead of a full-scale attack on Leningrad, it was decided to starve and bombard the city into submission.

Half rations, and less

Its population swollen by refugees fleeing the Nazi advance, Leningrad needed huge amounts of food each day. But the only routes left into the city were a small airstrip and a ferry via Lake Ladoga to the east. As winter arrived, the amount of food getting in was barely half what was needed – and worse was to come. By November, the besieged citizens were living on starvation rations.

Fear stalks the city

In desperation, people ate horses, cats, dogs, rodents – even grass. The only water supply was from the Neva, which ran through the city. Some even turned to cannibalism. It was said that people were afraid to leave their homes, in case they were killed and eaten. In the midst of all this suffering, there was also constant artillery and aerial bombardment. The streets were littered with dead bodies, killed by the bombs or from starvation. By winter, it wasn't possible to bury them, as the ground had frozen solid.

Citizens scurry between the dead and exploding artillery shells, in Leningrad's main street, Nevsky Prospekt.

Winter relief

But the winter freeze brought good news too. Lake Ladoga froze so solid, it was possible to drive heavy supply trucks over it. By January 1942, 400 trucks a day were coming into the city, taking out refugees on their return journey. The trucks often came under heavy fire, or crashed into craters and holes in the ice, but they saved the city from starvation.

In spring, the thaw cut off the truck supply route across the lake, although food continued to come in by boat. But the warmer weather bought further misery. As frozen corpses thawed and began to rot, an epidemic swept through the city, killing thousands.

INTERNET LINK

For a link to a website where you can find out more about what life was like in Leningrad during the siege, go to **www.usborne-quicklinks.com**

The end in sight

But the worst was over. As the ground softened, the bodies were swiftly buried, and a pipeline laid under the lake began to deliver fuel. Leningrad could sense it was winning, and celebrated with a concert in its Philharmonic Hall, performed by musicians recalled from the front. The music – the 7th (or Leningrad) Symphony – was written especially by Dmitri Shostakovich, one of its most famous citizens. The concert was broadcast and German soldiers who listened in became demoralized. Leningrad did not sound at all like a city on the brink of defeat.

PEARL HARBOR

One sleepy Sunday morning, on December 7, 1941, Japanese planes made a dramatic attack on the American naval base at Pearl Harbor, Hawaii. This one act changed the course of the war irretrievably. America declared war on Japan, and Japan's allies, Germany and Italy, declared war on America. The Axis powers would soon discover just what a formidable and determined opponent she would be.

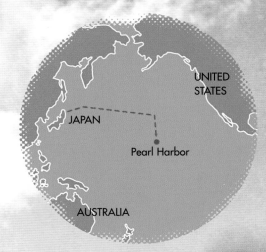

The Japanese launched their surprise attack on Pearl Harbor (route shown in red) from halfway across the Pacific Ocean.

A daring move

Pearl Harbor is a massive naval base in a natural inlet on Oahu Island, Hawaii. It was, and still is, the headquarters of the US Pacific Fleet. Also on the island are seven airfields, dry docks to repair ships, a submarine base and huge oil storage facilities. Japan was not at war with America at the time of the attack. But she hoped to land such a stunning blow on her Pacific rival that she would be able to seize vast swathes of territory before the United States recovered.

> INTERNET LINK
> For a link to a website where you can watch film footage and listen to radio broadcasts reporting the attack on Pearl Harbor, go to **www.usborne-quicklinks.com**

Disturbing the peace

The attack was timed to take place when American forces would be at their least alert. It worked like a dream: around 90% of all damage occurred in the first 10 minutes. A fleet of six aircraft carriers and 26 support ships had sailed from Japan 11 days earlier. Undetected, they arrived at their launch zone the night before, 450km (700 miles) north of Hawaii. Midget submarines, which had sneaked into the inlet, joined the attack. After half an hour of carnage and chaos, Japanese planes vanished from the sky.

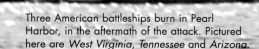

Three American battleships burn in Pearl Harbor, in the aftermath of the attack. Pictured here are *West Virginia*, *Tennessee* and *Arizona*.

Strike two

As American service personnel battled with fires and tended to the wounded, another 170 Japanese planes arrived for a second strike. For an hour they wheeled around the base, but this second attack was less successful. The Americans were now operating their anti-aircraft guns, and Japanese pilots faced determined opposition.

Easy targets

As a result of the Japanese attacks, 18 warships were sunk or damaged, 180 aircraft were destroyed, and 2,400 Americans were killed. They had all made easy targets: the ships in the inlet had been grouped in pairs and the planes in the airbases had been bunched together. The worst casualties occurred aboard the battleship *Arizona*. During the first attack, a bomb dropped right down her funnel, and set off an explosion which killed a thousand men in a single blinding flash.

Waking the sleeping tiger

The United States was outraged by the attack and declared war immediately. A stunned population heard their president, Franklin D. Roosevelt, describe December 7 as, "a date that will live in infamy." Overnight, the war was transformed from a European conflict into a global one. It was especially good news for Britain and Russia, who had been struggling to survive against Nazi Germany. Now they had America, the most powerful nation on earth, to fight beside them. Even the man who had been ordered to plan the Pearl Harbor raid, Admiral Isoruku Yamamoto, had grave misgivings. "I fear we have only succeeded in awakening a sleeping tiger," he told fellow officers.

Admiral Isoruku Yamamoto, Commander-in-Chief of the Japanese Combined Fleet, consults sea charts as he plans an attack.

JAPAN'S NEW EMPIRE

Following the devastating attack at Pearl Harbor, Japan's military leaders knew they had to act fast to create their new Japanese empire before America recovered its strength. In the lightning campaign that followed, the Japanese conquered most of the Asian Pacific seaboard, and looked set to invade India and Australia.

Japan's new empire (shown here in dark pink) took in mainland Asia and great swathes of the Pacific.

Runaway success

Before the attack, Admiral Yamamoto had promised, "a wild show for six months. But," he went on to say, "if the war drags on two or three years I cannot be confident of the outcome." His words were prophetic. The first six months saw Japanese successes that overshadowed even Hitler's victories. Their targets were the Allies' colonies in the Pacific and the Far East. Before the year ended, they had captured Hong Kong and invaded Burma, Malaya, Borneo and the Philippines. In February 1942, they defeated British troops in Singapore that outnumbered them almost three to one.

A friendly face?

Japanese propaganda described this sudden expansion of her empire as the 'Greater East Asian Co-Prosperity Sphere' and coined a slogan 'Asia for the Asiatics'. But, within days of occupation, the conquered peoples quickly came to realize that the Japanese were no better – and frequently worse – than the European powers that had previously ruled over them. In a deliberate policy to encourage citizens to surrender rather than fight, they were subjected to indiscriminate massacres and rape by the Japanese army.

Why Japan succeeded

Japan achieved these extraordinary victories by having several clear advantages over its enemies. At the beginning, the Japanese navy controlled the sea, and could protect the troop ships needed to ferry soldiers to these new territories. The forces defending many of the places they attacked were weak, and the Japanese army fought with greater ferocity, often defeating opponents who outnumbered them.

A Japanese soldier stands guard over American prisoners in the Philippines, on New Year's Day, 1942.

Show's over?

By May 1942, Japanese fighting forces had more than exceeded expectations. The plan now was to defend the newly conquered territories so fiercely that America and Britain would have to accept that they had lost them. But the Japanese had underestimated the United States, and the stunned outrage they had provoked. After inspecting the damage at Pearl Harbor, one American admiral vowed, "Before we're through with them, the Japanese language will be spoken only in hell." In spring 1942, America was about to strike back, and Japan's moment of triumph had passed.

UNDERGROUND RESISTANCE

The Germans and Japanese behaved with great brutality towards the nations they occupied and exploited. In the Pacific, conquered people were usually too shocked and frightened to offer further resistance. But in Europe and Russia – and to a lesser extent in Malaya, Burma and the Philippines – the occupying forces found that the citizens of the nations they so arrogantly ruled were prepared to fight back.

Resistance in the West

In Western Europe resistance was often low-key. People would walk out of cafés when German soldiers came in, or make other small gestures to make them feel unwelcome. But the French had groups of underground fighters, known as the French Resistance. Some lived ordinary lives in towns and villages, venturing out at night in secret to blow up German trains, or carry out hit-and-run raids on military bases or convoys. Others fled to forests and hills to live as outlaws in armed groups. They were known as the *Maquis*, after a French word for a kind of bush.

Other means

Resistance didn't just mean fighting Germans. Some people helped by hiding downed pilots, escaped prisoners-of-war, or fleeing Jews, as they made their perilous journeys to England. Others printed illegal newspapers, or discreetly sabotaged factory machinery, or stole military maps from under the noses of their enemy.

INTERNET LINK

For a link to a website where you can read fascinating stories of resistance fighters, go to **www.usborne-quicklinks.com**

Eastern Europe

Resistance was even fiercer in Eastern Europe, partly because the Nazis behaved with even greater savagery there. After the invasion of the Soviet Union, 88 million people lived under Nazi control. Bands of underground fighters, known as partisans, fought a protracted guerrilla war against them. Blowing up supply trains and railway lines was especially effective. Thousands of German troops had to be diverted from the front, to try to keep the partisans under control.

Fierce retaliation

Wherever resistance attacks took place, the Nazis reacted with vicious reprisals against the local people. In 1942, leading Nazi Reinhard Heydrich was assassinated in Prague by exiled members of the Czech army. As well as hunting down his killers, and hundreds of other suspects, the Nazis destroyed the Czech village of Lidice, executed the men and sent the women and children to concentration and death camps. In all, 5,000 were murdered in retaliation for the assassination.

Success in Yugoslavia

Perhaps the most successful resistance group of all was a band of Yugoslav partisans lead by Josip Tito, which grew to many thousands strong. They fought a constant campaign against the Germans for much of the occupation, taking over most of the northwest of the country. In October 1944, Tito's forces liberated the Yugoslav capital, Belgrade, driving the Nazis out. Yugoslavia became the only conquered country to free itself from Nazi rule without substantial help from abroad.

This band of Soviet partisans sheltering around a fire was photographed in 1943. Some are civilians who have taken up arms; others are soldiers who have fallen behind enemy lines.

THE HOME FRONT

Such was the scale and ferocity of the war, that many countries devoted almost their entire populations and resources to winning it. Women were recruited into factories and other areas of work previously reserved for men. For the citizens of the major fighting nations, the war became an inescapable part of their everyday lives – even for those who were lucky enough to escape the horror of bombing.

Hard times

During the invasion of Russia, 1,500 factories were moved east, away from the rapid German advance. Six million Russians, mainly women, were uprooted and sent to work in them. They had no choice in what they did, and had to work wherever they were sent. They built tanks like the very effective *T-34*. Produced in their thousands, away from the threat of German bombing, these tanks were crucial in helping the Soviets win their war against Nazi Germany.

Close to the front line, Soviet citizens toil to produce weapons in an underground factory, where they are safe from Nazi artillery and aerial attack.

This British woman carefully drills components for an RAF *Spitfire*, at an aircraft production factory in Southampton, England, in early 1940.

Arsenal of democracy

President Roosevelt declared that America would become the "arsenal of democracy" – arming itself and its allies in the fight against tyranny. American women flocked to factories to replace men called up for military service. Shipbuilding increased by 600%, and aircraft production by 500%. By 1944, one new plane was being built every five minutes. American armaments factories, like Russia's, were outside the range of enemy bombers.

This rate of production gave the United States a formidable advantage over Germany and Japan. Britain and the Soviet Union both used large quantities of American weapons. In Britain too, millions of women were recruited to help the war effort. Along with building planes and tanks, and making shells and ammunition, women worked on farms, as mechanics at airbases and vehicle depots, and as doctors and nurses in military hospitals.

INTERNET LINK

For a link to websites where you can hear radio broadcasts, see video clips and discover more about daily life in Britain and the United States during the war, go to www.usborne-quicklinks.com

The good to bad life

In the first few years of the war, the Germans plundered their conquered territories, and German citizens enjoyed luxury goods in their shops. But, when the tide of the war turned against Germany, goods became scarce and the constant threat of bombing made life much more difficult. Hitler was still reluctant to allow German women to work in factories. This was partly due to Nazi attitudes to women, summed up by the pre-war slogan: *Children, Church and Kitchen.* The Nazis felt that these were the most suitable roles for women. So, although some German women worked in industry, much of the work was carried out by slave workers from prisoner-of-war camps or conquered peoples.

Gas attack

Most civilian populations expected to be bombed both by high explosives and gas. In Britain, people were expected to carry gas masks at all times. But, fortunately, gas was never used on civilians.

These British children are taking part in a gas mask drill in February 1941. They are all evacuees from London and are being looked after in Windsor, to the west of the capital.

Evacuation

The fear of bombing led to mass evacuation of children from British and German cities, as soon as war broke out – although Berlin itself was not evacuated until 1943. The Japanese also sent city children to live with families in the countryside. This spared many thousands of lives, as Japan's mainly wooden cities were bombed with merciless ferocity.

These schoolchildren evacuees are boarding a train to take them away from a Japanese city. The trip almost certainly saved their lives. Japan's cities were attacked with even greater savagery than Germany's.

THE WAR IN NORTH AFRICA

Between 1940 and 1943, the hot, sandy deserts and shores of North Africa became a crucial battlefield. From this desert war, two great generals emerged on opposing sides: Bernard Montgomery and Erwin Rommel. For them, the desert was a perfect place to wage war. There were very few towns and civilians to get in the way, and they could move their forces around almost like pieces on a chessboard.

Soldiers of the 8th Army, dug into makeshift stone and sand shelters, look on as Afrika Korps vehicles burn in the flat desert landscape.

Italy joins the war

In June 1940, Italy joined Germany in the war, and in September attacked British forces in Egypt. The British responded by launching successful attacks on Italy's African colonies: Libya, Ethiopia and Italian East Africa.

Rommel to the rescue

With his ally facing humiliation, Hitler sent German Afrika Korps troops to help, led by the formidable Erwin Rommel, fresh from victories in France. His resourcefulness and cunning earned him a nickname: *the Desert Fox*. Rommel compared fighting in the desert to fighting at sea, saying, "No admiral ever won a naval battle from the shore." He risked capture and death by directing battles right from the front line.

Successes and failures

Between 1940 and 1942, the desert war went back and forth over the north coast of Africa. After initial British successes, the Afrika Korps made a determined advance, gradually beating the British 8th Army back as far as the Egyptian border.

Rommel's new rival

In summer 1942, the exhausted and demoralized 8th Army was given a new commander, General Bernard Montgomery. 'Monty' (as he was known) was eccentric and often rude. But he also had a gift for inspiring confidence in his troops.

Vichy 1940 - 42
Axis occupation
Allied occupation

ITALY
MOROCCO
ALGERIA
TUNISIA
Mediterranean Sea
LIBYA
El Alamein
EGYPT

Fighting took place along the whole of the North African coastline between 1940 to 1943. The Battle of El Alamein decided once and for all who would be the victor in the desert war.

'The Devil's Garden'

During the summer, both sides established strong defensive positions around the Egyptian town of El Alamein, near Alexandria. The Afrika Korps had surrounded themselves with so many deep minefields and booby traps, the area was known as the Devil's Garden.

By October 1942, Rommel had retired to Germany, ill with exhaustion. Most of his planes had been transferred east to fight the Soviets. On October 23, Montgomery launched a massive attack. It began with a thousand-gun bombardment, so intense the acting German commander suffered a fatal heart attack. Then, 230,000 8th Army troops and 1,230 tanks picked their way across the minefields to fight.

Rommel returned to find his army in a retreat that did not stop for 2,250km (1,400 miles). After the battle, British prime minister Winston Churchill commented, "...this is not the end. It is not even the beginning of the end. But it is, perhaps, the end of the beginning." This major British victory was followed by Allied landings in Morocco and Algeria in November. Caught between these two armies, the Afrika Korps surrendered in May 1943.

INTERNET LINK
For a link to a website where you can follow the battles in North Africa with animated maps, go to
www.usborne-quicklinks.com

LIFE IN OCCUPIED TERRITORIES

Like all empire builders, the Axis powers sought to exploit the resources – and the people – of the countries they conquered. As the war began to turn against them, they did so with increasing ruthlessness.

This Eastern European recruitment poster, urges Croatian and Bosnian men to join the Nazi SS.

Bad company

In every conquered country, food and raw materials were taken at will. In Europe, the Nazis confiscated art and luxury goods – either for their own private collections, or to fill the shops at home. Road signs were written in German, even in Russia, which didn't even share the same alphabet. Nazi propaganda, in radio, cinema and street posters, became an inescapable fact of life.

The Nazis believed the people they conquered in the East were racially inferior. In Poland and parts of Russia, children with blonde hair and so-called 'Aryan' looks were taken away to be brought up in Germany. Russians, who were regarded as little better than animals, were treated especially badly. They were addressed by a number, rather than by name, and made to wear that number on their clothes. Much worse was to follow. For example, when Soviet soldiers liberated the village of Parichi, near Bobruysk, they uncovered the bodies of children bled dry to provide blood transfusions for wounded German officers at a field hospital there.

Slave workers

Hundreds of thousands of people in eastern Europe and Russia were transported to Germany to work in armaments factories. Picked at random from towns and villages, they were whipped into cattle wagons or freight cars. If they survived the journey, they faced 18-hour days manufacturing tanks, aircraft or machine guns, for companies such as Daimler-Benz, Krupp and Siemens.

Japanese control

In the first six months of the war, Japan occupied over a million square miles (160 million km) of territory, with a population of over 150 million people. Unprepared for such staggering success, the Japanese relied on bullying and intimidation to control their new subject peoples. Everyone was ordered to bow to Japanese soldiers and officials. Those who did not risked anything from a slap in the face to decapitation. The Japanese language was taught in schools, and even the year was changed to fit in with the Japanese calendar – which made it 2602 instead of 1942.

Nazi collaborators

Not everyone resented their new masters. There were many who co-operated with the Nazis – either for their own selfish reasons, or because they shared their anti-Semitic ideas. In most of the conquered nations, they helped round up local Jews. The SS recruited over 300,000 young men who were considered sufficiently 'Aryan' to join them. In France, an auxiliary police force, the *Milice*, worked with the Germans to suppress the French Resistance.

Paris, during the German occupation of 1941-1944. This café, *La Place Blanche*, was reserved exclusively for the use of German soldiers.

THE BATTLE OF THE ATLANTIC

As the world's richest nation, the United States could produce more ships, planes and arms than any other country. This gave the Allies a great advantage. But, before they could be put to use, these weapons, and the men to fight with them, had to cross the Atlantic Ocean. For most of the war, the Atlantic was a bleak battleground between German submarines and Allied ships, in a desperate struggle for control of the supply route to Britain.

This map of the Atlantic shows in red where most ships were sunk by U-boats.

Convoys

British and other Allied merchant ships set off from North America in large groups known as convoys. They were protected by small warships – destroyers, corvettes and frigates – and, for some of their journey, by aircraft. The destroyers carried a detection device known as *asdic* – which used sound and its echo to locate submarines underwater.

Wolf packs

Waiting for them, especially as they neared the end of the journey, was a fearsome selection of German warships, aircraft and mines. But the greatest danger came from submarines, or U-boats, which roamed the Atlantic in groups known as wolf packs. They usually attacked on the surface, where asdic couldn't find them, and at night where they were less easily seen. The submarines used powerful cannon or torpedoes to sink the ships.

Life at sea

Life aboard a submarine was uncomfortable and dangerous. Men slept in bunks or hammocks right next to torpedoes or among engine room machinery. There were no facilities to shower or do laundry, and voyages could last six to eight weeks. Attacking convoys was such dangerous work that submariners called their vessels iron coffins.

Watery graves

For the first three years of the war, the U-boats were very successful. In a single night, October 18-19, 1940, for example, two convoys were attacked by six U-boats and 32 ships were sunk. In 1942, they claimed an average of 96 ships a month. The Allies couldn't afford such losses.

This photograph was probably taken from another U-boat, during a fierce storm in the North Atlantic. Men from the submarine crowd onto the conning tower, for a break away from the vessel's stifling interior.

INTERNET LINK
For a link to a website where you can play a game to lead a convoy across the Atlantic and outwit German U-boats, go to
www.usborne-quicklinks.com

Striking back

But the Allies fought back with new equipment and weapons. Escort ships were fitted with much-improved radar, which enabled them to detect U-boats on the surface. This was so effective that submarines were forced to attack from underwater – which was more difficult. New aircraft with a longer range were able to target U-boats out in the middle of the Atlantic. The Allies also managed to crack the secret code used by U-boats to reveal their positions. Forewarned of an attack, the convoys were able to defend themselves more effectively.

Ships by the yard

In March 1943, at the height of the so-called Battle of the Atlantic, U-boats sunk 105 Allied ships. But American shipyards were building 140 cargo ships a month, which enabled them to keep supplying their allies. The German navy, on the other hand, was being gradually worn down. Submarine losses were increasing, and new ones couldn't be built fast enough to replace them.

By 1944, when the Allies were preparing to invade France, the Battle of the Atlantic was almost over. Nearly two million soldiers and two million tons of military supplies had crossed the Ocean, with very few men lost. In the closing stages of the war, the average U-boat lasted only one or two missions before it was sunk. Nearly 1,200 U-boats fought in the war, and two out of three of them were sunk, with a loss of 30,000 out of 40,000 men.

A depth charge fired from an American escort destroyer

These lucky few German submariners have escaped from their sinking vessel and await rescue by a Canadian ship.

PROPAGANDA

Throughout the war, governments on both sides tried to present information about what was happening on the battlefronts, or in the conquered territories, in a way that would maintain support for them and the war. This is known as propaganda. The Axis powers often presented outright lies as straight news; the Allies were usually more truthful. But they, too, were happy to tell lies if it suited their purpose.

This image showing the Nazi idea of the ideal 'Aryan' German boy was used on a poster to recruit fire crews to combat the damage caused by air raids.

Passing on the message

Today many people get their news from television and the Internet, but neither was available at the time of the Second World War. Instead, public opinion was formed by newspapers and radio, as it still is today, and by newsreels – news shown in cinemas before the main film. Posters were also used to publicize a political message. On the front lines, all sides dropped leaflets on enemy forces, encouraging them to desert or surrender.

Controlling the media

Germany, Japan, Italy and the Soviet Union were all ruled by 'totalitarian' governments, who exercised an iron grip over their people. This meant the media in these countries was totally controlled by the government, which had to approve every piece of news. It was not so tightly regulated in Britain and her empire, or in the United States – but editors were expected to judge for themselves what was 'in the national interest' to pass on to the public.

Jugend im Luftschutz

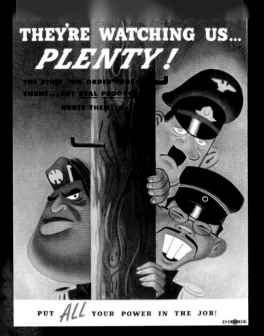

Not afraid to use crude racial caricatures, this American poster warns home front workers to beware of enemy spies.

This American leaflet, dropped in China, shows an American airman trampling on a Japanese soldier.

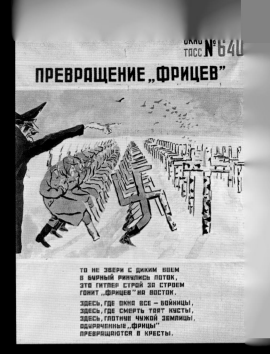

This Soviet leaflet was distributed to Soviet soldier Under Hitler's orders, German troops are turned into Nazi swastikas and march to their graves.

Masters of propaganda

Nazi Propaganda Ministry chief, Dr. Joseph Goebbels, summed up his aim as, "to arouse outbursts of fury … to organize hatred and suspicion – all with ice cold calculation." Germans were constantly reminded – by newsreels, radio broadcasts and newspapers – that communists and Jews were their greatest enemies, and that it was Germany's natural right to conquer land in the east. When the war turned against Germany, the job of the propagandists was made harder. After announcing Russia's defeat in 1941 and the fall of Stalingrad in 1942, they later had to acknowledge these stories had been false. Many Germans began to doubt the information their government gave them.

The Japanese crusade

The Japanese government told its citizens that its conquest of Pacific Asia was a crusade to liberate the east from European colonialists. When Japan occupied the Philippines, their radio claimed the locals had greeted them with cries of, "the angels are here!" The cruelty of the Japanese army, infamous for rape and massacre in conquered cities, was never mentioned.

Hitler the buffoon

The British and Americans told their own lies to but never on the same scale. British newspape tried to present the disaster at Dunkirk as a gre victory. American propaganda slyly let on that Hitler's real name was the unattractive-soundin *Schicklegruber*. A newsreel showing a jubilant Hitler reacting to the news of the French surrer in June 1940 was doctored to look as if the Führer was dancing a delighted jig. The British people were encouraged to believe that Hitler was a maniac who chewed the carpet when h was angry. The purpose of such stories was to make the German leader look like a buffoon, rather than a formidable monster.

Truth or lies

The best propaganda simply told the truth. When German soldiers were transferred from France to fight at Stalingrad, Russian planes dropped leaflets, with a simple, chilling message: "Men of the 23rd Panzer Division, welcome to the Soviet Union. The gay Parisian life is now over. Your comrades will have told you what things are like here, but you will soon find out for yourselves."

THE HOLOCAUST

Right from the start, the Nazis had reserved a special hatred for the Jews — blaming them for all of Germany's ills, especially defeat in the First World War and the economic upheavals that followed. Before war broke out in 1939, over 735,000 German and Austrian Jews suffered from fierce persecution, and the majority fled abroad. After the startling German victories at the beginning of the war, millions more Jews fell into the clutches of the Nazis.

Map showing the location of the main Nazi death camps

A German firing squad executes Jewish men at Drohobycz, in Poland.

From migration to mass killing

The Nazis had always intended to drive the Jews from Germany and their conquered territories to make them *Judenfrei* – or *Jew-free*. At first, they thought this could be achieved by forced emigration to limited areas in Polish and Russian cities, known as *ghettos*. Another suggestion was that all the Jews might be herded off to a faraway island, such as Madagascar, off the coast of Africa. But, as the war progressed, this idea was increasingly seen as impractical.

Whenever the Germans conquered new territory in the east, squads of uniformed SS men, known as *Einsatzgruppen* (or Special Action Squads), would arrive in their wake to search for Jews. Some Jews were sent to a ghetto – but mostly they were killed, usually by being shot. In a mass killing, in September 1941, at Babi Yar, near Kiev in the Soviet Union, 33,000 Jews were shot over three days. By the end of the year, over a million Jews had been killed in such massacres.

The Final Solution

These random killings were time-consuming and messy, and difficult to keep secret from the local people – and the rest of the world. On January 20, 1942, Nazi leaders decided on a more efficient way of eliminating Jews. At the Wannsee Conference, held in a villa outside Berlin, it was decided to send all Jews in Nazi territory to special death camps, to be gassed to death. This was known as *die Endlösung* – the Final Solution.

Acting directly on the orders of Hitler and the head of the SS, Heinrich Himmler, the Final Solution was masterminded by SS General Reinhard Heydrich, and the head of the *Gestapo* Jewish Affairs Section, Adolf Eichmann. Death camps were built in Poland, which had the densest Jewish population in Europe. Plans were drawn up to transport millions of people to the camps in freight trucks and cattle wagons.

The head of the SS – Reichsmarshal Heinrich Himmler.

Nightmare journey

From Norway to the Caucusus, Jews were rounded up and packed into freight trains. Many died on the journey, from lack of food or water, and disease. In some camps, such as Auschwitz, they were split into two groups – those who would be worked to death, and those who would be killed at once. In other camps, such as Belzec, Sobibor and Treblinka, Jews were killed as soon as they arrived.

Revolt and rebellion

Jews sent to the death camps were told they were going to be 'resettled' – but, after a few succeeded in escaping, the terrible truth reached others outside. A small group left in the ghetto in Warsaw, the Polish capital, rose up in rebellion. They managed to fight off the Germans for almost a month – from April 19 to May 16, 1943.

But the rebellion was crushed and the deportations continued. In Sobibor, 600 Jews tried to escape; 300 survived and joined the local partisans. In October, 1943, nearly all Denmark's 6,000 Jews were smuggled out to neutral Sweden, when it was discovered that the Nazis intended to deport them. But these were only tiny victories. It is estimated that between five and a half and six million Jews died in what became known as the Holocaust.

" The Führer has ordered that the Jewish question be settled once and for all… Every Jew that we lay our hands on has to be destroyed. "

Heinrich Himmler in conversation with Rudolf Höss, the commandant of Auschwitz, in the summer of 1941.

AUSCHWITZ-BIRKENAU

Busiest of all death camps was the vast complex of Auschwitz-Birkenau, near the Polish town of Auschwitz. Between the summer of 1942 and the last days of 1944, perhaps more than a million people were murdered there. The site had been chosen because it was at the heart of the Nazi empire, and had excellent rail connections – ideal for transporting Jews from all over the conquered territories.

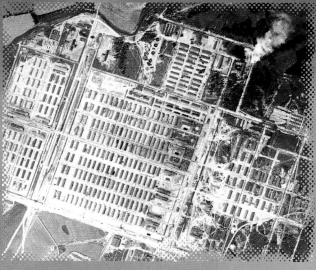

From this photo of Auschwitz-Birkenau, you can see just how huge the camp was. The long dark strip on the left was where arriving Jews were deposited from the trains and selected for work or immediate extermination. It was known as *the ramp*.

A glimpse into hell

The aerial photograph on the right shows Auschwitz-Birkenau at 11am on August 25, 1944, when the last Polish Jews from the Lodz ghetto were being gassed. It is estimated that around 437,000 Hungarian Jews had been killed here earlier that summer. On the far side of the photograph, you can just make out smoke from a burial pit. This was where bodies were dumped to be burned, when the camp crematoria were overloaded.

New arrivals at Auschwitz-Birkenau have just disembarked from their cattle trucks, and are being 'selected' by German officers. You can identify the other inmates by their characteristic striped uniforms.

The ramp

Trains ran directly into the camp, and arrivals were subjected to 'selection' by officers and doctors. The fittest and strongest were placed on one side. The rest – the sick, the old, and women with their children – were chosen for immediate extermination. In the picture below, those on the left are heading for the gas chamber. Those on the right will become slave workers, and survive for a few months more.

The gas chambers

Those selected for death were told they were being sent to a shower block – which was actually a large gas chamber located next to a crematorium. There were four main gas chambers and crematorium facilities at Auschwitz-Birkenau. Victims were herded into the chamber, hundreds at a time, then poisoned with a cyanide gas called Zyklon B.

'Canada'

The people who had been chosen to die were disposed of with typical Nazi efficiency. Their heads were shaved and the hair was used for insulation in aircraft and submarines. Clothes, shoes, spectacles, suitcases and other belongings were sent to Germany. Gold teeth and wedding rings were removed and melted down. After cremation, the ashes were used as fertilizer. A section of the camp near the gas chambers was used for storage. With ghoulish irony, the inmates named it 'Canada' – a land of plenty and prosperity.

A pile of shoes, taken from victims of the gas chambers

Liberation day

As the Red Army approached from the East, 67,000 of the camp's dwindling inhabitants were rounded up and marched back to Germany. When the Soviets finally arrived on January 27, 1945, they found around 2,800 sick and frail survivors.

These ragged inmates were photographed by a Soviet journalist when Auschwitz was liberated in January, 1945.

INTERNET LINK

For a link to a website where you can take a virtual tour of Auschwitz, go to **www.usborne-quicklinks.com**

169

Here, rows of B-17 Flying Fortresses are being made ready for the air war in Europe, at a Boeing factory in Seattle, Washington.

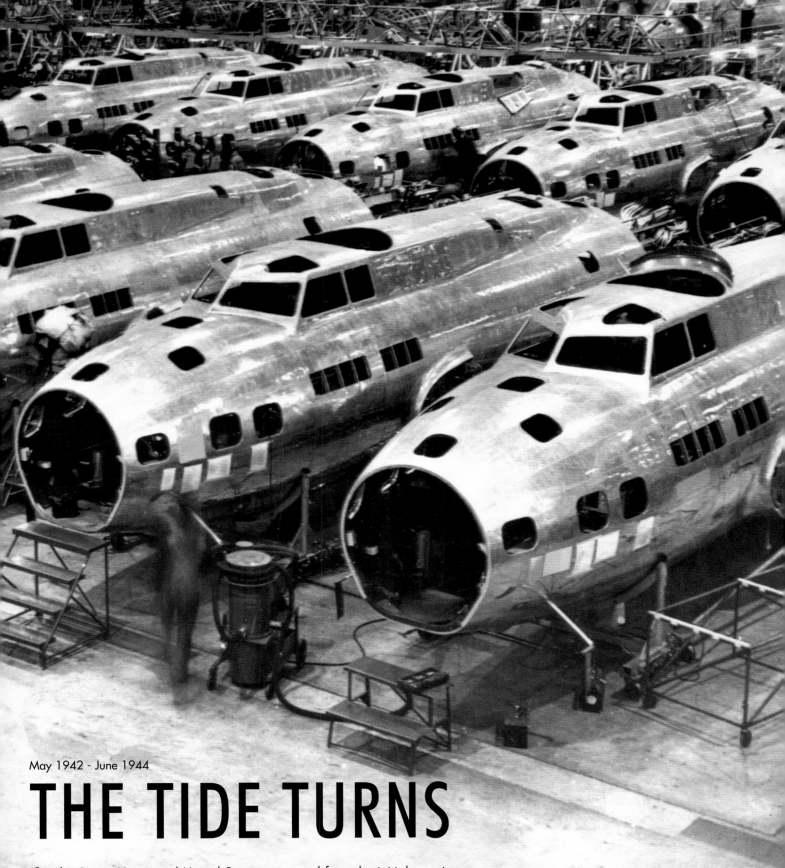

May 1942 - June 1944

THE TIDE TURNS

As the Soviet Union and United States recovered from the initial surprise attacks that had brought them into the war, they began to throw their huge industrial weight behind the war effort. America's ability to produce more tanks, aircraft, ships and guns than any other nation ensured the Allied victory.

CORAL SEA AND MIDWAY

In the spring of 1942, Japan was at the height of its power. Its assault on the Pacific was so successful, that plans were now laid for the invasion of Australia via New Guinea, and Hawaii via the island of Midway. Meantime, the US Navy was making a determined recovery from Pearl Harbor. The Japanese were about to discover the true potential of their formidable enemy.

Separated by thousands of miles of ocean, the battles at Coral Sea and Midway stopped Japan in its tracks.

America hits back

The overall damage inflicted at Pearl Harbor could have been much worse. Only two of the 18 warships hit were totally destroyed; within six months the rest were refloated and repaired. Better still, three aircraft carriers – the most important ships stationed at Pearl Harbor – had been out at sea during the attack – and escaped without a scratch.

Like all navies, the Japanese ships communicated with each other, and their high command, using secret code. But the Americans had broken this code. They found out that a large Japanese fleet was preparing to invade the southern tip of New Guinea, and they prepared an ambush.

Making history

In the Battle of the Coral Sea, on May 4-8, 1942, neither fleet actually set eyes on each other. For the first time in history, all the fighting was done by planes from aircraft carriers. Two valuable Japanese aircraft carriers were put out of action; several other warships and around 100 carrier planes were lost. The United States lost one aircraft carrier, two other ships, and 65 planes. The battle was inconclusive, but it seriously halted the Japanese advance. From now on, there would be a slow retreat back to Japan.

Meeting at Midway

The following month brought another trial of strength. A Japanese fleet of 145 ships, including eight aircraft carriers and 11 battleships, was heading for the American island of Midway. They were commanded by Admiral Yamamoto, who hoped to draw the American fleet into a decisive battle. But, once again, Japanese radio messages were intercepted, and the Americans were waiting.

On June 4, 1942, US aircraft launched a massive attack on the Japanese fleet, both from US aircraft carriers and airfields at Midway. The Japanese fought back. But Yamamoto had split his massive invasion force into small groups, and fatally underestimated American naval strength. It was to be his undoing.

INTERNET LINK
For a link to a website where you can see film footage and a slide show of the Battle of the Coral Sea, go to
www.usborne-quicklinks.com

Men abandon the US aircraft carrier *Lexington*, during the Battle of the Coral Sea. Amazingly, not one life was lost during the evacuation of the ship.

Five minutes that changed the world

Around 10:30 in the morning, in what might have been the most momentous five minutes of the war, three Japanese aircraft carriers were destroyed. Another was badly damaged and sank later in the day, as well as two cruisers and three destroyers. The Americans lost an aircraft carrier, *Yorktown*, and a single destroyer. Again, neither fleet actually saw each other. All the fighting was done from the air.

The Battle of Midway was the turning point in the Pacific War. The Japanese navy had been fatally undermined – and her expansion plans were postponed. From now on, the US Navy would be the dominant power in the Pacific.

THE BATTLE OF STALINGRAD

In June 1942, the German army lurched deep into the south of Russia. In the summer heat, with the vast Russian Steppe baked hard beneath their tank tracks and truck wheels, they swept forward in a great cloud of dust. By August they had reached the Caucusus Mountains, and the suburbs of Stalingrad. Defended by a ragged force only half their size, the Germans were convinced the city would fall in little more than a day.

A model city

Previously known as Tsaritsyn, Stalingrad had been renamed after the Soviet leader, because he had defended it in the Russian Civil War. It was a major transport hub, with important factories and steel works, and a population of 500,000, spread out 32km (20 miles) along the banks of the Volga. Leading the German attack was General Friedrich von Paulus, commander of the 200,000 men and 500 tanks of the 6th Army and 4th Panzer Army. Facing him was General Vasily Chuikov, commander of the 50,000 strong Soviet 62nd Army. On August 23, tanks and infantry began their first probing attacks on the outskirts of Stalingrad, while 600 *Luftwaffe* bombers attacked the city. Over 40,000 civilians were killed on that first day.

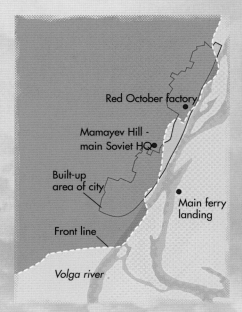

Stalingrad in September 1942, showing some of the key places in the battle. The red area is occupied by the Germans.

174

Brutal battleground

By late September, the city was nearly in German hands. But the fighting was extremely brutal, and the Russians showed no sign of giving up. Most of Stalingrad had been reduced to rubble, but it created perfect cover for the defenders. The Germans had to fight for the city room by room – rather than street by street. Chuikov told his men that every soldier was his own general – free to fight as best he could in the ruins of the city.

Breaking point

By early October, Chuikov had lost thousands of men and was under such stress he had developed painful eczema on his hands. Von Paulus, who had expected a quick victory, now had an uncontrollable tic in one eye. He launched a final all-out assault on the tangled remains of factories and steelworks in the industrial area of the city. But the Russians had been strengthened by reinforcements and were prepared. The assault failed.

In sharp winter sunshine, Soviet troops advance through the ruins of Stalingrad.

Counter attack

By now the German 6th Army was exhausted. Winter was fast approaching, and the troops were ill-equipped for cold weather fighting. Outside the city, a million Soviet troops, with strong artillery, tank and aircraft support, prepared to counterattack. The ground where they decided to strike was well chosen. It was held by soldiers of Germany's allies: Italy, Rumania and Hungary. Unlike the well-trained, battle-hardened German troops, these men had no desire to be in Russia at all. Once, when a whole battalion of Italians had surrendered without firing a shot, a Soviet interpreter asked why they hadn't fought. "We did not fire back because we thought it would be a mistake," replied a sergeant.

INTERNET LINK

For a link to a website where you can see photographs taken during the Battle of Stalingrad, go to www.usborne-quicklinks.com

175

THE DEATH OF AN ARMY

The Soviet counterattack came from both north and south of Stalingrad – cutting through with ease the Italian and Rumanian armies who were defending territory outside the city. In less than a week, the Soviet armies met up in the village of Sovietsky. Von Paulus and 250,000 German, Rumanian and Croatian soldiers were hopelessly surrounded.

Plea to retreat

Von Paulus immediately sent a message to Hitler, asking for permission to get out of Stalingrad before his army was destroyed. He could not have been franker: "Army heading for disaster. It is essential to withdraw all our divisions…"

But while Hitler and his generals discussed von Paulus's predicament, they were joined by the vain and bombastic head of the *Luftwaffe*, Hermann Goering. He convinced Hitler that the vast quantities of fuel, food and ammunition needed by the German 6th Army could be supplied by air to two airfields just outside the city. Von Paulus was told to hold fast, and so began the agonizing disintegration of his exhausted army.

Desperate failure

Goering's plan was a disaster. He didn't have enough planes to carry the supplies, and what planes he had were being reduced in number every day by Soviet fighters. Freezing fog often prevented flying and, even on the best days, only half the supplies needed arrived at the two airfields. Thousands of badly wounded men, awaiting a flight back to Germany, froze to death in flimsy tents alongside the runways.

Hitler ordered one of his best generals, Field Marshal Erich von Manstein, to break through the Soviet forces to open up a corridor to supply the 6th Army. His forces attacked from the south on December 12, 1942.

While the attack was diverting the Russian army, von Paulus again asked Hitler for permission to break out. He was refused. By December 23, it was clear that von Manstein had failed. The Soviet forces now surrounding Stalingrad were too strong.

Unhappy Christmas

Von Paulus's army was doomed. On Christmas Day alone, nearly 1,300 men died from frostbite, starvation and disease. The Soviet forces sensed victory, and harried them mercilessly. In January, the Soviets offered generous surrender terms. Von Paulus's men were roaming the streets, desperately searching for food and warmth. He also had 20,000 wounded soldiers in need of medical attention – but, incredibly, his loyalty to Hitler made him refuse. And so the battle dragged on.

INTERNET LINK
For a link to a website where you can listen to reports from Stalingrad as the Germans surrendered, go to **www.usborne-quicklinks.com**

The battle lost, von Paulus and other German commanders surrender to the Soviets. The agony of their futile struggle shows on their faces.

Soviet troops attack German positions, deep in the ruins of the 'Red October' metalworks factory in Stalingrad.

Promotion and ruin

With the battle almost over, Hitler promoted von Paulus to the rank of Field Marshal. No German Field Marshal had ever been captured, so this was a strong hint that von Paulus should commit suicide. He didn't. He was captured on January 31; the 6th Army surrendered on February 2.

As an unaccustomed silence fell over the city, Russian soldiers began to fire captured German signal flares into the air, and bright reds and greens lit up the smoking ruins of the city. Stalingrad lay in ruins: 41,000 homes, 300 factories, 113 schools and hospitals – 99% of its buildings – had been destroyed. But a great Russian victory had been won. The German defeat at Stalingrad would later be seen as the greatest turning point of the war.

THE SECRET WAR

Knowing what your enemy is going to do is a priceless asset for a military commander. During battles, armies use reconnaissance patrols and aircraft to try to discover what the other side is doing. But it's even better to know in advance what the enemy intends to do. Codebreakers, spies and informants can provide this information – often at great personal risk. But the world of espionage is dark and cunning, and what appears to be vital information can turn out to have been deliberately planted by the enemy to mislead…

Their man in Tokyo

Plans for many of the greatest battles of the war were reported by spies before they happened. Richard Sorge was a German journalist who worked for the German embassy in Tokyo. But, unfortunately for the Germans, Sorge was secretly working for the Soviets, and was sending frequent reports back to Moscow.

When Sorge discovered that the Japanese had no intention of joining the Germans in their attack on the Soviet Union in June 1941, the Soviets were able to transfer crack army divisions from their eastern border to their western front line. This ensured that the Soviet Union was saved from defeat. Sorge also warned them about the Pearl Harbor attack, but the Russians didn't pass on the information to the United States. He was arrested in November 1941, and executed in 1944.

This is the Japanese identification document carried by Richard Sorge.

Enemies in both camps

Rudolph Rössler (codenamed 'Lucy') was a Swiss citizen with several German military friends who detested their own Nazi government. They sent Rössler a constant stream of information which he sometimes passed on to the Allies. The invasions of Denmark and Norway, German tactics during the invasion of France, *Operation Barbarossa,* and subsequent Nazi campaigns in Russia, all came through 'Lucy'.

The Germans had a spy in Turkey – codenamed 'Cicero' – who was the manservant of the British Ambassador there. He spied for money and passed on to the Nazis details of the Normandy Landings. He was was paid in forged banknotes. Luckily for the Allies, his reports were disbelieved.

An amazing coincidence

Intelligence organizations can sometimes be too cautious. In May, 1944, a crossword compiler for the *Daily Telegraph* was interrogated by two intelligence officers, on suspicion of being a spy. In the month before the D-Day landings, his crossword had contained several secret codewords relating to the invasion: *Utah*, and *Omaha* (the two American landing spots), *Mulberry* (the makeshift piers to be used on the beaches) and *Neptune* (the naval operation on D-Day). Eventually they accepted that it was just an extraordinary coincidence. The full story only emerged in 1984. The crossword compiler was a teacher who had asked his pupils to suggest words. One of his pupils lived next to a camp of soldiers making ready for the invasion and had picked up the words by eavesdropping on their conversations.

The world of espionage is full of twists and turns, and it is easy to make mistakes, as British Intelligence showed when they interrogated the compiler of the *Daily Telegraph* crossword.

INTERNET LINK

For a link to a website where you can try sending secret messages using a virtual Enigma machine and learn some codebreaking tricks, go to **www.usborne-quicklinks.com**

Codebreakers

Any message sent by radio can be picked up by an enemy listening in, so throughout the war both sides used codes. Perhaps the most difficult one to crack was the German ENIGMA code, which was constantly being updated. But, thanks to the extraordinary efforts of Polish and British codebreakers, for most of the war the Allies were able to uncover some of the German plans in advance. The war in North Africa, the Battle of the Atlantic, the invasion of Sicily and Italy, and the Normandy Landings were all Allied victories won with the help of ENIGMA codebreakers. The Americans broke Japanese codes too, enabling them to intercept Japanese naval forces during the crucial Battle of Midway in 1942, and to shoot down a plane carrying Admiral Yamamoto in 1943.

German codebreakers also cracked the British codes used to transmit convoy routes. In 1942, 2,000 convoy signals a month were being picked up by the German navy and passed on to U-boat commanders searching for targets. The code was changed when the British discovered it had been broken.

Bletchley Park, Buckinghamshire, where British Intelligence translated German signals encoded by the ENIGMA machine, shown here on the right.

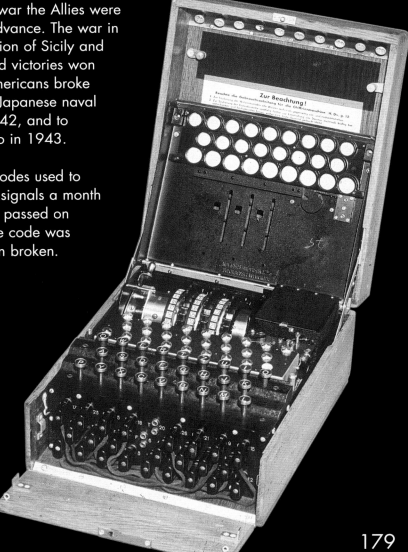

KURSK

In the winter months after Stalingrad, the German army fought to regain its momentum. In March 1943, the Germans recaptured the Soviet city of Kharkov. Then another great opportunity presented itself. A huge bulge in the front line around the city of Kursk offered them the chance to enclose and destroy three Soviet army groups at once. A victory like that might turn the war on the Eastern Front to Germany's advantage once more.

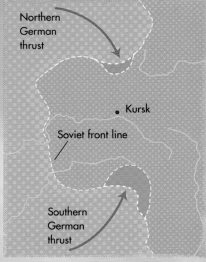

The Germans tried to link up at Kursk. The red shaded areas show how far they got.

Another gamble

The attack on Kursk came with great risks. At this stage of the war, the armies on both sides were equally matched. But the Soviets were now beginning to overtake the Axis forces with tanks, artillery and aircraft. Still, Hitler had owed his military success so far to a series of audacious gambles, so perhaps he would succeed again at Kursk?

New tanks

The attack could have taken place in early spring, but German commanders decided to wait for the arrival of two powerful new tanks: the *Panther* and the *Tiger*. More able to withstand direct hits, with more powerful guns, these new models promised to annihilate the standard Soviet tank – the *T-34*.

Soviet tanks and soldiers prepare to launch an assault during the Battle of Kursk.

Despite these advantages, when describing the imminent assault on Kursk to his Eastern Front commanders, Hitler complained, "Whenever I think of this attack, my stomach turns over."

A fatal delay

Their tanks in place, the Germans began their assault on July 5. But, in the weeks before the attack, the Soviets had been busy. Informed by spies that an attack was coming, they had reinforced their positions with deep minefields, 20,000 extra field guns and over a thousand *Katyusha* rocket launchers. The clash that followed would be the greatest tank battle in history.

Making history

In the flat grasslands of Central Russia, 6,000 tanks, 5,000 aircraft and two million men fought to win control of the war. This small section of the front contained more than the entire fighting force in Western Europe over 1944-45. As the tanks trundled towards each other, the sky was filled with opposing aircraft. The Soviet air force, having recovered from virtual annihilation in the first days of the war, flew 28,000 missions over the battlefield.

All-out carnage

The battle raged for eight days, most of the time in torrential rain. The carnage was horrific: about 90,000 men were killed or wounded. The Soviets lost over 2,300 tanks, the Germans around 400. The German tanks had been alarmingly effective, and more difficult to destroy, but they suffered breakdowns and other problems which blunted their usefulness.

Sunk in despair, a dead comrade sprawled behind him, this German soldier was photographed by his Soviet captors during the fighting in Kursk. German forces were completely outnumbered by the Soviets.

INTERNET LINK

For a link to a website where you can see photographs taken at the Battle of Kursk, go to **www.usborne-quicklinks.com**

Diversion from the south

For all the Soviet losses, the Germans could not penetrate their deep defensive positions. Soviet tanks were quickly replaced. Five days into the battle, another one began thousands of miles away, when British and American troops invaded Sicily. Hitler ordered an immediate transfer of some of the forces from Kursk. After a few more days, it became clear the Germans had failed. From this moment, the war would be one long retreat back to Berlin.

Scorched Earth

Immensely destructive fighting like this caused such damage that, by the end of the war, the Soviet Union had lost about 30% of its entire wealth. In retreat, both sides destroyed anything they could that might be useful to the enemy. This desperate tactic was known as *scorched earth*.

ALLIED BOMBING IN EUROPE

Until the beginning of the 20th century, wars were waged between opposing armies on the ground. But in the Second World War, the use of bomber aircraft led to the deaths of thousands of civilians, hundreds of miles from the front lines. The war began with squadrons of German bombers laying waste to city districts. But, from 1942, British and American aircraft were able to destroy entire German cities in massive thousand-bomber raids.

Allied strategy

When US forces began to arrive in Britain in 1942, plans were made for a great bomber offensive against Germany. The British specialized in lumbering night bombers, such as the *Lancaster*, *Halifax* and *Stirling,* which attacked cities in a tactic known as area bombing. Their aim was to 'dehouse' the German population, and undermine civilian support for the Nazis and the war.

The Americans had more heavily armed, better protected bombers, such as the *B-17 Flying Fortress* and the *B-24 Liberator*. These were used in daytime attacks to bomb specific industrial and military targets, such as factories or railway yards. "The more *Flying Fortresses* we have, the shorter the war is going to be," said a US Air Force commander, Curtis LeMay. But it wasn't that simple.

A squadron of *B-17 Flying Fortress* bombers is flying somewhere over Europe, on March 20, 1944.

This drifting black smoke is caused by anti-aircraft shells set to explode at the same height as the bombers.

Heavy losses

Heavy bombers such as the *Flying Fortress* were very expensive – $250,000 each – but they were highly vulnerable to both day and night fighters. German anti-aircraft fire was often radar-controlled and very accurate. The US lost over 8,000 heavy bombers and about 40,000 men. On one raid alone, against ball-bearing manufacturing plants in Schweinfurt, Germany, in October 1943, 60 of the 300 bombers sent on the mission were shot down. At the height of the war, RAF losses averaged 10% a raid – a chilling statistic for bomber crews who had to complete 30 missions before they could be reassigned to noncombat postings.

Maximum impact?

The losses only began to decline with the introduction in 1944 of long-range fighter escorts, such as the *P-51 Mustang*. But the effects of the bombing campaign are more difficult to calculate. Rather than destroying civilian morale, the bombing raids actually increased support for the Nazis. The aircrews were called 'terror fliers' by German propaganda. Like the British during the Blitz, the bombed German people were determined to carry on in defiance.

The bombing had a limited effect on the production of weapons in Germany, which continued to rise throughout 1944. But what the campaign did do was to divert much-needed resources away from the German front lines. By 1944, a quarter of all German artillery

A British pilot prepares for takeoff in a *Lancaster* bomber. Unlike most American bombers, which had a pilot and co-pilot, British bombers had only one pilot.

and ammunition was being used against Allied bombers. More importantly, almost all the remaining strength of the *Luftwaffe* was diverted to defending Germany's skies. This left German soldiers on all fronts with very little air support.

INTERNET LINK

For a link to a website where you can watch a movie that combines animations, photographs and audio clips, to get a glimpse of what it was like to be in a bomber and one of the bombed, go to **www.usborne-quicklinks.com**

BOMBS

War always speeds up scientific and technological progress – and the Second World War was no exception. In 1939 bombs carried by bombers were the main method of attacking enemy cities from the air. But by 1945 pilotless missiles and rockets had been developed to do this.

Different shapes and sizes

Throughout the war, bombers dropped simple high-explosive bombs, similar in design to the ones used in the First World War. The German *Luftwaffe* dropped 1,800kg (4,000lb) bombs on Warsaw and London, which detonated when they hit the ground. The blast from the explosion could knock down an entire building. Bombers also dropped incendiary bombs. These burst into flame when they landed, setting fire to buildings.

A lone firefighter tries to extinguish the flames in a street in Narvik, Norway, which was destroyed by German incendiary bombs in April, 1940.

INTERNET LINK

For a link to a website where you can watch video clips of V weapons being launched and in flight, go to **www.usborne-quicklinks.com**

B-29 bombers in July, 1945. Their target is the docks in the Japanese city of Kobe.

Near the end of the war, German scientists invented two new kinds of missiles, aimed at London and southern England, called the *V-1* and *V-2*. (The 'V' stood for *Vengeance*.) The *V-1* was a pilotless missile, which carried an explosive warhead and flew like a plane. It was powered by a jet engine, which cut out when it reached its target, and the missile plummeted to Earth. *V-1*s flew slow enough for fighter planes to shoot them down.

Even more deadly

The *V-2* also carried an explosive warhead – but it was much deadlier than the *V-1*. Its rocket engine took it high into the atmosphere, and it came crashing down to Earth at great speed. The *V-2* flew faster than sound, so it would explode without warning, before anyone heard it coming. 1,115 of these rockets were launched on London, killing 2,754 and wounding more than twice that number.

This *V-2* rocket dwarfs the group of German technicians surrounding it. The development of weapons like this led directly to the exploration of space in the 1950s and 1960s.

BOMBERS

During wartime, weapon designers constantly try to keep one step ahead of the enemy. Improvements, which might take decades during peacetime, speed up considerably. Here are two of the most widely used bombers of the Second World War.

Most of the crew in the *Heinkel He-111* sat in the cabin at the front. It was unpressurized, so the crew had to wear oxygen masks.

Heinkel He-111

The German *Heinkel He-111* bomber was designed to support troops on the ground, and to fly short-range missions behind enemy lines. It had a crew of five, and was used extensively against Poland and Britain during 1939-1940. The plane had a range of 2,000km (1,243 miles) and could fly at 7,800m (25,590ft).

The two engines gave a top speed of 415kmph (258mph).

1,497kgs (3,300lbs) of bombs could be carried in the bomb bay between the wings.

Boeing B-29 Superfortress

The American *Boeing B-29 Superfortress* was designed to fly long-range missions to attack enemy cities. It had a crew of 10, a range of almost 6,000km (3,700 miles) and could fly at 11,018m (36,150ft). It was used to bomb Japan between 1944 and 1945.

Four engines gave a top speed of 575kmph (357mph).

INTERNET LINK

For a link to a website where you can watch a video clip of *B-29s* in flight and take a virtual tour of the plane, go to **www.usborne-quicklinks.com**

The tail gunner operated a powerful cannon.

The gunners sat here.

This is one of the seven single machine guns, or cannons, that protected the *Heinkel* from enemy fighters.

Happy landings

One major breakthrough in aircraft design was to place a wheel at the nose rather than the tail. This gave the pilot a much better view on takeoff and landing. The two small illustrations below are drawn to scale, so you can see how much bigger the *B-29* is compared to the *He-111*.

The silhouette of a *He-111*

Tail wheel

The silhouette of a *B-29*

Nose wheel

Ten machine guns and one cannon, placed on top and underneath the aircraft, protected the *B-29* from enemy fighters. Most of the machine guns were operated by remote control.

The pilots, engineer, bomb aimer and radio operator sat here. The compartments were pressurized, so members of the crew did not have to wear oxygen masks.

9,072kgs (20,000lbs) of bombs could be carried in two bomb bays in the undercarriage.

BATTLE OF THE TITANS

For nearly a hundred years, the heavily-armed battleship had been the world's most powerful weapon. All the major fighting nations in the war had their own fleets. But now there was a new arrival in the navy arsenal: the aircraft carrier. Carrying up to a hundred aircraft each, the carrier proved to be more than a match for even the mightiest battleship.

INTERNET LINK
For a link to a website with photographs of aircraft carriers from the Second World War, go to
www.usbornequicklinks.com

Big is best

The most powerful battleships ever built were two identical Japanese ships named *Yamato* and *Musashi*. Designed in the late 1930s, these titans of the sea weighed 71,000 tons each, were 263m (862ft) long, with a crew of 2,500. The *Yamato* was the flagship of the Japanese fleet, from which the commander-in-chief directed battle. It had three main gun turrets, each containing three guns which fired massive shells 45cm (18 inches) wide. It also carried another 24 smaller guns, and 146 anti-aircraft guns.

Apart from this extraordinary firepower, the *Yamato* was shielded by a 40cm (16 inch) protective layer of thick steel, with over a thousand watertight compartments to stop water from flooding through the ship. *Yamato* fought at the battles of Midway and Leyte Gulf and was eventually destroyed in April 1945, on the way to defend the Japanese island of Okinawa. It took eleven torpedoes and seven bombs to send this great ship to the bottom of the East China Sea. Significantly, these were delivered by a force of 179 aircraft, from nine American carriers.

The great battleship *Yamato*. Each of her three big gun turrets weighed more than a destroyer.

A new kind of warfare

Aircraft carriers had first been built during the First World War, but it was only in this war that they were put into action. British and US carriers were used to protect their convoys from enemy submarines and warships. Aircraft from the British *Ark Royal* weakened the powerful German battleship *Bismarck* and enabled the British to catch and sink it.

But it was in the Pacific that aircraft carriers proved most crucial. The attack on Pearl Harbor would have been inconceivable without them, as would the American campaign to oust the Japanese from their Pacific conquests. In a single day in July 1945, US carrier aircraft destroyed a battleship, three aircraft carriers, a cruiser and twelve other ships.

Planes on the crowded flight deck of *USS Hornet* have their wings folded to allow them to be stored below.

Floating towns

Typical of the US carriers used in the Pacific was USS *Essex*, which could carry up to 100 planes. There were 24 similar carriers built during the war. Because aircraft carriers were so deadly, they were the principal target of enemy attack, and had to be surrounded by an escort of battleships, cruisers and destroyers. Preparing an attack from a carrier was an immensely complex operation, involving a crew of 3,500. Planes had to be filled with fuel, armed with machine-gun bullets, bombs and torpedoes, and taken from hangers inside the carrier and up to the flight deck. Heavy torpedo bombers were placed at the stern, to give them the greatest length of deck to take off from.

WOMEN ON THE FRONT LINE

During the Second World War, women were killed in greater numbers than in any previous war – as victims of bombing, resistance reprisal massacres or in extermination camps. But in places where the war was fought with the fiercest determination, many women took an active role, becoming combatants too.

Abandoning traditional roles

Millions of women, especially in the Allied nations, made an invaluable contribution to the war effort by working in factories producing tanks, aircraft and munitions. But women were also employed near, or actually on, the front line. Thousands of female nurses worked in field hospitals close behind the fighting, where they could be victims of artillery or air attack. Even in Germany, where the Nazi Party disapproved of women taking on traditionally male roles, teenage girls manned the anti-aircraft guns aimed at the British and American bombers. Women also took on jobs as engineers, repairing aircraft, tanks and trucks, and as air raid wardens and ambulance crews.

An air raid warden rescues a young girl from the wreckage of a London building bombed by the Germans during the Blitz.

Resistance fighters

The British and Americans didn't expect women to fight in combat, but the British made an exception with those who volunteered for the Special Operations Executive (SOE). This was a branch of the British secret service which trained agents to fight alongside men and women in resistance groups in Nazi-occupied Europe. One of them was Odette Sanson, a French woman living in London when the war broke out. She landed in the south of France in 1942 to assist French Resistance fighters in the area. Odette was captured, but managed to deceive the Germans into thinking she was married to a relative of Winston Churchill's. This did not stop her from being tortured, but it almost certainly saved her from execution – a fate that befell several other SOE women who were captured by the Nazis.

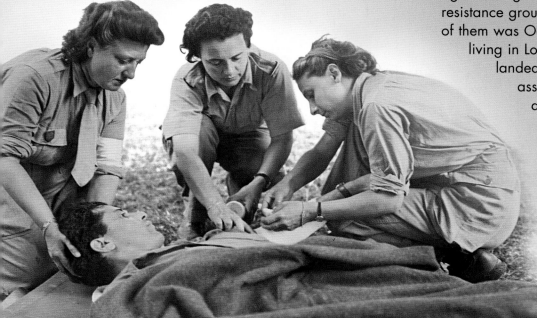

Three Allied nurses tend to a wounded soldier near the front line in France, August 1944. Women did not usually take part in combat on the Western Front, but were still close enough to the fighting to be killed.

Soviet women fighters

On the Eastern Front, Soviet women were unavoidably much closer to the war than their contemporaries in Britain and America. As the Germans approached Moscow and Leningrad, thousands of women and children were transported to the outskirts to dig massive anti-tank ditches. Soviet women worked as medical assistants or radio operators right on the front lines, and fought as combat soldiers – dying alongside their male comrades in tanks and trenches. Polish women also fought with men in the Warsaw Uprising in summer 1944, and others took part in bitter partisan and guerrilla campaigns behind the Eastern Front.

This Russian girl parachuted behind enemy lines, and has just been captured by German soldiers. She faces certain execution.

Air aces

Early in the war the Soviets were losing pilots at a rate of 50% a year, so women were allowed to join the air force too. By the end of the war, over one in ten Soviet combat pilots were women. There were three all-female air regiments, flying fighters and bombers, with their own female ground crews to fuel, arm and repair their planes. There were mixed squadrons too. Lilya Litvak flew with her lover Alexei Salomaten, until he was killed in combat. She destroyed 11 or 12 aircraft before she was shot down by German fighters sent to hunt for her.

INTERNET LINK

For a link to a website where you can read fascinating stories about women secret agents, go to **www.usborne-quicklinks.com**

A Soviet woman pilot poses proudly next to her fighter plane.

ISLAND FIGHTING

In the summer of 1942, Allied troops began the troublesome task of clawing back the territory seized by Japan in the first six months of the Pacific War. Early battles suggested the Japanese would fight fanatically to hold on to what land they had captured, in the hope of reaching a compromise with their more powerful enemy. In the savage fighting that followed over the next three years – on sandy beaches and in dense, torrid jungles – tiny, unheard-of islands would earn an infamous place in the history of the Second World War.

The blue arrows show the two-pronged American assault against the Japanese. The area shaded dark blue shows the limits of Japan's new empire.

Operation Cartwheel

The Allied plan to reconquer the Pacific was a two-pronged assault known as *Operation Cartwheel*. General Douglas MacArthur led one prong, through New Guinea and on to the Philippines. The second, led by Admiral Chester Nimitz, was heading for Japan via the tiny islands of the central Pacific: the Marshall Islands, the Marianas, Iwo Jima and Okinawa.

Avoiding trouble

The Allies had much stronger naval and air forces, which allowed them to cut off supplies to Japanese strongpoints. So, wherever possible, Japanese garrisons were bypassed – left, as Chester Nimitz famously remarked, "to wither on the vine." The 100,000 strong Japanese force, at Rabaul in the Solomon Islands, was one example.

Guadalcanal

Following the US naval victories at Coral Sea and Midway, the Marines launched their first land assault, at Guadalcanal, in the Solomon Islands. Here the Japanese were building a large airbase, which would give them the potential to disrupt shipping between the USA, Australia and New Zealand.

Australian troops also joined in the fighting, which lasted from August 1942 to February 1943. Both sides suffered heavy casualties, but the Allies had more equipment and soldiers. Throughout the war, this gave them a decisive edge against their opponents.

As soon as the land fighting began, the Japanese soldiers proved both determined and ruthless. When they were certain of defeat, most would kill themselves rather than surrender. At Guadalcanal, wounded Japanese soldiers waited for American medics to attend to them, then blew themselves and their helpers to pieces with hand grenades.

Tarawa Atoll

To the south, across a vast swathe of empty ocean, lay Tarawa Atoll, a chain of small but heavily-fortified islands. In November 1943, on one of these islands – a narrow strip just four miles long, named Betio – 5,000 Japanese defenders fought to the last 17 men against invading US Marines. The Americans suffered 3,000 casualties in three days, with a thousand of them dying on the island.

INTERNET LINK
For a link to a website where you can watch film footage and see photographs of the Battle of Tarawa, go to
www.usborne-quicklinks.com

Under attack from Japanese machine-gun fire, American soldiers wade towards a beach on Makim Atoll, in the Gilbert Islands, during November 1943.

A different climate

In spring 1943, US troops invaded the island of Attu, in the Aleutians. Attu was Japan's most northerly conquest, and the fighting took place in bitter Arctic conditions. The 2,500 Japanese holding the island fought with the usual determination. By the time the Americans recaptured it, there were only 28 Japanese soldiers left alive. In August, 29,000 US Marines and 5,200 Canadians attacked the nearby island of Kiska. The assault was preceded by a heavy bombardment by bombers and battleships. The invaders met no resistance. What they didn't know was that the 6,000 Japanese troops defending the island had left weeks earlier.

ENTERTAINING THE TROOPS

Every general knows that the mood of his troops – their morale – is as important as their equipment and fighting skills. Civilians at home also need to feel they are on the winning side, and are contributing to victory. In the Second World War, both sides made great efforts to entertain their citizens, to keep their spirits up.

Star turns

On the Allied side, the war made lasting stars out of singers such as Vera Lynn and Dinah Shore, comedians Bob Hope and George Formby, and band leaders Glenn Miller and Tommy Dorsey. Already famous, they became associated forever with the intense and unforgettable war years. To us today, because of changing musical fashions, and overuse in TV documentaries, popular songs from the war often sound trite and sentimental. But when Vera Lynn sang, *"We'll meet again... don't know where, don't know when,"* it pulled at the heartstrings of millions of people separated from friends and relatives, who they might easily never see again.

Sheet music for *"We'll meet again"* – a tune that was very popular with Allied soldiers

INTERNET LINK

For a link to a website where you can listen to music from the Second World War, go to **www.usborne-quicklinks.com**

Front line tours

Most of the big stars of the war were known mainly from their radio performances, although many also toured hospitals and factories and performed behind front lines. Some lesser known performers took greater risks and did shows much closer to the action, improvising as well as they could in fields, barns and bunkers.

The Soviet Union had over a thousand touring companies who entertained front line troops with sentimental ballads, dances, comedy routines and poetry readings. One Soviet entertainer recalls coming under German mortar attack during a show. On another occasion, the soldiers twice went off to fight, before returning to watch the rest of the show. American entertainment was provided by USO (United Services Organization); British by ENSA (Entertainments National Service Association) – although wits soon called it *Every Night Something Awful*.

Escape to Hollywood

Many films from the war years were propaganda pieces – created to record victories, or spur their audiences to greater efforts and sacrifices. Along with such action films as *In Which We Serve* and *Guadalcanal Diary*, were romances such as *Casablanca*, and comedies such as Charlie Chaplin's *The Great Dictator*.

Enemy radio

Enemy broadcasts were popular too – although in Germany and Japan those caught listening could face imprisonment or even execution. US soldiers in the Pacific listened to *Tokyo Rose* (American-born Iva Ikuko Toguri), whose flirtatious, silky voice was a siren call for men missing their sweethearts at home. British listeners tuned into the Nazi propaganda broadcasts of William Joyce, to laugh at his biased reporting of the war. His sneering, upper class voice earned him a nickname: *Lord Haw-Haw*.

Just behind the front line, a troupe of actors and musicians entertains Soviet soldiers, using a *T-34* tank as a makeshift stage.

SPECIAL FORCES

Some operations in the war were simply too dangerous or difficult to expect ordinary soldiers to carry them out. So special groups of highly-trained volunteers were used instead. Dropped behind enemy lines by boat, glider or parachute, these special forces stirred up havoc, before vanishing into the night.

Commandos

Formed after Dunkirk, British commando units swiftly became legendary. They were so effective that Hitler ordered any commando captured should be shot, rather than held prisoner. Commandos specialized in hit-and-run raids in occupied Europe. One raid in 1942, at St. Nazaire in France, destroyed a vast dry dock which was being used to repair German battleships. But of 611 commandos and sailors taking part, only 214 returned home. Another raid, in 1943, destroyed a German atomic weapons research laboratory in Norway.

The SAS (Special Air Service) was formed during the war, to assist British forces in North Africa. Its sabotage activities behind enemy lines were so successful that German soldiers were sent to kidnap the SAS leader, Lt. Col. David Stirling. They succeeded. Stirling spent the next two and a half years in prisoner-of-war camps. After escaping four times, he was sent to the infamous Colditz Castle in Germany. Field Marshal Montgomery described the young Stirling as, "quite mad, quite, quite mad. However in war there is often a place for mad people."

INTERNET LINK
For a link to a website where you can find an illustrated account of the mission to rescue Mussolini, go to www.usborne-quicklinks.com

American special forces, who were under the command of General Merrill, patrol the Burmese jungle in June 1944.

196

Long-term fighters

Most special forces operations rarely lasted more than a day, but some groups were formed to fight long-term campaigns. In Burma, occupying Japanese forces had to contend with two distinct guerrilla forces working way behind their front line. The Chindits, named after a mythical Burmese lion, were led by British Major General, Orde Wingate. The other unit – known as Merrill's Marauders – was commanded by US Brigadier General Frank D. Merrill. These groups struck at supply columns and bases and seriously undermined the Japanese army in Burma.

Scarface Skorzeny

Otto 'Scarface' Skorzeny

One of the boldest raids of the war was when German commandos snatched Mussolini from a ski resort hotel in the Italian Abruzzi Mountains, where he was being held prisoner. They used gliders to land silently, right next to the hotel, bursting in on Mussolini and his captors, without having to fire a shot. The ex-dictator was quickly bundled into a small aircraft and flown to Hitler's headquarters. Leading the attack was SS Captain Otto Skorzeny, who was nicknamed 'Scarface' because of a duelling injury.

In October 1944, Hitler feared his ally Hungary was about to surrender to the approaching Soviet army. He ordered Skorzeny, and a special unit of SS troops, to kidnap the son of the Hungarian leader, Admiral Horthy. Horthy had told his people their country was no longer at war, but this announcement was swiftly contradicted. Perhaps Skorzeny's greatest coup was when he used captured US vehicles and uniforms to disguise German troops in the Ardennes in December 1944. They destroyed supply dumps, and ambushed unsuspecting US units, causing widespread panic and confusion.

Mussolini, during his rescue by Skorzeny's glider troops

THE ITALIAN CAMPAIGN

In February 1945, as his world collapsed around him, Adolf Hitler complained, "It is quite obvious that our Italian alliance has been of more service to our enemies than to ourselves." Most Italians hadn't wanted their country to be involved in the war in the first place. As defeat loomed, the Italian government rose up against their leader Mussolini, and made peace with the Allies.

This map of Italy shows important cities and battles during the fighting that took place between 1943 and 1945.

The first steps into Italy

The Allied victory in North Africa in the spring of 1943 offered the Allies the chance to invade Italy from the south. On July 10, British, Canadian and American troops landed in Sicily. Within five weeks the island was theirs, and preparations were made to invade Italy itself. For the Italian government, the writing was on the wall. Mussolini was deposed and imprisoned, and secret surrender negotiations began with the Allies. This was a tricky business, as Italy was full of German troops. A surrender agreement was signed on September 3, 1943, the same day British troops crossed the Strait of Messina to the Italian mainland.

Six days later, the US army landed further north, at Salerno. For Germany, the Italian surrender made little difference. German soldiers simply disarmed the Italians and changed from being allies to behaving like an occupying force. Where possible, Italian soldiers changed sides. Within a few months, 350,000 of them were fighting with the Allies – rather than against them.

American artillery men advance through the dusty roads of Sicily, in September 1943.

Slow progress

Italy is a narrow, mountainous country, with many rivers crossing its interior. This made it easy to defend and difficult to attack. After early Allied success in the south, the Germans established a solid defensive line about 100km (60 miles) south of Rome. So Allied commanders decided to launch attacks along the coast instead. But the landing craft needed for such assaults were in short supply. The campaign to drive Japan from its Pacific empire was in full swing, and equipment in England was being stockpiled for the coming invasion of France. Allied soldiers landed at Anzio on January 22, 1944, but were hemmed in by strong German forces.

However, a few months later, two decisive victories finally enabled them to break through the German defensive ring and push further north. A group of mainly Polish forces overran a German strongpoint in the ancient hilltop monastery of Monte Cassino – destroying the 1,500-year-old historic site in the process. Within three weeks, the undefended Italian capital of Rome was in Allied hands. On June 6, the Allies landed at Normandy in France, and the war in Italy became something of a sideshow. But, by the end of the war, Allied forces in Italy had reached the River Po, and only the far north of the country remained in German hands.

INTERNET LINK
For a link to a website where you can watch a slide show of photographs taken during the Allied invasion of Sicily, go to www.usborne-quicklinks.com

A grisly fate

Hitler had many appalling traits, but he could be very loyal to his friends. This included the imprisoned Mussolini, who he had rescued by German commandos. The Italian dictator, now a shadow of his former self, set up a new government in German-occupied Italy. It was called the Salo Republic, after the small northern town he made his headquarters. But Mussolini was now just a puppet – completely under Nazi control. In April 1945, he and his mistress, Clara Petacci, were captured and swiftly executed by Italian partisans. Their bodies were hung in a city square in Milan, to be spat and shot at by vengeful Italians.

WAR IN THE PACIFIC

The Allied campaign to clear the Pacific of Japanese forces gained an unstoppable momentum in 1944. But Japan was not yet a spent force. While many of its island fortresses were isolated and starved into submission, those that were attacked fought almost to the last man. And Japan's navy was still among the most powerful in the world.

The battle for the Philippines

In May 1944, US forces invaded Biak – an island north of New Guinea, and a vital stepping stone for their planned reconquest of the Philippines – and went on to take the Marianas Island chain. The Japanese counterattacked by sending a large fleet under Admiral Ozawa Jisaburo to repel the invaders. Ozawa's force contained four of Japan's largest aircraft carriers, and 326 planes took off to attack Admiral Marc A. Mitscher's US fleet. They were heading for disaster.

A US Marine searches for Japanese soldiers in the rubble of a destroyed defensive position on Saipan Island, June 1944.

The Turkey Shoot

On June 19, American pilots shot down 219 of these Japanese planes near the Marianas Islands, losing only 30 of their own. Planes fell out of the sky, like birds shot down by hunters, in an air battle that became known as the Marianas Turkey Shoot.

That same day, US submarines sank two Japanese aircraft carriers – and, the following day, US dive bombers sank a third. By the end of the battle, Admiral Ozawa had only 35 planes left. The impressive Japanese carrier force that had struck such a stunning blow at Pearl Harbor had been all but destroyed.

Vital islands

By August 10, American forces had cleared the islands of Saipan, Tinian and Guam, in the Marianas. The fighting had been hard. At Saipan, 32,000 Japanese troops had fought to the death. Another 22,000 Japanese civilians stationed on the island committed suicide.

The loss for Japan was extremely serious. American control of the islands gave them airbases from which their B-29 Superfortress bombers could attack Japan's major cities – only 2,000km (1,300 miles) to the north.

A last gamble

In October 1944, a vast US invasion fleet of 700 ships and 200,000 troops stormed towards Leyte in the Philippines, ready to tackle the Japanese garrison of 70,000 troops. In a final, desperate attempt to counteract this threat and repel the invasion, the Japanese navy mustered what was left of its forces. The two sides met at the Battle of Leyte Gulf. The battle posed a terrible risk for the Japanese. If they lost, their oil supplies in the East Indies would be cut off to them, and their naval power would be destroyed.

A Japanese *kamikaze* plane, set ablaze by anti-aircraft fire, narrowly misses a US aircraft carrier, sailing close to Saipan Island.

From October 23–25, the United States and Japan fought the greatest sea battle in history – over a vast area of the Pacific Ocean about the size of France. Although it was touch and go at times, the Americans eventually outflanked the Japanese. Japan lost 26 ships, including *Musashi*, one of the world's biggest battleships, and the United States lost seven ships.

The suicide pilots

The stakes at Leyte Gulf had been so high that the Japanese navy's defeat virtually guaranteed that Japan would lose the war. But Japan was not going to surrender easily. During the battle, American sailors were horrified to see that Japanese pilots had deliberately begun to crash their planes into American ships.

A *kamikaze* pilot wraps the Japanese flag around his head, as he prepares for his one-way mission.

This dramatic, last-ditch use of suicide pilots, who the Japanese named *kamikaze* (meaning 'divine wind'), had never been seen before. But, over the following year, 1,228 Japanese airmen – mostly young and inexperienced – would deliberately sacrifice themselves in this way. And it was effective too. Altogether the *kamikaze* pilots managed to sink 34 American ships – and damage a further 288.

INTERNET LINK
For a link to a website where you can listen to US radio broadcasts reporting the progress of war in the Pacific, go to
www.usborne-quicklinks.com

201

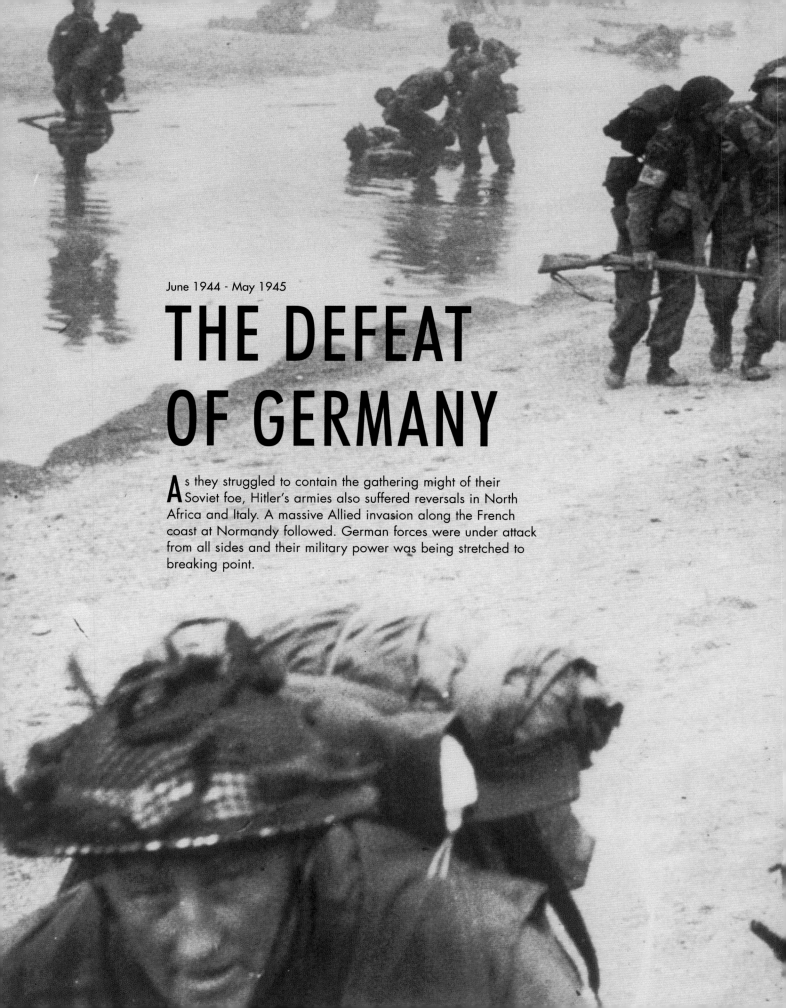

June 1944 - May 1945

THE DEFEAT OF GERMANY

As they struggled to contain the gathering might of their Soviet foe, Hitler's armies also suffered reversals in North Africa and Italy. A massive Allied invasion along the French coast at Normandy followed. German forces were under attack from all sides and their military power was being stretched to breaking point.

British troops arrive on Sword Beach, during the Normandy Landings of June 6, 1944. It is 8:45 in the morning, and they are still under enemy fire, as they mill around in the chaos of the opening hours of the invasion of Western Europe.

PREPARING FOR D-DAY

From 1941 until June 1944, most of the fighting took place in the Soviet Union and the Pacific. But, in England, the Allies had spent two years building up a powerful force, to invade and liberate Western Europe from the Nazis. People joked that the only thing stopping the island sinking under the weight of all the men and equipment were the anti-aircraft barrage balloons that flew over every military base.

Commander-in-chief, General Eisenhower, visits parachute troops on the eve of the invasion. Within hours, these men were fighting and dying in France.

Expecting visitors

The Germans knew an invasion was inevitable – they had been expecting it for some time. From Norway to Spain, they had built concrete fortresses and heavy gun positions, and sewn the beaches with barbed wire, mines and anti-tank obstacles.

The Atlantic Wall, as it was known, looked formidable – but it had weaknesses. It was too long to defend strongly at any single point, and it was mostly held by second-rate soldiers. But there were still strong German forces in France, who would hurry at once to stop any invasion.

Where to start?

American general Dwight D. Eisenhower was given the enormous task of directing the invasion of Canadian, British and American troops, codenamed *Operation Overlord*. He would have to break the Atlantic Wall, allow his men to land, then transport troops, tanks and other equipment – at great speed – before the Germans could throw them back into the sea. He also had to decide on a landing point. Calais was nearest, but it was strongly defended, and right in the north of France. Normandy, though further, offered a more direct way into the rest of France, and the entire south coast of England could be used as a launch point.

Getting ashore

British general Bernard Montgomery planned to land at five points along a 100km (60 mile) stretch of coast. Troops would arrive by sea in landing craft; others by parachute or glider. Once they captured a beachhead, they had to be able to land further troops and supplies at great speed. The ports were too well defended to attack, so the Allies had to make their own landing jetties. Two huge ones, codenamed *Mulberries*, were built from concrete sections, to be towed across the channel. PLUTO (a vast Pipe Line Under The Ocean) was laid down to provide fuel for vehicles.

Special weapons

Special weapons were developed to help the Allies in those first crucial hours. *Sherman* tanks were fitted with propellers and canvas 'floatation collars' – to allow them to float ashore. Other tanks had rotating flails of steel chains attached to their fronts, to destroy mines buried on the beaches. Some tanks carried giant spools of fabric to be unravelled on soft sand, to allow other vehicles to get off the beach without sinking. But most fearsome of all were *Churchill* tanks fitted with napalm flame throwers. These could shoot a jet of fire 110m (360ft) towards enemy positions.

Faking it

Finally, the Allies pulled off an amazing confidence trick. Fake fuel and equipment dumps, as well as landing craft and airfields, were built in Kent – just across the Channel from Calais – to fool German reconnaissance aircraft and make the Germans think the invasion was really heading there instead. Radio signals for a non-existent new invasion army, based in Kent, buzzed across the airwaves. Even a small invasion fleet was assembled. When everything was ready, Eisenhower and his staff – and hundreds of thousands of soldiers, sailors and airmen – had to wait for the crucial moment to proceed.

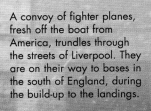

A convoy of fighter planes, fresh off the boat from America, trundles through the streets of Liverpool. They are on their way to bases in the south of England, during the build-up to the landings.

INTERNET LINK

For a link to a website where you can find out about the machines invented for D-Day and follow an animated map of the landings, go to
www.usborne-quicklinks.com

THE D-DAY LANDINGS

The timing of the Normandy Landings was crucial. Tides, weather, moonlight – all had to be right. By early June, everything was ready, but unseasonable storms lashed the Channel. Then, forecasters predicted a lull on the night of June 5-6. Eisenhower, his troops already packed into invasion ships and barges, could wait no longer.

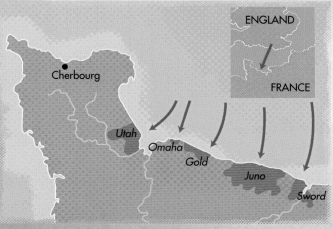

The arrows on this map show the direction of assault on the first day of the Landings. Each beachhead had its own codename, shown here.

From sky and sea

On June 5, a fleet of 5,000 ships moved out from the ports of southern England to assemble off the Normandy coast. That night, troops crowded into gliders and planes, and ground crews armed the fighters and bombers that accompanied the invasion force. In all, 9,000 aircraft took part. French Resistance forces were tipped off, via a coded message. Throughout France, railway lines and telephone exchanges were blown up – to hamper German forces heading for the coast. The invasion began at 12:16am on June 6 – known as D-Day – when three British gliders packed with troops landed just outside Caen, on the edge of the invasion zone. Their task was to capture vital roads and bridges or destroy enemy strongpoints.

Beach landings

For many soldiers in the landing crafts, the invasion began in a blur of seasickness, freezing spray, and noise from the guns of Allied warships and thousands of planes flying low overhead. By preventing attacks on the invaders, the planes were crucial to success. At 6:30am, the first seaborne troops landed at the poorly defended *Utah* beach. By nightfall, 23,000 US troops had come ashore with only 200 casualties. *Omaha* beach would be much more difficult. Right from the start, landing craft were subjected to heavy artillery and machine-gun fire.

Mixed fortunes

Around 1,000 Americans were killed at *Omaha* beach; it was to be the worst bloodshed that day. British and Canadian troops landing further east had mixed fortunes. The beach landings were easier, but they met heavy German opposition as they tried to move inland. By the evening, 150,000 Allied troops had landed in Normandy. Casualties had been relatively light – only 2,500 men in total were killed.

American war photographer Robert Capa took this close-up of *Omaha* beach, in a series of photographs that made him famous.

INTERNET LINK

For a link to a website where you can read eyewitness accounts and newspaper clippings from the D-Day landings, go to **www.usborne-quicklinks.com**

Wrong again

Hitler was told of the Allied landings when he woke around midday. He was delighted. "As long as they were in Britain we couldn't get at them. Now we have them where we can destroy them." But his commanders on the ground were divided on what to do. Field Marshal von Rundstedt, commander-in-chief of all Germany's western forces, wanted to let the Allies build up their forces before he attacked in strength. This, he hoped, would allow him to destroy more of his enemy's troops. His second-in-command, Erwin Rommel, wanted an early attack, to destroy the Allies on their beachheads.

The die is cast

But the Germans were still convinced that the main attack would come at Calais, so they held back reinforcements. The Allies also completely dominated the skies, annihilating German troops and tanks as they headed up to Normandy. By the end of June, Eisenhower had 850,000 men and 150,000 vehicles ashore. His gamble had paid off. There was no doubt now that Germany would lose the war. The only question was how much longer it would take.

The very first troops to land on *Omaha* beach are already pinned down by murderous machine-gun fire from the high cliffs beyond the beach.

207

HITLER — THE MILITARY COMMANDER

J udged solely in terms of his impact on the world, Hitler was one of the most impressive military commanders in history. Nazi propaganda portrayed him as a military genius, and early German successes demonstrated his ability. But self-delusion was one of his greatest defects and as a commander he was deeply flawed. The German people paid a terrible price for his blunders.

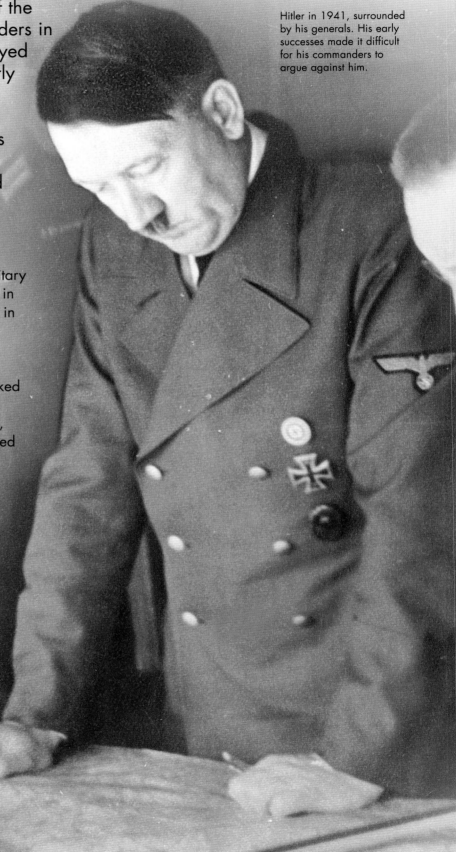

Hitler in 1941, surrounded by his generals. His early successes made it difficult for his commanders to argue against him.

A flawed force

The Nazis spent the 1930s building a military force that was probably the most effective in the world. Their troops were brainwashed in Nazi ideology, and they had exceptional weapons which they used with great skill.

But, right from the start, Hitler deeply disliked and distrusted many of his generals. He thought them cautious and narrow-minded, while they felt he was reckless, and resented his interference with their battle plans.

For example, Hitler followed the battle for Stalingrad with a street map spread out before him, issuing orders from a distance concerning the day-to-day running of the battle. His decisions that soldiers should stand firm, when battlefield commanders wanted to retreat, lost the German army hundreds of thousands of men, as well as valuable equipment.

General Heinz Guderian wrote this damning epitaph: *"He had a special picture of the world, and every fact had to be fitted into that ... world. As he believed, so the world must be; but in fact it was a picture of another world."*

Hitler visits the Polish front, during the opening stages of the war. As the war turned against him, such visits became increasingly rare.

Bad planning

Military equipment was often in short supply. But Hitler was so sure of victory in the Soviet Union in 1941 that he ordered the production of weapons and ammunition for the army to be drastically reduced. Instead he switched resources to the air force and the navy, to defeat the British. Army weapons production resumed in 1942, but equipment did not reach troops until late summer.

Strategic errors

Hitler's greatest blunders were on a much larger scale, though. His decision to risk war with Britain and her empire was taken with no real thought of how such a substantial enemy was to be defeated. He fatally underestimated the strength of the Soviet Union, and his invasion of that vast country was to become his undoing. In December 1941, just when it became clear that the war there was going badly wrong, he declared war on the United States: the world's most powerful nation. Germany may have had the world's best army, but it had to fight the three strongest powers on earth.

Hitler's twisted ideology also placed huge demands on Germany's military strength. In 1943 and 1944, massive efforts were put into the transportation of millions of Jews to death camps, deploying trains, soldiers and other resources that could have been effectively used to help his beleaguered armies.

The July assassination plot

Whether it was because most Germans were in thrall to Hitler's vision of world domination, or because the *Gestapo* (the Secret Police) was so effective, there was little resistance to the Nazis inside Germany. Some generals had long despised the ex-corporal who treated them with such contempt, but it was only in 1944 that a serious plot was hatched to kill Hitler.

Led by glamorous war hero Colonel Claus von Stauffenberg, the plotters intended to kill him with a briefcase bomb planted in his headquarters. Then they planned to seize control of the country with the Home Army – units of the German army stationed in Germany. The bomb blew Hitler's trousers to tatters, but it failed to kill him. In the wake of the assassination attempt, 7,000 people were arrested, and between two and three thousand of them were executed.

Hitler (middle) with von Stauffenberg (far left), in Rastenburg, East Prussia, on July 15, 1944. Stauffenberg is carrying a bomb to kill Hitler. But, on this occasion, he was not able to set it off.

INTERNET LINK
For a link to a website with an account of the 1944 assassination attempt on Hitler, go to **www.usborne-quicklinks.com**

FIGHTING FOR FRANCE

Despite their huge numbers, it took the Allies over six weeks to break out from their Normandy beachheads. But, when they did, the German army that had fought so fiercely to hold back the invaders, crumbled before them. Ahead lay the French capital, Paris.

Fighting for France

The fighting in Normandy had been tough. High hedges and narrow roads made defending easy for the Germans. Thousands of dead cows, killed in artillery and aerial bombardment, lay all around, adding to the chaos and stench of death. But, by July 24, US troops under General Omar Bradley broke out south of Saint-Lo. By August the Germans were in full retreat, and a further Allied invasion from the Mediterranean added to their problems. Allied troops finally met up in central France in mid-September.

"Paris must be destroyed!"

Major General Dietrich von Choltitz had been given the unenviable task of defending Paris. In early August, Hitler had summoned him and ordered that if the German army had to abandon the city, "it must be utterly destroyed … nothing must be left standing, no church, no artistic monument." With this in mind, German engineers placed demolition charges in major buildings, and prepared to destroy Paris.

A French Resistance fighter, identifiable by his armband, joins Allied troops in street fighting on the way to Paris.

Second thoughts

Von Choltitz was a loyal, even ruthless general, who had served the Nazis well. But he found his orders too much to stomach. By a window high up in his Parisian headquarters, he spent a wistful evening staring out on this beautiful city. Below, a woman in a bright red dress cycled by. "I like these pretty Parisians," he told an aide. "It would be a tragedy to have to kill them and destroy their city."

Twists and turns

As the Allies drew closer to Paris, Eisenhower decided to bypass it. He did not want his troops to have to fight in the city, and ruin its historic buildings. Inside the capital, events were acquiring their own momentum. The police went on strike, and French Resistance groups rose up to confront their German occupiers. Barricades were set up in the streets, and sporadic fighting broke out. Fearing a bloodbath, Eisenhower changed his mind, and US and Free French forces headed for the city. Meanwhile, von Choltitz, at great risk to his own life, sent out a message to the approaching troops, telling them he was willing to surrender.

The Allies enter Paris

On August 25, 1944, Allied troops poured into the city. Some were greeted by cheering Parisians, who showered them with flowers and kisses. Others met sporadic but determined German resistance. Von Choltitz officially surrendered at 2:30pm. But, as the streets filled with cheering crowds, German snipers fired on them from the rooftops. It would be another 24 hours before they were flushed out from their hiding places.

On to Germany

The Allies continued their advance into the early autumn. The Belgian cities of Brussels and Antwerp fell on September 3, and the first American patrols crossed into Germany on September 11. But then the Allies came up against three significant obstacles: two great rivers – the Meuse and the Rhine – and a formidable line of concrete bunkers and antitank barriers, known as the West Wall. It was a good place to stop. After such a rapid advance, forward units were running short of supplies. For the moment, the war in the West came to a halt.

German officers, who have surrendered during the liberation of Paris, eye their captors warily.

INTERNET LINK

For a link to a website where you can listen to the sound of Parisians celebrating the German surrender, and read eyewitness accounts, go to www.usborne-quicklinks.com

Crowds who took to the streets to celebrate the liberation of Paris are fired on by German snipers.

MOTHER OF INVENTION

Creativity has always blossomed in wartime. The development of new weapons and tactics can give one side a crucial advantage over the other. During the Second World War, scientists worked around the clock to produce extraordinary new weapons, machines and medicines – all in a fraction of the time it would have taken to produce them in peacetime.

The first jet planes

A British engineer named Frank Whittle invented a jet engine in 1930. But the British government wasn't interested in his idea at the time. It was the Germans, operating completely independently, who first flew a plane powered by a jet rather than a propeller.

The Germans went on to design the highly effective *Messerschmitt Me-262*, the first jet fighter to be used in combat and the most sophisticated fighter plane of the war. At 870kmph (540mph), it flew considerably faster than Allied planes. The *Me-262* was the most deadly adversary for American bombers. But, fortunately for the Allies, it wasn't introduced until 1944 and only a few were ever built. If they had been produced in greater numbers, it might have changed the course of the war. But Hitler insisted the new jet should be fitted with bombs and used to support ground troops. It was only used as a fighter plane when this proved to be a failure.

Two British scientists at work on the mass production of life-saving penicillin

Magic medicine

Since the late 19th century, scientists had known that some fungi could destroy bacteria which cause infections. But they weren't able to put this knowledge to use. In London in 1940, Australian Howard Florry and German refugee Ernst Chain managed to extract a substance from the fungus *penicillium* which they named penicillin. Tests showed penicillin could be used to fight infections in wounds. Within three years, this new drug was being mass-produced in great vats, saving the lives of thousands of Allied soldiers.

The German jet-propelled *Messerschmitt Me-262*

Creating oil from coal

Military forces always need vast quantities of fuel, for their tanks, ships and planes, and for vehicles to transport their soldiers and artillery. The Germans had no fuel supplies of their own, and relied on the oil deposits of their ally Rumania. But this was never enough to supply all their needs. So, German scientists devised a technique to produce oil from a raw material Germany had a lot of: coal. This process, which involved mixing pulverized coal with high pressure hydrogen gas, was extremely effective. By 1944, 25 synthetic petroleum plants were producing at least half of all Germany's fuel.

Inventions that didn't work

As the war progressed, revolutionary new weapons were developed – from radio-guided missiles, to bouncing bombs designed to leapfrog over anti-torpedo nets. But not all these inventions worked. One, known as the *Panjandrum*, was designed to smash through concrete fortifications on the heavily defended coastline of France. It consisted of two enormous metal wheels, with two tons of explosives in its stubby axle. The wheels were driven by rocket engines placed all along the rim. It looked like a gigantic Catherine Wheel – and it was a disaster. Once unleashed, it was impossible to predict which way it would go!

This is a very rare photograph of the *Panjandrum*, during one of its farcical trials on an isolated British beach. On the outer rim of the wheel, you can make out the rocket engines that were supposed to drive it along.

INTERNET LINK

For a link to a website where you can find out more about some of the inventions and discoveries made during the war years, go to www.usborne-quicklinks.com

Simple ideas

Some of the best new ideas didn't rely on complicated machines at all. British bombers used a very simple and effective technique to confuse enemy radar about where a bomber attack was heading. They dropped reams of thin strips of tinfoil known as *Window*. These were picked up by German radar operators as a signal on their screens which looked like thousands of bombers.

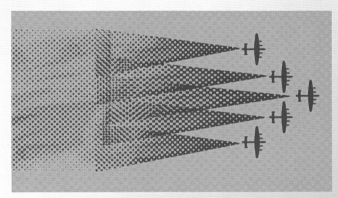

This diagram shows a small formation of British bombers dropping *Window* tin foil to confuse German radar operators.

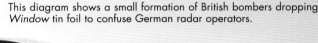

SPECIAL RELATIONSHIPS

The two great partnerships of the war fought in very different ways. The Allies – principally the United States, the Soviet Union and Britain – cooperated closely. But the main Axis powers – Germany, Italy and Japan – made almost no effort to work together. This was to have a major effect on the outcome of the war.

Common bonds

The fact that Britain and the United States shared a language and democratic culture contributed greatly to their wartime cooperation. But they also worked well with their other principal ally – the totalitarian communist regime of Soviet Russia. When told of the Nazi invasion of the Soviet Union, the famously anti-communist Winston Churchill remarked: "If Hitler invaded Hell, I would at least make a favourable reference to the Devil…" All three countries recognized that – whatever their differences – nothing was more important than defeating the Nazis.

Churchill, Roosevelt and Stalin (left to right) meet to decide the fate of the world, in the Soviet town of Yalta, on the Black Sea in February 1945.

The Atlantic alliance

The United States and Britain had worked together even before Pearl Harbor, as President Roosevelt wanted to help in the war, without involving American troops. In the Lend-Lease Act of 1941, the US government put aside seven billion dollars to supply weapons and equipment to Britain. When the Axis powers declared war on the United States, Churchill and Roosevelt met up at once to forge a common strategy. They decided Germany should be defeated first, and then Japan. US and British forces fought together effectively in the Mediterranean and Europe. Their efforts were coordinated by a group of top military men, known as the Combined Chiefs of Staff, all under a single commander-in-chief. The Americans conducted their own campaign in the Pacific, where the British played a smaller part.

Close collaboration was not as necessary with Soviet forces, as they were fighting in different parts of the world. Nonetheless, the United States and Britain sent millions of dollars' worth of military equipment, food and supplies, to help the Soviets.

Vital meetings

The three Allied leaders, Roosevelt, Churchill and Stalin, met during the war – to ensure they worked well together, and to agree what would happen at the end of the war. At Teheran, in 1943, they discussed the invasion of Western Europe. At Yalta, in 1945, Stalin promised the Soviet Union would help the United States to defeat Japan. The three leaders also accepted that, after the war, Eastern Europe would be ruled by regimes loyal to the Soviets, but Western Europe and the Mediterranean would be left under the control of democratic governments.

This American poster celebrates the Allied war effort. Among other flags you can see those of the United States, Britain, the Soviet Union, China and Australia.

An Italian propaganda poster celebrating the Japanese attack on Pearl Harbor

The other side

By contrast, the Axis powers barely worked together at all, even when they were fighting on the same battlegrounds. Most German soldiers despised their Axis comrades, as they felt they fought badly. But the truth was that most of them had been sent to fight a war they had no desire to be in. Italian and German cooperation with the Japanese was almost non-existent. The Japanese didn't even forewarn them of the Pearl Harbor attack, and Japan didn't declare war on Germany's greatest enemy, the Soviet Union. Throughout the war, American ships flying the Soviet flag sailed to Russia's Pacific coast with weapons and supplies, and none were ever attacked by Japanese submarines.

INTERNET LINK
For a link to a website where you can watch archive film footage of a meeting between the three Allied leaders, go to **www.usborne-quicklinks.com**

GERMANY'S ILL-FATED CITIES

Throughout the war, people lived in fear of bombing – and with good reason. Cities such as London, Warsaw and Rotterdam were badly damaged by German bombers at the start of the war. As the war progressed, the Allies concentrated their huge industrial resources on building thousands of bombers and began attacking German cities with increasing intensity.

Cologne and Hamburg

On the night of May 30, 1942, for the first time in history, a stream of over a thousand bombers – 110km (70 miles) long – took part in a single raid on the city of Cologne. Fewer than 500 people were killed, but 45,000 were made homeless. The Allies found that incendiary bombs could be made more effective if high explosive bombs were dropped first. This worked to chilling effect in Hamburg, on the night of July 24-25, 1943. Incendiary fires merged into one great conflagration. As hot air rose into the sky, cold air was sucked into the middle of the blazing city, creating a firestorm, which melted windows and set alight the asphalt streets. Tornado-like winds sucked cars and people into the flames. Even those seeking safety in bomb shelters suffocated for lack of oxygen.

The destruction of Dresden

The most infamous raid of the war was on the city of Dresden. Firestorms raged for a week, killing at least 35,000 people, mainly women and children, and destroying 25,000 of its 28,500 inner-city houses. (The casualty figure even may have been higher because the city was full of refugees fleeing from the advancing Russian army.) "We did not recognize our street anymore. Fire, only fire, wherever we looked," recalled a German child who survived, "there were burning vehicles and carts with refugees, people, horses, all of them screaming and shouting in fear of death." Even the zoo was destroyed. One keeper remembers having to shoot the big cats in case they escaped and went looking for people to eat.

Hamburg citizens wade through the ruins of their city, in July 1943. Hamburg was the first city to suffer destruction by firestorm.

Right or wrong?

The commander of British bomber forces, Air Marshal Arthur Harris, reported: "Dresden was a mass of munitions works, an intact government centre, and a key transportation point to the East. It is now none of these things." This was all true – yet the bombing of this historic and beautiful city remains one of the most controversial Allied actions of the entire war. Critics claim that the city had little military value, and that as many as 135,000 may have died. Some suggest raids like these constitute 'war crimes' – just like the German massacres of civilians or the wholesale destruction of the Jews.

Those defending the raid support Harris's assertion that Dresden was a weapons manufacturing city, and an important rail link for German troops heading for the Eastern Front. But even British Prime Minister Winston Churchill was alarmed by the scale of the destruction. As the war drew to a close, he worried that, "we shall come into control of an utterly ruined land."

A stone figure on top of Dresden Town Hall looks down on the devastated city, after the firestorm of February 13-14, 1945.

TO GERMANY'S EASTERN BORDER

After Kursk there was only one possible conclusion to the war in the East. Although the German army was a superbly trained and organized fighting force, it couldn't match the sheer weight of Soviet forces pitted against it. 1944 was to become known as 'the year of ten victories' in the Soviet Union.

A scorched earth retreat

The Germans conducted a 'scorched earth' retreat through territory they had marched through so confidently two or three years before. Their arrogance and brutality had stirred up a vengeful force against them. Now they felt, said one soldier, "like a man who has seized a wolf by the ears, and dare not let go." The Soviets advanced relentlessly, but they did so at a terrible cost. The Germans still fought very effectively. Wherever they clashed, the Red Army suffered far higher casualties. But they still had more men. By 1944, their army numbered six million, with another million in reserve. The German forces amounted to a dwindling three and a half million.

INTERNET LINK
For a link to a website where you can find film footage, eyewitness accounts and more from the Warsaw Uprising, go to www.usborne-quicklinks.com

The Soviets fight back

On June 22, 1944, three years to the day after the Nazi invasion, four Soviet armies launched a massive assault against German Army Group Centre. Outnumbered ten to one, and with strict orders from Hitler not to surrender, the Germans were wiped out. By late July, Soviet troops were a mere 13km (eight miles) from the Polish capital, Warsaw. Moscow Radio was urging the Poles to rise up and help them in the liberation of the city.

A Polish rebellion

Inside the heavily defended capital, 40,000 men of the Polish underground rose up in rebellion. Under the command of General Tadeusz Komorowski, they formed part of the Home Army. In four days, they seized three-fifths of the city, but disaster quickly overtook them. The Germans struck hard against the approaching Soviet forces, driving many of them back 100km (60 miles). German reinforcements poured into Warsaw, intent on destroying the Polish rebels. Brutal house-to-house fighting followed; over 200,000 civilians were killed. By the end of August, Poles were hiding in cellars, parched and starved, many weak from dysentery. Still, men, women, and even children, continued to fight against the Germans with great determination.

From bad to worse

Many of the German forces were desperate men too – with little to lose. They included soldiers from punishment battalions, and Russian deserters who had been persuaded to fight against their own country. These men behaved with merciless barbarity towards anyone they captured. Gradually, the Polish resistance was limited to the northern district of Warsaw. As their strength ebbed away, their only hope was that the Red Army would arrive to capture the city. But although Churchill and Roosevelt had asked Stalin for help, this never came.

Some historians believe Stalin deliberately denied them help – because the Home Army was loyal to the Polish government in exile in London, and he didn't want them to return to rule Poland. The Soviets claimed, with good reason, that they themselves were running short of supplies and faced tough opposition outside the city. But, surprisingly, given the ruthless way the Nazis usually dealt with rebellions, the Home Army managed to negotiate a surrender. On October 3, 15,000 of them marched off to prisoner-of-war camps.

Crouching behind the grand pillars of the Warsaw Opera House, German soldiers come under attack from the Polish Home Army.

INTO GERMANY FROM THE WEST

As 1944 drew to a close, American, British and Canadian forces stood ready to pour into Germany. But they were overstretched, exhausted and poorly coordinated. An autumn offensive at Arnhem, intending to open the way to Berlin, failed. In December, the German army counterattacked in force, causing US general George Patton to observe, "We can still lose this war."

Seizing bridges

Following the great victories in France and Belgium, British Field Marshal Montgomery suggested a bold strategy to reach Berlin quickly. Allied forces would seize important bridges in the Netherlands, then press through north Germany to Berlin.

General Eisenhower, the Allied Supreme Commander, was against the idea. He preferred an advance across a broad front. But Montgomery was given the chance to put his plan into operation. It almost worked. Bridges at Eindhoven and Nijmegan were captured by parachute troops, but the most northerly bridge, Arnhem, could not be held. Of 10,000 British paratroops dropped to seize the bridge, barely 2,000 managed to escape back to Allied lines.

A German tank passes columns of US prisoners during the Battle of the Bulge, December 17, 1944.

The Battle of the Bulge

Seriously weakened by five years of war, the German army was still a formidable fighting force. As the Allies closed in, the Germans fought back with even greater ferocity. On December 16, a sudden, unexpected German counterattack began. New tanks, kept for such an offensive, lurched through fog and snow in the thick forest of the Ardennes in Belgium.

A great bulge developed in the Allied line, as US troops retreated in confusion. Panic spread when it was discovered that the Germans were using special commando units dressed in US army uniforms. But December 23 brought clear blue skies, perfect for the Allies' great strength: their air power. German tanks and troops were mercilessly battered by planes carrying rockets and bombs, and the advance ground to a halt. The battle had been Hitler's last chance to turn the tide of the war, and it had failed. In early 1945, the Allies moved into Germany in force.

INTERNET LINK
For links to websites where you can find photographs, maps and eyewitness accounts of the Battle of the Bulge, go to
www.usborne-quicklinks.com

Germany in chaos

The Allies were hampered by two major obstacles: the Ruhr area had been deliberately flooded, and the great Rhine river blocked the way east. But in March they crossed the river and were advancing swiftly, sometimes covering 80km (50 miles) a day. In April, German forces in the Ruhr were encircled and 400,000 were taken prisoner – the greatest capitulation of the war in the West so far.

Germany was in chaos. Soviet troops had invaded, and millions were fleeing from them in terror. Squads of fanatical Nazis were executing any soldier who dared suggest surrender. Hitler, directing what was left of his forces from a bunker in Berlin, grew increasingly out of touch with reality. Before the war, he had said, "We may be destroyed, but if we are, we shall drag the world with us … a world in flames." He intended to keep his word.

Orders were given to destroy everything in the Allies' path: bridges, power stations, hospitals. "If the war is lost, the German nation will also perish," Hitler told his minister Albert Speer. "There is no need to take into consideration the basic needs of the people. Those that remain after the battle are those who are inferior; for the good will have fallen."

THE FALL OF BERLIN

In the last weeks of the war, farce mixed with tragedy. Hitler, directing non-existent armies from his bunker in central Berlin, grew increasingly shrill and deranged. Stalin was determined to take Berlin – whatever the cost. And millions of soldiers – on all sides – wondered if, having got this far, they would be the ones to die in this last great battle.

As smoke rises over the rubble-strewn streets of Berlin, a Russian soldier flies the Soviet flag from the roof of the German parliament, right in the middle of the city.

No escape

Throughout late 1944, Soviet forces had been pressing west through Eastern Europe. By February 1945, they were waiting on the River Oder, just outside Berlin, building up their strength for an assault. The Americans were close too, but Eisenhower had already decided the expected cost in casualties was not worth the prestige of capturing the capital. Stalin had no such scruples. 2,500,000 men, 6,000 tanks, 41,000 guns and 7,500 aircraft lay ready and waiting. Facing them was the tattered remains of the German army. Alongside these war-weary veterans were newly conscripted old men, and boys so young they could barely pick up a rifle, who wore helmets that were too big for their heads.

Panic in the streets

As the Soviets approached, millions of Germans fled, leaving behind a shattered capital. Already ruined by bombing, it was to be further destroyed by fearsome artillery barrages, and street-to-street fighting. An aura of unreality descended. Executed soldiers dangled from lampposts, hung for desertion to deter others from doing so. People staggered drunkenly through the chaos, trying to blot out the awful reality of what was about to happen. One possibly true story from this time tells that, after a final performance of Wagner's *Götterdämmerung*, members of the audience filed past boys of the Hitler Youth who carried baskets of cyanide suicide capsules provided for them.

The battle for Berlin began on April 16. By April 24, the city was surrounded by Soviet troops. As they advanced into the suburbs, German army communication lines broke down completely. To find out how near the Russians were, officers in central command posts had to ring outlying districts via the city's public telephone network. When a voice answered the phone in Russian, they knew the end was a little nearer.

Wrong place, wrong time

During their invasion of the Soviet Union, the Nazis had behaved with great inhumanity towards both Soviet citizens and soldiers. For the Soviets entering Berlin ('the lair of the Fascist beast' – according to Soviet propaganda), the time for revenge was at hand. Unfortunately, those who suffered most were civilians. With over two million Soviet soldiers now in Berlin, thousands of women who had stayed on in the capital were raped.

The final act

Hitler spent the last few weeks in an underground bunker in central Berlin. In a feverish, hysterical atmosphere, he found time to marry his mistress, Eva Braun, and to denounce the German people in an unapologetic final political testament. They had, he said, shown themselves unworthy of the faith he had placed in them. Then, in the nearest he came to taking any of the blame for the disaster he had brought his country, this most ruthless and barbaric of leaders declared he had not been ruthless enough: "Afterwards, you regret the fact you have been so kind."

On April 30, 1945, Hitler took cyanide and shot himself in the head. Eva Braun killed herself too. Their bodies were burned, without ceremony, outside the bunker. A week later, on May 8, the war in Europe was over.

In one of the most famous photographs of the war, US Marines plant the stars and stripes on top of Mount Suribachi, Iwo Jima, on February 23, 1945. The capture of this small island was hugely significant, as it was the first piece of Japanese home territory to fall into American hands.

February - September 1945

THE DEFEAT OF JAPAN

In December 1941, Britain and the United Sates had agreed that Germany was their principal enemy and should be defeated first. As that task neared completion, American forces also began closing in on mainland Japan. The Japanese hoped the fanatical tenacity of their fighting forces would save them, but they were unprepared for the terrible weapon that would be soon unleashed against them.

IWO JIMA AND OKINAWA

As the war in Europe reached its inevitable conclusion, US forces in the Pacific began their final island battles before the invasion of Japan. In February and April, 1945, they invaded two formidably defended Japanese islands: Iwo Jima and Okinawa. The Japanese knew they couldn't hold the islands, but they hoped to inflict such dreadful casualties on the invaders that President Roosevelt would be forced to negotiate a compromise peace.

Iwo Jima

Barely 20 square km (8 square miles) in area, Iwo Jima was defended by 21,000 Japanese soldiers, who had been ordered to fight to the death. This was, after all, the first piece of Japanese home territory to be invaded in 4,000 years. The tiny island was an ugly slab of black volcanic rock and scrub. It had once been used as a fighter airbase, but had been turned into a formidable fortress of concrete gun emplacements and pillboxes, linked together by tunnels.

Approaching the island from Hawaii, trailing 110km (70 miles) along the ocean, was an invasion fleet of 800 vessels and 300,000 men. 100,000 of them were marine combat troops, and the invasion was set for February 19.

A US Marine dashes forward under a hail of machine-gun fire, during the battle for Okinawa, in May 1945.

Concentrated carnage

Shortly after the first American landing craft hit the island beaches, Japanese forces began a withering bombardment. For the next month, American soldiers and marines would have to struggle for every inch of the island. Because their Japanese opponents were so well hidden, the Americans usually didn't see them until they were dead. The fighting ended on March 16. Of the defenders, only 216 surrendered; the rest fought to the death. 6,000 Americans were killed; 17,000 wounded.

Worse to come

The next target to be invaded was an even tougher nut to crack. Okinawa, a narrow island, 110km (70 miles) long, was only 500km (300 miles) from mainland Japan. Most of the 100,000 Japanese troops there were dug into three strong defensive ridges in the south of the island. They peered out from a dense well-concealed network of caves and tunnels, and they too had been ordered to fight to the last man.

On Easter Day, April 1, 1945, another gigantic armada began to land 172,000 US troops on Okinawa. The fighting that followed was the bloodiest of the entire Pacific War. Torrential rain lashed the island, reducing the battlefield to a muddy quagmire. With its well dug-in defenders and endless mud, the fighting reminded some marine veterans of the trenches of the Western Front during the First World War.

INTERNET LINK
For a link to a website where you can watch archive film footage of the fighting on Iwo Jima, go to **www.usborne-quicklinks.com**

A nightmare campaign

Eventually, with flame-throwers and high explosives blasting the Japanese from their positions, the Americans captured the island. It took three months and cost them 5,500 dead and 51,000 wounded. Japanese casualties were far worse, although a surprising 11,000 surrendered. During the campaign, the US fleet had stayed offshore, to resupply their forces inland, and bombard Japanese positions. But the Japanese had sent 800 *kamikaze* planes to bomb them, with devastating effect: they sank 32 US ships and damaged 368. The Americans had paid a great price to win these two small islands. Now they faced the invasion of Japan itself.

Just behind the front lines, men of the 77th Infantry division in Okinawa listen to the news of Germany's surrender on May 8, 1945. A minute later, they were back at their posts, killing or being killed.

THE MANHATTAN PROJECT

In the 1930s, scientists working in nuclear physics realized they could use the energy inside atoms of uranium and plutonium to create an immense explosive. Over the next decade or so, Allied and Axis scientists carried out research aimed at constructing the world's first atomic bomb. What they all knew for certain was that any nation who possessed such a weapon would be able to win the war.

Robert Oppenheimer – the scientist in charge of the Manhattan Project. Like many of his colleagues, he was very uneasy about producing the A-Bomb.

Selling the idea

Fearing that Germany, or even Japan, might win the race to build a working atomic bomb, Allied scientists tried to persuade American politicians to fund the development of their own. But the science behind it was so bizarre, they were not taken seriously. There are, for example, 200 million volts of electricity in a single atom of uranium. The world's greatest living scientist, Albert Einstein, even wrote to President Roosevelt to try to interest him in the project. But Einstein got a cool response. "What would America want with such a weapon?" reasoned the President.

International team effort

But war with Japan and Germany changed the President's mind. Funding was made available, and a brilliant American physicist named Robert Oppenheimer put together an international research team to develop a working atomic bomb. The enterprise was codenamed the *Manhattan Project* and based in a warren of laboratories in Los Alamos, a remote spot in the New Mexican desert.

INTERNET LINK

For a link to a website where you can find out about the people involved in the Manhattan Project, go to
www.usborne-quicklinks.com

This extraordinary photo shows the awesome power of the first ever atomic bomb explosion. Within .062 of a second, when the shot was taken, the fireball is already over 300m (900 feet) wide.

The Los Alamos laboratory in New Mexico, where the world's first atomic bomb was created.

A lucky break

In an amazing twist of Allied good fortune, many of the world's top atomic scientists were political or Jewish refugees from Germany and Italy. Hitler had seriously underestimated them. "If the dismissal of Jewish scientists means the annihilation of contemporary German science, we shall have to do without science for a few years," he claimed. Without them, or the Americans' vast resources, the Axis had no chance of building a bomb. But the Allies didn't know this. Their research was driven by the fear that Germany would beat them to it.

Vast expense

Research continued with desperate haste. 'Tickling the dragon' was the term scientists used to refer to their dangerous work. The Manhattan Project blossomed into a business as vast as the American motor industry, in its size and use of resources. It cost two billion dollars, and its factories and research laboratories were staffed by 600,000 people. Despite these vast sums and numbers, it remained a secret. Even the vice president, Harry Truman, didn't know about it until he became president, when Roosevelt died in April 1945.

The bombs

As explosives, uranium and plutonium are very powerful. An amount of either the size of a large orange is equivalent to 20,000 tons of TNT – the explosive most commonly used in Second World War shells and bombs. The bombs developed by the Manhattan Project worked like this:

Uranium bomb
A uranium projectile, shaped like this, is fired along a barrel into another quantity of uranium. On impact, there is a vast explosion.

Plutonium bomb
A ring of uranium projectiles, like this, are fired into a central core of plutonium, producing a similarly vast explosion.

A trial run

By the summer of 1945, the Manhattan Project scientists had produced two different atomic bombs. One, using the element uranium, they were sure would work. The other, using the man-made material plutonium, was more of an uncertainty. To test it, a tall tower was constructed at Alamogordo, in the New Mexican desert, and the bomb was placed on top. Successfully detonated on July 16, 1945, it sent a plume of radioactive smoke and sand 12,000m (40,000ft) into the sky. By this stage of the war, Japan was the only Axis power left fighting. US politicians were afraid that invading Japan would involve a terrible cost in American lives. The atomic bomb offered the opportunity to end the war – with one final, dramatic flourish.

Oppenheimer, together with an American general, stands at the exact point of detonation of the first atomic bomb. All that remains of the tower the bomb was placed on are a few twisted strands of metal, and the surrounding desert sand has been turned to glass.

HIROSHIMA & NAGASAKI

Throughout the summer of 1945, Japanese forces resisted their inevitable defeat with such ferocity that Allied planners feared the invasion of Japan itself would cost half a million lives. The atomic bomb presented an opportunity for the Allies to destroy their tenacious enemies in a single flash of terrible fire.

Where to go?

The Americans chose their targets carefully. They wanted to bomb a city that was an important military hub. They also wanted a target that had been relatively untouched by the bombing raids of the previous year, so they could see exactly how much damage their new weapon was capable of doing. This ruled out Tokyo, which had already been devastated by bombers in March, in a raid that had killed 100,000 and left fires burning for four days.

The city selected to be destroyed was Hiroshima, a military supply base with shipyards, weapons factories, and a population of 300,000. The pilot chosen for the mission was Col. Paul Tibbets, who would fly the *B-29 Superfortress Enola Gay* from Tinian airbase in the Marianas Islands. After being given the go-ahead, Tibbets and his crew were delayed by a whole five days, waiting for the weather to clear.

Beneath this fearsome mushroom cloud of radiated smoke and rubble lies the city of Hiroshima.

This aerial photograph of Hiroshima was taken a few days after the attack. The city has been almost entirely flattened by a single bomb.

A peep into hell

Enola Gay, and two other planes packed with scientific equipment, arrived over the clear blue sky of Hiroshima shortly after 8:00am on August 6. Their uranium bomb, codenamed *Little Boy*, exploded 576m (1,890ft) above the city. In the flash and blast that followed, factories, office blocks and homes were flattened. Commuters in trains were flung topsy-turvy into the air. Grass, flowers and trees in city parks burst into flames. People caught outdoors were vaporized. Only their shadows remained, caught in the superheated flash of the atomic detonation. Watching from above, "a peep into hell" was how *Enola Gay*'s tail gunner described the dreadful sight.

Horrifying destruction

About two-thirds of the city was destroyed in an instant – along with 80,000 of its citizens. Over the following months and years, another 80,000 died of radiation poisoning. The Japanese government was too stunned to react. Communications were totally destroyed between Hiroshima and Tokyo. When news of the annihilation eventually reached the Japanese capital, it was dismissed as an exaggeration.

Unlucky Nagasaki

On August 9, another *B-29*, *Bocks Car*, was dispatched from Tinian, carrying a plutonium type bomb, codenamed *Fat Man*. Their target was the great weapons arsenal of Kokura, but when they arrived it was covered by thick cloud. The city hovered on the brink of destruction – but the bomb aimer couldn't see his target. So the plane flew another hundred miles southwest, to the industrial city of Nagasaki, dropping the bomb over it at 11:00am. The damage wasn't as great as at Hiroshima – there was less to destroy – but just as many people died.

A double blow

The previous day, the Soviet Union had declared war on Japan, and invaded Manchuria. But still the Japanese government argued over surrender. Emperor Hirohito and most of his ministers wanted the fighting to stop. But this provoked a revolt among senior army officers, determined to fight to the end. Fortunately, the revolt failed. Fighting stopped on August 15, and a surrender was signed on September 2, 1945 – six years and a day after the war began.

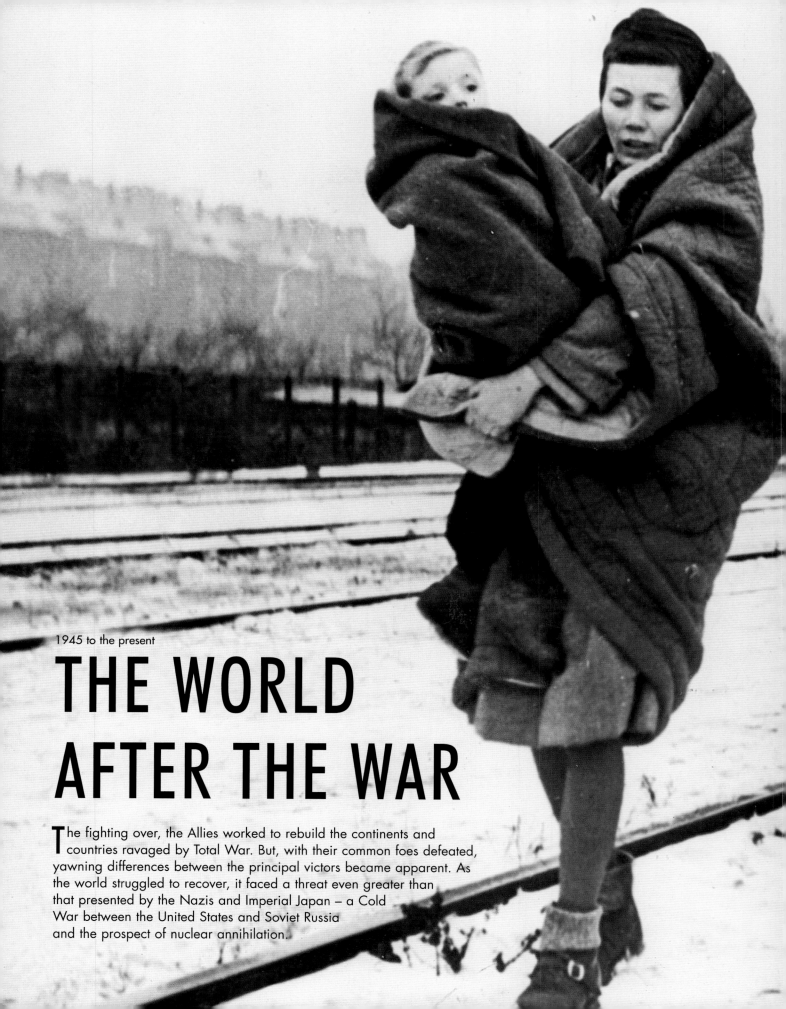

1945 to the present

THE WORLD AFTER THE WAR

The fighting over, the Allies worked to rebuild the continents and countries ravaged by Total War. But, with their common foes defeated, yawning differences between the principal victors became apparent. As the world struggled to recover, it faced a threat even greater than that presented by the Nazis and Imperial Japan – a Cold War between the United States and Soviet Russia and the prospect of nuclear annihilation.

Eight months after the war in Europe ended, German civilians were still trying to reach the West, to escape the vengeful Soviet occupation. The women and children in this photograph were all that remained of a party of 150 civilians who fled from Poland in the early winter of 1945.

THE END OF THE WAR

The official end of the war, September 2, 1945, was marked by a huge display of military might in Tokyo Bay. As the Japanese delegation left the USS *Missouri*, 450 US carrier aircraft in tight formation flew over assembled Allied warships. It was a fitting symbol, as US military strength, more than anything else, had won the war against the Japanese. Now, with peace declared in both Europe and Asia, the world faced an uncertain future.

Glory and disgrace

News of the end of the fighting provoked delirious scenes in the major cities of the victorious nations. In New York, two million people converged on Times Square. In London, a giant conga line stretched around Piccadilly and Oxford Street. In Japan, people wept openly in the street for their humiliated nation. The citizens of Germany contemplated their new circumstances in dazed despair. Until 1943, most German civilians had prospered from the fruits of the Nazi empire. Now, after two years of around-the-clock bombing, and invasion from east and west, they were left with a devastated country.

Waving the Allied flags of the Soviet Union, Great Britain and the United States, civilians join British and American servicemen in London's Trafalgar Square, to celebrate the end of the war in Europe. The war against Japan dragged on for another three months.

Displaced persons

The most immediate problem was what to do with the millions of people the war had uprooted. In Germany, there were five and a half million Soviet citizens who needed to be sent home. Among them were soldiers who had fought for the Nazis and faced certain execution at home. But, with a cruel logic, the Soviet authorities decided that many of the others, who had survived captivity as prisoners-of-war and slave workers, were 'traitors' too. So they returned home to long prison sentences. Millions of Germans had also fled west from the approaching Soviet armies in the East. In the months before and after the end of the war, as many as two million of these refugees may have died of starvation, disease and exhaustion.

Retribution

Representatives of the old regimes were rounded up. The Soviets shot any Nazi official from the rank of mayor and above, partly in reprisal for the Nazi practice of automatically executing any communist official they had captured in Soviet territory. In other European countries, those who had collaborated – cooperated with the German invaders – were punished too. In France, 120,000 collaborators were given prison sentences, and 2,000 were executed. Another 50,000 or so, who escaped 'official' justice, were murdered in the years after the war.

Changing hearts and minds

In Japan and Germany, people loyal to their former regimes faced re-education. This process was awkwardly known as demilitarization – or *de-Nazification*. In Germany, for example, citizens were taken to see the victims of nearby concentration camps, or shown films of recently liberated death camps such as Auschwitz.

These German civilians have been taken on a tour of a concentration camp, to show them the true nature of the Nazi regime.

The terrible price of war

With the fighting over, it was now possible to begin to estimate the human cost. Most historians accept the war claimed at least 50 million lives. The Soviet Union suffered the worst, with over 25 million military and civilian deaths. Shockingly, only 3% of Soviet men aged between 19 and 23 survived. German dead numbered three and a half million military men, and over two million civilians. Britain and her Commonwealth lost 420,000 men, the United States, 292,000. In Poland six and a half million – one in five of the population – perished. Three and a half million of these were Jewish victims of the Holocaust.

> ### INTERNET LINK
> For a link to a website where you can listen to the announcement of the end of the war, and hear the reaction from King George VI and the crowds on the streets of London, go to **www.usborne-quicklinks.com**

THE AFTERMATH OF THE WAR

As summer 1945 turned to autumn, the victors were left with the difficult task of winning the peace. They needed to rebuild Europe and Japan, and establish stable new governments in place of the fallen dictatorships. But those responsible for plunging the world into war had to be punished first.

Hitler's deputy, Hermann Goering, listens attentively during his trial at Nuremberg. Sentenced to death by hanging, Goering committed suicide by taking poison on the night of the execution.

The war trials at Nuremberg

In the 12 months following the war, top German and Japanese politicians and generals were put on trial for war crimes. In Germany, the location was Nuremberg – a city closely associated with great Nazi rallies. Death sentences were handed down to the worst offenders. Those hanged at Nuremberg had their bodies burned in the crematorium of infamous Dachau concentration camp, and their ashes scattered in a nearby river.

Slow recovery

As well as claiming millions of lives, the war had destroyed millions of homes, bridges, railway lines, hospitals, factories and offices. In the 'scorched earth' fighting of the Eastern Front, the Soviet Union lost a quarter of all its buildings, and 60% of its farm produce. Germany, too, suffered similar destruction. Other countries, though, had grown richer – especially the United States, which had provided so many of the weapons used to win the war. Canada, Australia and New Zealand – like the USA, untouched by bombing – also prospered.

Europe and Japan were hardest hit. The summer of 1945 also brought a drought which worsened already serious food shortages by causing a disastrous grain harvest. In Britain, bread was rationed for the first time, to make sure there was enough to feed the starving people of Germany.

Germany's fate

The First World War had ended with the vengeful Treaty of Versailles, which punished Germany severely. This bred a fierce resentment among the German people, which contributed to the rise of Hitler and led directly to the Second World War. Now, at the end of that war, the Allies were divided over the best way to treat the defeated German nation.

The Soviets wanted to strip Germany of its industry, and ship out factory machinery to help rebuild their own country. Before the war ended, US Treasury Secretary Henry Morgenthau proposed to turn Germany into a pre-industrial society, by demolishing its factories and flooding its mines. Such drastic measures would, it was hoped, prevent the country from ever being strong enough to go to war again. Fortunately though, other, more humane policies were adopted.

Rebuilding shattered economies

Britain and the United States realized, however, that the defeated nations needed to be nurtured as well as punished, to avoid another disastrous conflict in the future. In 1948, American Secretary of State George Marshall introduced the Marshall Plan, which offered economic aid to all European countries – regardless of which side they had been on. The Soviets refused to allow the countries they had occupied in Eastern Europe to receive this aid. But it played a vital role in helping the Western European countries, including Germany, to rebuild their shattered economies.

German civilians wait in line for soup rations in the ruins of Hamburg, a year after the war in Europe had ended.

From poverty to riches

Japan, too, suffered terribly after the war ended. Some people had to wear paper clothes and eat edible weeds just to survive. US General Douglas MacArthur was put in charge of ensuring that Japan became a stable and democratic society. He was extremely successful. By the time he left in 1951, he had introduced a new constitution, giving all adults the right to vote. He had also created the foundations that would enable Japan to become one of the world's most successful economies in the second half of the 20th century.

INTERNET LINK
For links to websites where you can watch video clips and see photographs of the war crimes' trials, and hear radio broadcasts from postwar America, go to **www.usborne-quicklinks.com**

THE WAR AND THE 20TH CENTURY

In scope and destruction, the Second World War was the most momentous event of the 20th century. In the last 2,000 years, only the Black Death in the Middle Ages had a more disastrous impact on the lives of those who lived or died through it. The shadow of the war haunted the rest of the century, and its effect on the world is still with us today.

Empires rise and fall

Before the war, Britain, France, Germany and Japan had all been world class military powers. Now they were eclipsed by the United States and Soviet Union – the world's two new superpowers. In the years after the war, Britain and France slowly came to terms with their status as second division powers, and gave up control over their once mighty global empires. This process of 'decolonialization' created scores of newly independent nations.

New enemies, new friends

The Nazis had always known their opponents were political opposites, and had hoped that the communist Soviet Union would fall out with its democratic British and American allies. As the world began to recover from the conflict, the Allies' alliance did crack, and a 'Cold War' broke out that would last for the next 45 years.

Redrawing the map

Soviet troops remained in Eastern Europe, and totalitarian communist regimes similar to the Soviet one were introduced throughout the region. Germany and its capital, Berlin, were divided into two – with the West under the control of the United States, Britain and France, and the East under Soviet control. In 1961, the East Germans built the Berlin Wall, to stop their citizens from escaping to the West, where they hoped for a better life.

INTERNET LINK
For a link to a website where you can explore the history of the Berlin Wall, go to **www.usborne-quicklinks.com**

Global hostilities

During the new Cold War, both the Soviets and Americans sought support from other nations. US troops were sent to Korea and Vietnam to prevent communist forces from taking over these countries. They succeeded in Korea, which is still divided into a communist North and capitalist, democratic South. But they failed in Vietnam. American fear of communism saw US troops based in Western Europe for the rest of the century.

The collapse of communism

The war gave the Soviet Union an opportunity to control Eastern Europe, and establish itself as the world's second most powerful nation. Only in the late 1980s, when the Soviet government tried to reform the communist system, did the Soviet Union collapse and give up its hold over Eastern Europe. For some, this meant freedom and the prospect of greater prosperity. Germany was reunited, and the hated Berlin Wall was destroyed. But for others, especially in Yugoslavia, which was ethnically divided, the communist collapse brought civil war.

After the Holocaust

After the war, many Jews who had survived the Holocaust joined others in Palestine, then under British control. When the British left in 1948, Jews in Palestine established the state of Israel. War broke out between Israel, the Palestinians and the surrounding Arab nations, which has continued, on and off, ever since. Israel has survived, not least because of massive help from the United States. The existence of Israel, and the refugee status of the Palestinians, has contributed directly to the rise of militant Islamic fundamentalism in recent times.

FACT FILE

THE WARS ON FILM AND TV

The two wars remain popular topics with both cinema and television audiences. Here are some productions that combine watchability with broad historical accuracy. All these are also available on video or DVD. Some feature harrowing depictions of violence which will not be suitable for younger viewers.

The First World War on film

Partly because it took place longer ago, and partly due to the limited availability and quality of moving images from the time, the First World War has never been as popular a topic for film and television makers as the Second World War. But there is still plenty here to choose from.

All Quiet on the Western Front
directed by Lewis Milestone, 1930

Several films of variable quality were made about the war during the 1920s and 30s, and this version of Erich Maria Remarque's famous novel has been the most enduring. Made soon after the advent of talking pictures, it is thought to be one of the most powerful anti-war films ever made.

Lawrence of Arabia
directed by David Lean, 1962

Peter O'Toole plays T.E. Lawrence, the British soldier who fought alongside Arab forces against the Turks. Visually ravishing, the film introduced cinema-goers to one of the lesser-known battlegrounds of the First World War – the Middle East. Tellingly, both of the region and the times, although the film is three and a half hours long, there are no female speaking parts.

Oh! What a Lovely War
directed by Richard Attenborough, 1969

The cream of British acting talent – Laurence Olivier, Maggie Smith, John Gielgud and Ian Holm – star in this unsettling musical, which juxtaposes the horrors of the war with the popular songs of the day.

Gallipoli
directed by Peter Weir, 1981

In this film, respected director Peter Weir painstakingly strives to recreate authentically the Australian experience of the Gallipoli landings in 1915. Mel Gibson and Mark Lee star as two soldiers caught up in the carnage.

The Trench
directed by William Boyd, 1999

Written and directed by the novelist and screen writer, William Boyd, *The Trench* is a tense, claustrophobic study of a group of soldiers in the final 48 hours before the calamitous first day of the Battle of the Somme.

A Very Long Engagement
directed by Jean-Pierre Jeunet, 2004

This breathtaking and beautiful film stars Audrey Tautou as Mathilde, a disabled young woman who is convinced her fiancé, reported killed in the war, is still alive. Told in post-war flashback, the film depicts the trenches in horrific detail, as well as the terrible social and psychological cost of the conflict on the French population. (Most definitely not recommended for younger readers.)

The First World War on TV

The Great War
1964

Narrated by Michael Redgrave, this 26-part series does a similar job to 'The World at War', and is considered to be one of the best documentary series on the conflict.

World War One in Colour
2003

Narrated by Kenneth Branagh, this six-part series uses computer technology to tint archive footage. This attempt to make the war more approachable to viewers unused to black and white images had a mixed critical reception.

Testament of Youth
directed by Moira Armstrong,1979

This moving television drama starring Cheryl Campbell brings to life Vera Britain's autobiographical book of the same name. Detailing the dreadful personal cost of the war on a young woman of the time, Vera reflects, "In the last four years my god, my king and my country have stripped me of everything I ever cared for." The series is currently only available in video format.

The Second World War on film

The Longest Day
directed by Ken Annakin, Andrew Marton and Bernhard Wicki, 1962

This spectacular and comprehensive depiction of the D-Day landings of June 6, 1944 was based on the Cornelius Ryan book of the same name. Unlike the more recent Saving Private Ryan, the film portrays events from the perspectives of all the participants – British, American, Commonwealth, French and German.

Memphis Belle
directed by Michael Caton-Jones, 1990

Although it occasionally lapses into sentimentality and cliché, this depiction of the final mission of a US bomber crew based in England, gives a strong impression of the everyday tensions and dangers of the air war over Europe. It is based closely on a true story.

Das Boot
directed by Wolfgang Petersen, 1981

This fascinating portrayal of the crew of a German U-boat during its final mission, shows the claustrophobic world of the submariner in all its grimy, terrifying detail.

Schindler's List
directed by Steven Spielberg,1993

Based on Thomas Keneally's book, *Schindler's Ark*, this tells the story of the Holocaust through the tale of German industrialist Oskar Schindler's attempts to save Jewish workers employed in his factory.

Enemy at the Gates
directed by Jean-Jacques Annaud, 2000

This account of the Battle of Stalingrad gives a good idea of the dreadful ordeal faced by both German and Soviet troops during this pivotal battle of the war.

Tora! Tora! Tora!
directed by Richard Fleischer, 1970

Taking its name from the Japanese radio codeword to signal that the attack had been a total surprise (Tiger! Tiger! Tiger!) the film captures the chaos of the day well. Although lacking the spectacular special effects of the more recent *Pearl Harbor* (2001), most critics agree that *Tora! Tora! Tora!* is a more accurate history.

Battle of Britain
directed by Guy Hamilton, 1969

An all-star cast reenacts the story of how Britain was defended by the Royal Air Force in the summer of 1940.

Band of Brothers
directed by Phil Alden Robinson and Richard Loncraine, 2000

A scrupulously accurate dramatic recreation of the experiences of a group of American soldiers fighting from Normandy and into Germany during 1944 and 1945.

The Second World War on TV

The World at War
directed by Jeremy Isaccs, 1973

With a poetic and mesmerizing narration by Laurence Olivier, and a haunting score by Carl Davis, this 32-part epic mixes contemporary newsreel film with interviews from surviving soldiers, politicians – and even Hitler's secretary.

The Nazis – A Warning from History
produced by Laurence Rees, 1997

This documentary series takes a fresh look at the Third Reich. Similar in style to the World At War in its mixture of archive footage and interviews with surviving eyewitnesses, the makers ask the ominous question, "Could it happen again?"

The War of the Century
produced by Laurence Rees, 1999

This series looks at the most fiercely fought and barbaric aspect of the war: the German invasion of the Soviet Union. The production makes fascinating use of recently released archive material, which had previously been forbidden to documentary makers by the Soviet Union.

Hell in the Pacific
produced by Jonathan Lewis, 1997

This four-part series covers the Pacific conflict from Pearl Harbor to Hiroshima and Nagasaki with first-hand accounts from participants. Lesser known areas of the war in the Pacific, such as Burma, are also covered.

WHO'S WHO

Many people played a vital role in the events of the two World Wars. Here are some of the leading personalities from both sides. Names shown in *italic* type have an entry of their own, and words in *italics* are explained in the glossary on the following pages.

The First World War

Allenby, Field Marshal Sir Edmund (Later Lord Allenby) (1861-1936) commanded the British *cavalry* on the *Western Front* until 1917. After that, he was the Allied commander-in-chief in the Middle East, where he led the final campaign against the Turks.

Brusilov, General Alexei (1853-1926) was a general in the Russian army. In 1916, he led a successful offensive against Austria-Hungary, and in 1917, *Alexander Kerensky* made him Russia's commander-in-chief.

Churchill, Winston (1874-1965) was Britain's First Lord of the Admiralty in 1914-15, and Minister of Munitions in 1917-18. He believed the navy could help to win the war on land, and was partly responsible for the disastrous Allied campaign in Gallipoli. In 1940, he became British prime minister.

Clemenceau, Georges (1841-1929) was the premier of France, 1917-1920. At Versailles, he was the most vocal in demanding strict punishment of the Germans, and was nicknamed 'the Tiger' because of his aggressive negotiating skills.

Enver Pasha (1881-1922) was a former officer in the Turkish army, who underwent part of his training in Germany. He became leader of the Young Turks in 1908, and was their minister of war from 1914.

Falkenhayn, General Erich von (1861-1922) was the German army's chief of general staff until 1916. *Kaiser Wilhelm II* held him responsible for huge numbers of German casualties at Verdun, and replaced him with *Hindenberg* and Ludendorff in August 1916. He was transferred to the Balkans, where he swiftly defeated Rumania.

Feisal, Emir of Mecca (1885-1933) led the Arabs against the Turks and continued to argue for Arab independence after the war. In 1920, he claimed the throne in Syria, but was thrown out by the French who held the *mandate* there. A year later, after an offer from the British, he became the first king of Iraq.

Foch, Marshal Ferdinand (1851-1929) led the French forces at the Battle of the Somme. In 1918, he took overall command, of the combined Allied forces on the *Western Front*, where he helped to bring the Allies to victory.

Franz Ferdinand, Archduke (1863-1914) was the heir to the Austro-Hungarian throne. His assassination by Gavrilo Princip led to the outbreak of the war.

French, Field Marshal Sir John (later Earl French of Ypres) (1852-1925) was a former cavalryman and commander-in-chief of Britain's overseas army – the British Expeditionary Force – at the outbreak of the war. He lost his job in December 1915, partly because one of his own generals, *Haig*, whispered to King George V that the army had lost confidence in him.

Haig, Field Marshal Sir Douglas (later Earl Haig of Bemersyde) (1861-1928) took command of the British army on the *Western Front* from *French*. His tactics have been attacked for their cost in human life, particularly at the Battle of the Somme.

Hindenberg, Field Marshal Paul von (1847-1934) was called out of retirement, aged 67, when the war broke out. With his right-hand man, General Erich Ludendorff, he masterminded Germany's final Spring Offensive on the *Western Front* in 1918. He was president of Germany from 1925 until his death, and appointed Adolf Hitler as his chancellor in 1933.

Jellicoe, Admiral of the Fleet Earl John (1859-1935) was commander-in-chief of the British Grand Fleet. At the Battle of Jutland, his tactics were criticized for being too cautious.

Joffre, Marshal Joseph (1852-1931) was commander-in-chief of the French army in 1914, and credited with having saved Paris.

Kemal, Mustafa (1881-1938) was a Turkish army commander, whose leadership at Gallipoli made him a national hero. After the war, he led the Turkish resistance to Allied occupation and set up a provisional government. In 1924, he abolished the Ottoman sultanate and became the first president of the Turkish Republic. In 1934, he was given the title *Atatürk* – meaning 'Father of the Turks' – by the Turkish National Assembly.

Kerensky, Alexander (1881-1970) became Russia's Minister of Justice after the fall of *Tsar Nicholas II*, then head of the Russian government. His unpopular decision to continue fighting the war, led to a second *revolution* in Russia. In November 1917, he and his government were overthrown by the Bolsheviks, and he spent the rest of his life in exile.

Kitchener, Field Marshal Lord, Earl Kitchener of Kartoum (1850-1916) was British Secretary of State for War, and built up the British army. He died in 1916, on a ship that struck a mine.

Lawrence, Thomas Edward (1888-1935) was a British *intelligence* officer, known as Lawrence of Arabia because of his fervent support for Arab independence. After the war, he published *Seven Pillars of Wisdom*, his account of the Arab Revolt. He died in 1935, after a motorcycle accident. Already a legend, his iconic status was confirmed when his story was made into a Hollywood movie, *Lawrence of Arabia*, in 1962.

Lenin (1870-1924) was born Vladimir Ilyich Ulyanov, but changed his name during his student days. In 1905, he played a leading role in a revolt against the Tsar. After that, Lenin lived in exile in Switzerland. In 1917, he returned to Russia to lead the Bolshevik *Revolution*, becoming the new head of government. He died of brain disease in 1924. His body was preserved and has been on public display in Moscow ever since.

Lettow-Vorbeck, Colonel (later Major General) Paul von (1870-1964) led the German army's campaign in East Africa. He used *guerrilla* tactics to fight an Allied force far bigger than his own, and was the only commander to last the entire war without ever being defeated. After the war, he served in the German parliament where he opposed the Nazis.

Lloyd George, David (1863-1945) was the leading member of the British government throughout the war. He became prime minister in 1916, and led the post-war peace talks in Paris, along with *Clemenceau* and *Wilson*.

Moltke, General Helmuth von (1848-1916) was responsible for putting the German army's Schlieffen Plan into action in August 1914. When it failed, he was replaced by *Falkenhayn*.

Nicholas II, Tsar (1868-1918) came to the Russian throne in 1894. During the war, he took command of the Russian army, while his wife, the Tsarina, managed affairs at home. Both were unsuccessful and became increasingly unpopular, until the Tsar was overthrown in March 1917. The following year, the Tsar and his family were executed by Bolshevik soldiers.

Nivelle, General Robert (1856-1924) replaced *Joffre* in command of the French Army on the *Western Front* in 1916-1917. But, when his ambitious offensive in the spring of 1917 failed, many of his troops *mutinied* and he was replaced by *Pétain*.

Pershing, General John Joseph 'Black Jack' (1860-1948) led the American army in Europe. After the war, he was given the title General of the Armies, a rank previously only held by President George Washington.

Pétain, General Henri Philippe (1856-1951) was credited with saving Verdun in 1916, and became a French national hero as a result. In May 1917, he became French commander-in-chief. During the Second World War, he led the French government in Vichy under German *occupation*. He was later found guilty of treason for collaborating with the Nazis, and died in prison.

Richthofen, Captain Baron Manfred von (1892-1918) was a German fighter pilot, known as the Red Baron, and the most successful air 'ace' of the war, with 80 confirmed kills. He was shot down over the *Western Front*, in April 1918, aged 25.

Scheer, Admiral Reinhard (1863-1928) masterminded the German naval attacks against Britain in the North Sea, and commanded the High Seas Fleet at the Battle of Jutland.

Smuts, General Jan (1870-1950) was a South African who fought in the Boer War against the British, but who led the Allied forces in Africa during the First World War. He became prime minister of South Africa in 1919.

Spee, Admiral Count Maximilian von (1861-1914) commanded the German fleet in the Pacific. He waged a form of naval *guerrilla warfare*, targeting the Allies' merchant ships and trading ports. His fleet was eventually defeated at the Battle of the Falklands, when Spee went down with his ship.

Wilhelm II, Kaiser (1859-1941) Emperor of Germany, 1888-1918. The Kaiser spent the early years of his reign building up the strength of his armed forces, especially the navy. Officially, Wilhelm was the head of the German military throughout the war. But, in reality, he lacked the necessary skill and experience, so was little more than a figurehead. At the end of the war, he was forced to *abdicate* and spent the rest of his life in exile in the Netherlands.

Wilson, Thomas Woodrow (1856-1924) President of the United States, 1913-1920. He kept his country out of the war until 1917, when German *U-boats* began sinking US ships. In January 1918, he produced a 14-point plan for peace, which provided the basis for the *Armistice* later that year. Mainly responsible for establishing the League of Nations, he was bitterly disappointed when the US Senate refused to join.

The Second World War

Chamberlain, Neville (1869-1940) was Prime Minister of Britain from 1937-1940. Chamberlain is remembered most for his failed policy of appeasement – addressing the problem of Nazi Germany's growing aggression by trying to reach a peaceful understanding. His approach earned him only contempt from *Hitler*. He resigned as German forces swept through Europe, and died before the year ended.

Chuikov, Lieutenant General Vasily (1900-1982) was a Soviet general who played a leading role in the battle of Stalingrad (1942-3), the re-capture of Poland (1944) and the Battle of Berlin (1945).

Churchill, Winston (1874-1965) Having spent the inter-war years warning of the dangers of Nazism and appeasement, Churchill was an obvious choice as Britain's wartime leader. He successfully courted America, whose support helped to ensure his own country would not fall victim to seemingly invincible German forces. His statesmanship, wit and stirring historic speeches inspired his countrymen and ensured his place in history as Britain's greatest prime minister.

Eichmann, Obersturmbannführer Adolf (1906-1962) was an SS German bureaucrat who organized the mass movement of Jews to *ghettos* and extermination camps in Nazi-occupied Europe. Escaping at the end of the war he was caught in Argentina in 1960 by Israeli agents, tried by an Israeli court for crimes against humanity, and hanged, in 1962.

Eisenhower, General Dwight D. (1890-1969) was one of America's most famous generals. He was the supreme commander of all Allied forces in Europe and directly responsible for the Normandy Landings of June 6, 1944. A likeable and popular man, he became the 34th President of the United States between 1953 and 1961.

Goebbels, Dr. Joseph (1897-1945) was a Nazi politician who held the position of Minister for Public Enlightenment and Propaganda throughout *Hitler's* regime. He was responsible for inciting anti-Semitic violence and the infamous *Kristallnacht* when Jewish synagogues, homes and business were attacked hundreds of Jews were killed, and another 30,000 were taken off to *concentration camps*. The result was a mass migration of Jews out of Germany and Austria. After *Hitler's* suicide, he was German Chancellor for one day, before committing suicide.

Goering, Reichsmarschall Hermann (1893-1946) was a leading member of the Nazi party and second-in-command to *Hitler*. Founder of the *Gestapo*, the Nazi Secret Police, he was also head of the German air force, the *Luftwaffe*. As the war turned against Germany, he became a bloated drug addict. One of the few Nazi leaders to be captured alive, he was tried and convicted of war crimes in Nuremberg, but committed suicide by taking a cyanide pill two hours before his scheduled hanging.

Guderian, General Heinz (1888-1954) was a military strategist who played a key role in training and employing German forces in *blitzkrieg* tactics which were successfully employed in Poland, Western Europe and the Soviet Union.

Harris, Air Marshal Arthur (1892-1984) was in charge of the bombing campaign against Germany from 1942-45, using the controversial tactic of 'saturation' bombing which killed thousands of civilians. Under his command, the RAF decimated Hamburg, Cologne and, most infamously, Dresden. Harris commanded immense respect from his men, but his bombing tactics were becoming controversial even before the war ended.

Heydrich, Obergruppenführer Rheinhard (1904-1942) was *Himmel's* deputy, and deputy chief of the *Gestapo*. He chaired the Wannsee Conference in 1942, which discussed and organized the fate of occupied Europe's Jews. In September 1941, he was made 'Deputy Protector' of Bohemia and Moravia. He died from injuries following an assassination attempt by the Czech resistance. In retaliation, the village of Lidice was razed and every man executed.

Himmler, Reichsführer Heinrich (1900-1945) was the head of the *SS* and *Gestapo* and driving force behind the Holocaust. He was in charge of the *concentration camps* and death squads and responsible for the final implementation of the plan to exterminate millions of people. At the end of the war, he tried to escape, but was caught by the British Army and swallowed cyanide.

Hirohito, Emperor (1901-1989) was Emperor of Japan from 1926 to his death in 1989. During the 1930s and 1940s, Japan became an aggressive, militaristic nation and waged war against China and Western nations. As his role was considered to be symbolic, he was not held responsible and, in 1946, he became a constitutional monarch.

Hitler, Adolf (1889-1945) was leader of Germany and the Nazi Party. He wanted to make Germany the world's dominant power by conquering Europe, colonising the lands to Germany's east and exterminating Jews and eliminating the *communists*. His regime was characterized by diabolical brutality and immense arrogance. In choosing unsuitable allies and taking on both Soviet Russia and the United States, Hitler ensured his own, and his country's, destruction.

MacArthur, General Douglas (1880-1964) was an American general who oversaw the war in the Pacific between 1942 and 1945, and the occupation of Japan, 1945-1951.

Manstein, General Erich von (1887-1973) was a German general. After success in Poland and France he failed to relieve *von Paulus's* army at Stalingrad. After the war, he was imprisoned as a war criminal.

Merrill, Brigadier General Frank D. (1903-1955) commanded the first unit of American special forces to fight in mainland Asia. His men, known as 'Merrill's Marauders', conducted *guerrilla* warfare in the jungles of Burma.

Mitscher, Admiral Marc A. (1887-1947) was an admiral in the US Navy who took part in raids on Japanese-held Pacific islands, the campaigns to capture the Marianas, Palaus and Leyte, and the Battles of the Philippine Sea and Leyte Gulf, in 1944. In 1945, as Commander of Task Force 58, he led assaults on Iwo Jima, Okinawa and the Japanese Home Islands.

Montgomery, Field Marshal Bernard (1887-1976) 'Monty', as he was known, commanded British forces at the Battle of El Allemein, and expelled *Axis* forced from North Africa. Working with *Eisenhower* he also commanded the land forces during the invasion of Normandy in 1944. Regarded with affection by many of his troops, he could also be famously overbearing, prompting *Winston Churchill* to say of him: "In defeat, unbeatable, in victory, unbearable!"

Mussolini, Benito (1883-1945) was Prime Minister and dictator of Italy, 1922-1943. He imposed a fascist, nationalistic regime on his country. He was a close ally of *Hitler*, and entered the war, disastrously, on the side of Nazi Germany in 1940. After the *Allies* invaded Sicily in 1943, he was overthrown and imprisoned, only to be freed by German commandos. After ruling a Nazi-controlled puppet state in the north of Italy he was captured by *partisans* as the war was ending. Shot near Lake Como, his body hung in a square in Milan, to be spat and shot at by his disillusioned countrymen.

Nimitz, U.S Admiral Chester (1885-1966) was Commander-in-Chief of Pacific Fleet, and was America's leading expert on submarines. He defeated the Japanese in the Battle of the Coral Sea, the Battle of Midway, and during the Solomon Islands Campaign. In 1944, he became Fleet Admiral of the US Navy.

Oppenheimer, J. Robert (1904-1967) was an American theoretical physicist. Director of the Manhattan Project he led the team which developed the nuclear weapons used to destroy Nagasaki and Hiroshima in 1945.

Patton, General George (1885-1945) was a US Army general who commanded troops during the invasions of North Africa, Sicily, France and in the Ardennes. Flamboyant and controversial, he died in a road accident in Germany in December 1945.

Paulus, General Friedrich von (1890-1957) was a German general who commanded the 6th Army at Stalingrad. Although he followed *Hitler's* orders not to withdraw when he still had the chance, he disobeyed *Hitler* by surrendering in 1943, and thereafter became a vocal critic of the Nazi regime.

Rommel, Erwin, Field Marshal (1891-1944) was one of the most distinguished military commanders in the German Army. He commanded the *Deutsches Afrika Korps*, and was nicknamed the 'Desert Fox' for his skilful campaigns in North Africa. He also commanded the German defences against the D-Day landings in Normandy. Following the *Allied* invasion, he was accused of involvement in the plot to assassinate *Hitler* and was given the choice of standing trial or committing suicide. He chose to take a cyanide pill.

Roosevelt, Franklin D. (1882-1945) was the 32nd President of the United States (1933-1945). He led his country through both the Great Depression and the Second World War. He was paralysed by polio from the waist down, but this didn't stop him from being re-elected on four separate occasions. Although he strove to avoid war before 1941, he helped Britain by supplying arms. Japan and Germany both declared war on the US in December 1941, an act that ensured their defeat. America's huge economic power virtually guaranteed that it and its allies would overcome their enemies. Roosevelt died three weeks before Germany's defeat.

Rundstedt, Field Marshal Gerd von (1875-1953) was a German soldier who played an active role in the fighting in Poland, France, Soviet Russia and the Ardennes.

Stalin, Josif Vissarionovich Dzhugashvili (1878-1953) led his country, the Soviet Union, to victory against the Nazis in what became known as *The Great Patriotic War*. In his ruthless inhumanity, Stalin could be *Hitler's* equal, although he was often shrewd enough to act on the advice of his generals, something *Hitler* rarely did.

Stauffenberg, Colonel Claus von (1907-1944) was a German officer and war hero who was one of the leading figures in the 1944 plot to kill *Hitler*. He planted a bomb during a military conference. It blew *Hitler's* trousers to tatters and partially deafened him but failed to kill him. Stauffenberg was executed that very evening.

Truman, Harry S. (1884-1972) was 33rd US President (1945-1953), successor to *Roosevelt* and the man whose decision it was to drop the first atomic bombs on Hiroshima and Nagasaki.

Yamamoto, Admiral Isoruku (1884-1943) was the architect of the Pearl Harbor attack which brought Japan into the war. He always doubted the wisdom of such an attack, and died when his plane was shot down by American aircraft.

Zhukov, Giorgiy (1896-1974) was regarded by many as the greatest Soviet general of the war. After directing troops at the siege of Moscow (1941), the counter attack at Stalingrad (1943), the battle of Warsaw (1944) and Berlin (1945) he accepted the German surrender at the end of the war.

GLOSSARY

This glossary explains some of the words you may come across when reading about the First and Second World Wars. If a word used in an entry has a separate entry of its own, it is shown in *italic* type.

abdication Giving up a position of power, usually that of king, queen or emperor.

aircraft carrier A large, long-decked warship from which aircraft can take off and land at sea.

airship A large air balloon which can be steered and is propelled by engines.

Allied Powers The countries that fought against the *Central Powers* in the First World War. The main Allied nations were Britain, France, Russia, Italy and the United States of America.

Allies The nations that fought against the *Axis* during the Second World War. The main Allied countries were Great Britain and its empire, the Soviet Union, the United States of America and France.

armada A large number of ships or aircraft.

armaments The weapons and *munitions* used by a military force.

armistice An agreement between warring nations or parties to stop fighting.

arms race The competition between nations to produce and stockpile bigger, better and more weapons than each other.

arsenal A stock of weapons and *munitions*.

artillery Large but transportable *armaments*, such as cannons and heavy guns used in land fighting.

Aryan A Nazi term for a 'pure-blooded' German.

atomic bomb An explosive weapon that releases enormous energy by splitting elements such as uranium or plutonium. Also called an A-bomb.

auxiliary A person who works to support the armed forces, but who isn't directly engaged in combat.

Axis The pact signed between Germany, Italy and Japan, on September 27, 1940, joined by other, smaller nations – Slovakia, Rumania, Hungary, Croatia and Bulgaria – who opposed the *Allies* in the Second World War.

barrage Steady *artillery* fire against an enemy force.

barrage balloon An elongated balloon tethered over a military target to support cables or netting that hinder low-flying enemy planes.

battalion A unit in the armed forces, comprising a large number of soldiers who are organized into several different groups and the leaders who control these groups. Usually numbering about 850 men.

battleship A large heavily-armed and fortified warship.

bayonet A long, sharp blade designed to be attached to the end of a rifle for use in hand-to-hand fighting.

blitzkrieg A fast-moving attack, using tanks, motorized troops and aircraft, used to great effect by the German army at the beginning of the Second World War. (The word means 'lightning war' in German.)

blockade An attempt by one warring party to obstruct the passage of troops, food and other supplies into land owned or controlled by their opponents.

bunker An underground defensive position or protective chamber.

cavalry Soldiers who fight on horseback.

cease-fire A period of truce, when opposing forces agree to stop firing at one another. A cease-fire is either temporary, or the first step in the process of making permanent peace.

censorship The control or suppression, often by a government, of information that may threaten its goals.

Central Powers The nations that fought against the *Allied Powers* in the First World War. The Central Powers were Germany, Austria-Hungary, the Turkish empire and Bulgaria.

civilian Anyone who is not a member of the armed forces.

colony A geographical area under the political control of another country.

commando A member of a small military unit specially trained to make quick, destructive raids by both land and sea in enemy territory.

communism A political system in which the state controls the wealth and industry of a country on behalf of the people.

communist Someone who follows the system of *communism*.

comrade A fellow member of a group, especially a squad of soldiers, sailors or aircrew.

concentration camp A guarded prison camp where *civilians* and political prisoners are held during wartime, usually under harsh conditions.

conscription Compulsory recruitment of *civilians* into the armed forces.

convoy ships Merchant ships that travel in a group across a sea, with warships to protect them from attack.

cooperative A system in which workers and consumers share ownership and profits of a business.

cruiser A large warship that is faster than a *battleship*, but with less firepower, and not as heavily fortified.

death camp A *concentration camp* where the captives are deliberately killed or worked to death.

democracy A political system in which citizens can freely elect people to represent them in government.

deport To expel someone from a country.

depression A period of steep price rises, when many businesses fail, leading to mass unemployment and poverty.

destroyer A small warship that is easy to direct and position. It can be armed with guns, *torpedoes* and depth charges.

dictatorship Government of a country or empire by a ruler who holds unlimited power.

dive bomber A military aircraft that releases its bombs during a sharp dive towards its target, to improve the chances of an accurate hit.

dreadnought A type of *battleship* mounted with guns and powered by turbines, named after the first of its kind, HMS *Dreadnought*.

dry dock A large, basin-shaped structure from which water can be drained, used for building or repairing a ship below its water line.

Eastern Front The *front lines* in central and eastern Europe which lay to the east of Germany and Austria-Hungary.

empire A group of countries or territories under the control of another country.

epidemic A widespread outbreak of a disease.

espionage The use of spies to obtain information, particularly political or military secrets.

evacuate To send troops or *civilians* away from a threatened area, for safety. During the Second World War, many *civilians* were evacuated from cities to rural areas.

evacuee Someone who has been evacuated.

exiled Sent away or banished from a country.

fascism A system of government usually run by a dictator, often characterized by extreme *nationalism*, in which opposition is suppressed by terror and censorship.

front line The boundary along which opposing armies face each other.

garrison A military base or fortification.

genocide The systematic extermination of a group of people based on distinctions of race, nationality, ethnicity or religion.

ghetto During the Second World War, this meant a densely populated, enclosed district of a city, such as the Warsaw Ghetto in Poland, set up by the Nazis to keep the Jewish population cordoned off from the "*Aryan*" districts.

glider An aircraft which has no independent power and is usually towed by another aircraft.

grenade A small explosive weapon thrown by a soldier.

guerrilla force A group of independent, armed *resistance* fighters.

guerrilla warfare The method of fighting by launching surprise attacks which are relatively small and scattered, usually used against a larger or more professional army.

Holocaust The term given to the Nazis' systematic slaughter on a massive scale of European Jews and other groups during the Second World War.

home front Anyone or anything in the home country during a foreign war. In times of *Total War*, the contribution and efforts of those on the home front is seen to play a vital role in the war's outcome.

howitzer A type of *artillery* cannon capable of firing *shells* high into the air to increase their range and impact.

hyperinflation An ongoing extreme rise in prices, causing the currency effectively to lose its value. Hyperinflation often leads to a period of financial *depression*.

incendiary bomb A bomb that is designed to burst into flame on impact.

infantry Soldiers who fight mostly on foot.

inflation An ongoing rise in prices, combined with an ongoing decline in the purchasing power of money.

intelligence Secret military information about an enemy, often gathered by *espionage*.

jihad An Islamic holy war waged against non-Muslims.

kamikaze A Japanese word meaning "divine wind" which referred to a plane loaded with explosives to be piloted in a suicide attack.

Luftwaffe The name of the German air force before and during the Second World War

machine gun A gun that can fire bullets very quickly without needing to be reloaded.

mandate A territory controlled and administered by a member state of the League of Nations after the war.

Maquis Mainly rural *guerrilla forces* of the French resistance movement during the Second World War. They were named after a French word for the type of scrubby vegetation in which they were reputed to hide.

Marine A member of the US Marine Corps, an American body of sea-going troops.

marine A type of soldier who operates on land and sea.

merchant ship A non-military ship which transports goods to be bought and sold.

missile A weapon that is thrown or fired.

mobilization Action taken in preparation for going to war; 'mobilizing the troops' means organizing soldiers and getting them into position ready for combat.

morale The collective spirit or confidence of a group of people, especially in the armed forces.

munitions Military equipment including *artillery* and ammunition such as bullets, bombs and *shells*.

mutiny A revolt against the person or persons in charge by those who are supposed to obey them.

napalm An explosive mixture of polystyrene, benzene and gasoline which burns fiercely.

nationalism The belief that nations benefit from acting independently, rather than in cooperation with other nations. Extreme nationalism results in the belief that one nation is superior to all others.

no-man's-land The stretch of open, unoccupied land separating the *front lines* of two warring sides.

occupation Seizing and taking control of an area.

occupy To seize and take control of an area.

officer Usually a senior member of the armed forces.

over the top In *trench warfare*, the act of climbing over the *parapet* of a *trench* into *no-man's-land* in order to charge at the enemy.

parapet The top edge of a *trench* wall facing the enemy, usually lined with sandbags.

partisan A member of a *guerrilla force*.

patriotism Loving one's country and being prepared to fight for it.

periscope A vertical tube with prisms at each end that allows you to see something from a position a long way below, used in submarines and sometimes in trenches.

pillbox A low-roofed concrete structure on which a machine gun or antitank gun is positioned.

private The lowest rank of soldier in the armed forces.

propaganda Information that is systematically spread to promote or damage a political cause.

racism The belief that race is responsible for differences in ability and character and that a particular race is superior to others. Extreme hatred of another race is often a feature.

radar A system that uses radio waves to detect and determine the distance of airborne objects.

radiation Energy given off by atoms. With some materials, such as uranium and plutonium, this radiation can be harmful.

radioactivity The emission of *radiation* from atoms.

rationing Strict control of how much food and other goods someone is allowed.

reconnaissance An exploration and inspection of an area to gather information.

Red Army The army of the Soviet Union.

reparations Payments made by Germany to several Allied nations after its defeat in the First World War, justified as being compensation for causing the war.

reprisal An act of retaliation or revenge.

resistance Relating to secret organizations that fought to overthrow the enemy forces occupying their country, especially in France.

revolution The overthrow of a leader or government by the people, usually as a result of violent struggle.

sabotage To damage or destroy property and utilities in order to hinder an enemy's progress.

salient A piece of land held by one warring party that bulges into its enemy's territory.

scorched earth Military tactic that involves destroying anything that might be useful to the enemy, while advancing though or withdrawing from an area.

seaboard Land bordering on the sea.

secret service A government agency engaged in *intelligence*-gathering activities.

sentry A person charged with the job of keeping guard and watching for danger.

shell A hollow *missile* containing explosives.

shell shock Mental illness or breakdown caused by participation in active warfare. Doctors now recognize this as a form of post-traumatic stress disorder.

shrapnel Small pieces of metal scattered by the explosion of a bomb, *shell* or mine.

Slavs A race of people occupy ing large parts of Eastern and Northern Europe, including Bulgarians, Russians, Serbo-Croats, Poles and Czechs.

sniper A rifleman who takes shots at enemy soldiers from a concealed position.

SS An elite unit of the Nazi party that served originally as Hitler's personal guard and as a special security force in Germany and the occupied countries. SS stands for the German word *Schutzstaffel*, which means 'protection squad'.

stalemate A situation where neither side can win, and no further action can be taken.

stormtrooper Originally a member of the Nazi Party Militia, the SA. (SA stands for *Sturmabteilung*, which means 'assault unit' in German.) More widely, the term refers to highly mobile troops used in *Blitzkrieg* tactics.

submarine A ship that can travel under the water for long periods, widely used for the first time in the First World War.

'Tommy' A nickname used to refer to British soldiers, from 'Thomas Atkins' – commonly used as a sample name when demonstrating how to fill in military forms.

torpedo A self-propelled, explosive device which travels though water and can be launched from a plane or ship.

Total War A type of warfare which involves entire nations, including *civilians* on the *home front*, rather than just those directly engaged in the fighting.

trench A deep, fortified ditch.

trench warfare A type of warfare in which opposing armies dig *trenches* facing one another along most of the *front line*. *Trenches* are easy to defend but difficult to attack, so trench warfare often ends in *stalemate*.

U-boat A German *submarine*. The name comes from *unterseeboot*, which means 'undersea boat' in German.

Vichy France During the war, the part of France under the control of a government that cooperated with Germany.

warhead The front of a *missile* or *torpedo* that carries an explosive charge.

Western Front The *front lines* which lay to the west of Germany, in Belgium and Northern France.

Zeppelin A tube-shaped *airship* invented by the German, Count Ferdinand von Zeppelin, and used for *reconnaissance* and bombing during the war.

INDEX

252

INTERNET LINKS

Throughout this book, we have recommended interesting websites where you can find out more about the World Wars and watch movie clips, see battle reconstructions and view interactive exhibits. To visit the sites, go to the Usborne Quicklinks website, where you will find links to all the sites.

1. Go to **usborne.com/quicklinks**

2. Type the keywords for this book: **world wars**

3. Type the page number of the link you want to visit.

4. Click on the links to go to the recommended site.

Websites to visit

Here are some of the things you can do on the websites recommended in this book:

• View animated timelines and maps of the major battles of the wars
• Watch film footage of soldiers digging a trench on the Western Front
• Hear archive radio bulletins, reporting on the progress of the Second World War
• Listen to eyewitness accounts of the Holocaust

Site availability

The links in Usborne Quicklinks are regularly reviewed and updated, but occasionally you may get a message that a site is unavailable. This might be temporary, so try again later, or even the next day. Websites do occasionally close down and when this happens, we will replace them with new links in Usborne Quicklinks. Sometimes we add extra links too, if we think they are useful. So when you visit Usborne Quicklinks, the links may be slightly different from those described in your book.

Staying safe online

Make sure you follow these simple rules to keep you safe online:

Always ask an adult's permission before connecting to the internet.

Never give out information about yourself, such as your real name, address, phone number or school.

If a site asks you to log in or register by typing your name or email address, ask permission from an adult first.

If you receive an email from someone you don't know, don't reply to it. Tell an adult.

Net help

For information and help using the Internet, go to the Net Help are on the Usborne Quicklinks website. You'll find information about "plug-ins" – small free programs that enable your browser to play sound, videos or animations. You probably already have these, but if not, you can download them for free from Quicklinks Net Help. You can also find information about computer viruses and advice on anti-virus software to protect your computer.

Adults

The websites described in this book are regularly reviewed, but websites can change and Usborne Publishing is not responsible for the content on any site other than its own.

We recommend that children are supervised while on the Internet, that they do not use internet chat rooms, and that filtering software is used to block unsuitable material. You can find more information on Internet safety at the Usborne Quicklinks website.

ACKNOWLEDGEMENTS

Every effort has been made to trace and acknowledge ownership of copyright. If any rights have been omitted, the publishers offer to rectify this in any future editions following notification. The publishers are grateful to the following individuals and organizations for their permission to reproduce material on the following pages: (IWM=Imperial War Musiem, t=top, m=middle, b=bottom, l=left, r=right)

Cover: 'Bomber's Moon' (1962), Oil on canvas, by Alan Moore, © Australian War Memorial (ART27553).

p1© Corbis Historical/Getty Images; **pp2–3** © Bettman/Getty Images; **pp4–5** MPI/Archive/Getty Images; **pp6–7** © Hulton Archive/Getty Images; **p6** (bl) © Bettman/Getty Images; **p7** (br) © Hulton-Deutsch Collection/CORBIS/Corbis via Getty Images; **pp8-9** © David Hughes/Robert Harding/Getty Images; **p10** Scherl/SV-Bilderdienst; **p12** (bl) © Christel Gerstenberg/CORBIS, (tr) IWM Q81824; **pp12–13** The Naval Historical Foundation, Washington, USA; **p14** (tr) IWM Q81831, (br) IWM Q91840; **p15** © Time Life Pictures/Getty Images; **p16** (tr) © Topical Press Agency/Hulton Archive/Getty Images; **pp16–17** © Bettmann/CORBIS; **p17** (br) © Gunn & Stuart/Hulton Archive/Getty Images; **p18** (tr) IWM Q65817, (b) IWM Q53248; **p19** (t) Robert Hunt Library, (br) Robert Hunt Library; **pp20–21** Jacques Moreau/Archives Larousse, Paris, France/Giraudon/The Bridgeman Art Library; **p22** (tr) IWM Q57380; **pp22–23** © Topical Press Agency/Hulton Archive/Getty Images; **p23** (tr) IWM Q57287; **p24** (tr) IWM ART1656; **pp24–25** Roger-Viollet/Topfoto; **pp26–27** IWM Q49104; **p28** (tr) IWM Q27870; **pp28–29** IWM CO747; **p29** (tr) © Hulton Archive/Getty Images; **p30** (tr) Mary Evans Picture Library, (br) © Hulton-Deutsch Collection/CORBIS; **pp30–31** IWM CO872; **p32** (tr) IWM Q19538; **pp32–33** © Spencer Arnold/Hulton Archive/Getty Images; **p34** (tr) IWM PST2734, (b) © Bettmann/CORBIS; **p35** (t) © Hulton Archive/Getty Images, (b) IWM; **p36** (tr) © akg-images/ullstein bild, (bl) TopFoto; **p37** © Hulton Archive/Getty Images; **pp38–39** Robert Hunt Library; **p40** (bl) IWM PST2756; **pp40–41** IWM Q20896; **pp42–43** IWM Q45776; **p43** (tr) IWM Q15681; **p44** (tr) IWM Q23732; **pp44–45** © Hulton-Deutsch Collection/CORBIS; **p45** (tr) © Hulton Archive/Getty Images; **p46** (b) © Cheryl Koralik/Photonica/Getty Images; **pp46–47** (t) Armin T. Wegner © Wallstein Verlag, Germany. All rights reserved. Used by Permission; **p47** (br) © TopFoto; **pp48–49** © MPI/Hulton Archive/Getty Images; **pp50–51** © Hulton-Deutsch Collection/CORBIS; **p52** (b) IWM Q51650; **p53** (t) IWM Q11586, (br) IWM Q55085; **p54** (tr) The Art Archive/Private Collection Newbury, (b) IWM Q8382; **p55** © Hulton Archive/Getty Images; **p56** (tr) © Bettmann/CORBIS; **pp56–57** © CORBIS; **p57** (br) © Mary Evans Picture Library/Alamy; **p58** (tr) SHEILA TERRY/SCIENCE PHOTO LIBRARY; **pp58–59** IWM Q58481; **p59** (bl) IWM Q27226; **p60** (bl) IWM Q28440, (tr) IWM PST3521; **pp60–61** © Hulton-Deutsch Collection/CORBIS; **p62** (tr) Mary Evans Picture Library; **pp62–63** © CORBIS; **p64** (tr) © Bettmann/CORBIS; **pp64–65** IWM Q115126; **pp66–67** © Hulton-Deutsch Collection/CORBIS; **p68** (tr) © Hulton Archive/Getty Images; **pp68–69** Musee d'Histoire Contemporaine, B.D.I.C., Paris, France, Archives Charmet/The Bridgeman Art Library; **p70** (tr) © Hulton Archive/Getty Images; **pp70–71** IWM Q18121; **p72** (l) IWM Q27025A; **pp72–73** IWM Q23584; **p74** © David Wall/Alamy; **p75** (tr) IWM Q107381, (ml) © George Hall/CORBIS; **p76** (bl) IWM Q754; (tr) Hulton Archive/Getty Images; **pp76–77** IWM Q70167; **p78** IWM Q24047; **p79** (tr) IWM Q70742, (br) IWM E(AUS)715; **p80** (b) © CORBIS, (tr) IWM PST2766; **p81** (t) IWM Q27255, (br) IWM Q106252; **p82** © TopFoto; **pp82–83** (t) RIA Novosti Photo Library; **p84** © Underwood & Underwood/CORBIS; **p85** (bl) The National Archives, UK, (r) © Blue Lantern Studio/CORBIS; **p86** (tr) IWM Q46094; **pp86–87** IWM Q58863; **p87** (r) IWM Q24168; **pp88–89** IWM Q69408; **p90** (bl) © Bettmann/CORBIS, (tr) IWM ART5219/Reproduced with kind permission from the Nevinson estate/The Bridgeman Art Library; **p91** RIA Novosti Photo Library; **p92** (tr) © Bettmann/CORBIS; **pp92–93** © Bettmann/CORBIS; **p93** (bl) © Hulton-Deutsch Collection/CORBIS, (tr) TopFoto; **p94** © Three Lions/Hulton Archive/Getty Images; **p95** (l) © Bettmann/CORBIS, (tr) Courtesy of The Library of Congress, LC cph-3g03859, (br) © CORBIS; **p96** (tr) IWM Q5943; **pp96–97** IWM E(AUS)001220; **pp98–99** © Bettmann/CORBIS; **p100** (tr) US National Archives and Records Administration; **pp100–101** (b) The Art Archive/IWM; **p101** (tr) © Time Life Pictures/Getty Images; **p102** (bl) IWM Q12616, (tr) IWM Q13213B; **pp102–103** Australian War Memorial, Negative Number B00256; **p104** (bl) © Hulton-Deutsch Collection/CORBIS, (tr) IWM Q43225; **pp104–105** © Hulton-Deutsch Collection/CORBIS; **pp106–107** IWM Q9580; **pp108–109** © Bettmann/CORBIS; **p109** (tr) IWM HU55555; **p110** (tr) © Underwood & Underwood/CORBIS; **p111** (bl) © Bettmann/CORBIS; **p112** (tr) Library Kings College Cambridge/RCB/V/1 folio 17: 'The Soldier'; **pp112–113** IWM Q005242; **p113** (r) IWM Q79045; **p114** (tr) © Hulton-Deutsch Collection/CORBIS; **pp114–115** © Bettmann/CORBIS; **p115** (tr) Mary Evans Picture Library; **p116** (tr) IWM ART16695; **pp116–117** IWM ART1921; **p117** (l) © John Springer Collection/CORBIS; **p118** (tr) © American Stock/Hulton Archive/Getty Images; **pp118–119** IWM ART1460; **p119** (tr) The Art Archive/Private Collection/Dagli Orti/© DACS 2017; **p120** (tr) Mary Evans Picture Library; **pp120–121** IWM Q42446; **pp122-123** U.S. National Archives and Record Administration; **p124** (tr) © Bettmann/CORBIS, (bl) © CORBIS; **p125** (tr) © Getty Images/Keystone, (br) © CORBIS; **pp126–127** © Getty Images/Fox Photos; **p127** (tl) © Bettmann/CORBIS, (mr) © Getty Images/Keystone, (bm) © popperfoto.com; **p128** (tr) © Getty Images/MPI; **pp128–129** © Ewing Galloway/CORBIS; **pp130–131** © Getty Images/Keystone; **p131** (m) © CORBIS; **p132** (ml) © Getty Images/Topical Press; **pp132–133** © Getty Images/Three Lions; **pp134–135** © Getty Images/Hulton-Deutsch; **pp136–137** © Hulton-Deutsch Collection/CORBIS; **p136** (b) © Bettmann/CORBIS; **p138** (tr) © Getty Images/Time Life Pictures; **pp138–139** © Hulton-Deutsch Collection/CORBIS; **p139** (br) © CORBIS; **pp140–141** IWM CH26;

Many of the photographs in this book were originally in black
and white and have been digitally tinted by Usborne Publishing.

Usborne Publishing Ltd. has paid DACS' visual creators
for the use of their artistic works.

Half-title page: A German lancer
Title page: *Martin B-26* bomber planes in flight over Belgium

Picture research: Ruth King
Cartography: Craig Asquith
Digital imaging: Keith Furnival
Editorial Consultant: Paul Dowswell
Additional editorial contributions: Elizabeth Dalby, Rachel Firth,
Sarah Khan, Hazel Maskell and Abigail Wheatley

**For more information about Imperial War Museums,
go to: www.iwm.org.uk**